Texas

Mary G. Ramos and Dick J. Reavis
Photography by Kevin Vandivier

COMPASS AMERICAN GUIDES
An imprint of Fodor's Travel Publications

Travel
977.64,
Fodor's
2004

Compass American Guides: Texas

Editors: Chris Culwell, Daniel Mangin
Designer: Siobhan O'Hare
Compass Editorial Director: Daniel Mangin
Compass Creative Director: Fabrizio La Rocca
Compass Senior Editor: Kristin Moehlmann
Photo Editor and Archival Researcher: Melanie Marin
Map Design: Mark Stroud, Moon Street Cartography
Production Editor: Linda Schmidt

Cover photo: Kevin Vandivier, Twin V Ranch

Third Edition
ISBN 0–676–90502–1
ISSN 1543–1673

Compass American Guides, 1745 Broadway, New York, NY 10019
PRINTED IN CHINA
10 9 8 7 6 5 4 3 2 1

To my dear, encouraging mother, Esther Koger Gassett; to my inspiring high school English teacher, Vera Lazenby Beck; but most of all, to my wonderful husband, Charles Ramos, for his abiding love, support, wit, and wise counsel. —M.G.R.

To the original Dick Reavis, my dad, without whose inspiration and hard work the previous editions of this guide wouldn't have been possible. —D.J.R.

C O N T E N T S

Sidebars and Topical Essays

Literary Extracts

Maps

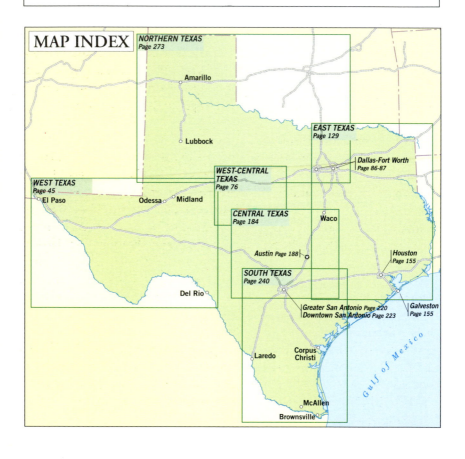

MAP INDEX

NORTHERN TEXAS
Page 273

Amarillo

EAST TEXAS
Page 129

Lubbock

Dallas-Fort Worth
Page 86-87

WEST-CENTRAL
TEXAS
Page 76

WEST TEXAS
Page 45

El Paso   Odessa   Midland

CENTRAL TEXAS
Page 184

Waco

Austin Page 188

Houston
Page 155

SOUTH TEXAS
Page 240

Del Rio

Greater San Antonio Page 220
Downtown San Antonio Page 223

Galveston
Page 155

Laredo

Corpus
Christi

Gulf of Mexico

McAllen

Brownsville

O V E R V I E W

Texas has long been associated with oil, cowboys, egotistical millionaires, and anything big. Big is the operative word because Texas *is* big—big enough to encompass tropical swamps, sandy beaches, towering desert mountains, and endless grain fields. The Lone Star State goes from sea level to over 8,700 feet without stopping for breath, and from an average 56 inches of rain a year on the coast to fewer than 9 in the west. The super-sized population includes rustlers and oil magnates as well as Austin hipsters and immigrants from Mexico, Vietnam, and the Middle East.

WEST TEXAS

The most dramatically beautiful region of Texas is the Trans-Pecos—the part of Texas that juts out to the far west and contains the state's highest mountains and most spectacular river canyons. The Trans-Pecos, the Rio Grande gorges, the El Paso borderlands, and the mysterious Marfa lights all exist in this most desolate of regions, where in some counties there are fewer people than square miles.

DALLAS AND FORT WORTH

Dallasites used to call Fort Worth a cowtown, and Fort Worthians were frequently heard to say that their city is "where the West begins and Dallas is where the East peters out." Over the years, the rivalry has been replaced by a spirit of collaboration that has resulted in a commuter rail line connecting the two cities and a cooperative effort to market the region to international big business. The warming trend between the two cities has not, however, diminished their individuality. Dallas is a mix of bankers, boosters, cowboys, and glitz, and Fort Worth prides itself on being a rambunctious Old West town. Wealthy residents of both cities have financed world-class art museums and architecture.

EAST TEXAS

East Texas doesn't look like Texas at all to people who grew up watching Western movies. This part of Texas is lush and green with pine and oak trees, deep woodlands, even occasional swamps. More a part of the American Southeast than it is of the West, East Texas encompasses bayous, beaches, Baptists, bass fishing, and year-round barbecues.

HOUSTON AND GALVESTON

Houston, the state's largest city and the nation's fourth largest, is an international capital of commerce, technology, and oil. The city's superb museums exhibit treasures from the dawn of civilization to the present day, and draw from the many ethnicities—Spanish, Native American, Vietnamese, among many others—that comprise Houston's diverse cultural population. Galveston's large natural harbor has seen prosperity and ruin. Its colorful history of pirates and tycoons, oil magnates and hurricanes can be traced in the city's fine antebellum estates, recovered pirate treasures, and mammoth Seawall.

CENTRAL TEXAS

With its history of German and Czech settlement and liberal politics, and the academic and artistic bent of Austin, the state capital, Central Texas is the least stereotypically "Texan" part of Texas. The "heart of Texas" includes the state's most bucolic area—the Hill Country, to which tourists make pilgrimages in fall for the brilliant foliage and in spring for the wildflowers. Limestone bluffs are coursed by spring-fed streams; crowned with live oaks, junipers, and fragrant Texas mountain laurel; and riddled with caves that serve as summer nurseries for millions of bats. The winged creatures also hang out, so to speak, in Austin, which has over the years become a mecca for politicians, students, young musicians, and high-tech workers.

SOUTH TEXAS

South Texas is best known for its agriculture and Mexican heritage. In San Antonio, a Latino cultural capital, millions come annually to enjoy colorful festivals and stroll the River Walk, a redeveloped downtown area along the banks of the San Antonio River. White sand beaches rim the curve of the Gulf Coast from Houston all the way down to Brownsville at the southern tip of the state. Highways in southernmost Texas are lined by ranks of stately palm trees. The land is thick with vegetable fields and citrus orchards, and the skies are alive with hundreds of species of birds that flock here from north and south. South Texas upstream along the Rio Grande is the rough, arid Brush Country, set about with scrubby, thorny mesquite trees and cacti and looking like an extension of northern Mexico.

THE PANHANDLE AND NORTHERN TEXAS

The great expanse of the High Plains is the defining feature of the state's far northern landscape. Great crops of cotton are grown on the plains, but cattle raising is the chief industry and cowboy culture is the region's primary attraction. Lubbock is home to Texas Tech University, and Amarillo has livestock auctions and Stetson-wearing cowboys. Though the region lacks the greenery of East Texas and the spectacular mountains of West Texas, Palo Duro Canyon, which divides the South Plains and the North Plains, is considered by many Texans to be the most beautiful natural setting in Texas.

TEXAS FACTS

Nickname: The Lone Star State (because of the design of its flag)

Capital: Austin

State motto: Friendship

State flower: Bluebonnet

State tree: Pecan

State bird: Mockingbird

State fish: Guadalupe bass

State insect: Monarch butterfly

State plant: Prickly pear cactus

State reptile: Texas horned lizard

State song: "Texas, Our Texas"—lyrics by William J. Marsh and Glady Yoakum Wright, music by William J. Marsh (1929)

Entered Union: December 29, 1845 (the 28th state)

The state's name is the Spanish pronunciation of a Caddo Indian word meaning "friends" or "allies."

Counties: 254

Largest county: Brewster County (Trans-Pecos region; 6,193 square miles)

Smallest county: Rockwall County (North Central Texas; 148.6 square miles).

Miles of roads/highways: 300,000

Airports: 592 (including 27 commercial ones)

POPULATION

State: 21,518,555 (2002 estimate, State Demographer's Office)

Population density: 79.6 per square mile

Cities of 100,000 population or more: 24

Cities of 50,000 population or more: 50

Cities of 10,000 population or more: 210

Labor force: 10,325,000

Five Largest Cities by Population

Houston 1,980,950	Austin 678,198
Dallas 1,201,759	El Paso 573,787
San Antonio 1,182,840	

This map, compiled by Stephen F. Austin in 1837, depicts the Texas-Mexico border along the Nueces River well north of today's Rio Grande, identified on this map as the Rio Bravo.

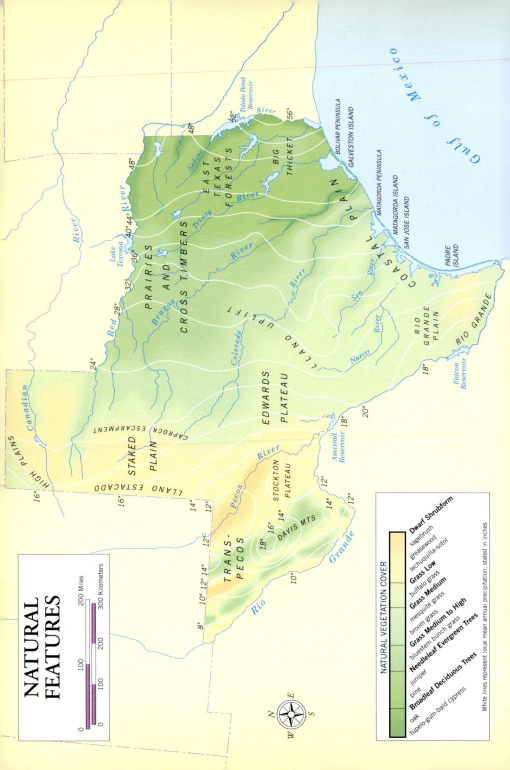

NATURAL FEATURES

200 Miles
300 Kilometers

Gulf of Mexico

BOLIVAR PENINSULA
GALVESTON ISLAND
MATAGORDA PENINSULA
MATAGORDA ISLAND
SAN JOSE ISLAND
PADRE ISLAND

Toledo Bend Reservoir
Sabine River
Trinity River
River
Brazos
Colorado
San River
Nueces
River
Red River
Canadian River
Lake Texoma
Pecos River
Rio Grande
Amistad Reservoir
Falcon Reservoir

EAST TEXAS FORESTS
BIG THICKET
COASTAL PLAIN
PRAIRIES AND CROSS TIMBERS
LLANO UPLIFT
EDWARDS PLATEAU
CAPROCK ESCARPMENT
STAKED PLAIN
LLANO ESTACADO
HIGH PLAINS
TRANS-PECOS
STOCKTON PLATEAU
DAVIS MTS
RIO GRANDE PLAIN
RIO GRANDE

52" 56"
48"
48"
44"
40"
36"
32"
28"
24"
16"
16"
14"
12"
12"
8" 10" 12" 14"
16" 18"
14"
12"
12"
14"
18"
20"
18"
18"

NATURAL VEGETATION COVER

Dwarf Shrubform
sagebrush
greasewood
lechuquilla-sotol

Grass Low
buffalo grass

Grass Medium
mesquite grass
broom grass

Grass Medium to High
bluestem bunch grass

Needleleaf Evergreen Trees
juniper
pine

Broadleaf Deciduous Trees
oak
tupelo-gum-bald cypress

White lines represent local mean annual precipitation, stated in inches

GEOGRAPHY AND CLIMATE

Area: 267,277 square miles
Land area: 261,914 square miles
Water area: 5,363 square miles
Rivers: 11,247 named streams; combined total length of 80,000 miles
Highest Point: Guadalupe Peak, 8,749 feet
Lowest Point: Gulf of Mexico coastline, sea level
Highest recorded temperature: 120° F, recorded at Seymour on
      August 12, 1936, and at Monahans on June 28, 1994
Lowest recorded temperature: –23° F, recorded at Tulia on February 12, 1899,
      and at Seminole on February 8, 1933
City with greatest normal precipitation: Orange, on the Gulf coast,
      with an average of 58.3 inches per year
City with least normal precipitation: El Paso, at the westernmost tip of Texas,
      with an average of 8.8 inches per year

INTERESTING FACTS

- Second-most populous state, behind California
- Second largest U.S. state, after Alaska
- Second-highest birth rate, behind Utah (17.3 births per 1,000 population)
- Population living in urban areas (2000 U.S. census): 84.8%
- Median age: 32.3 years
- Home ownership rate, 2000: 63.8%
- Gross state product, 2000: $771.7 billion
- First in the nation in number of farms (227,000) and land in farms
  (131 million acres)
- Public and private colleges and universities: 142, including the University of
  Texas at Austin, with more than 52,200 students; Texas A&M University,
  with more than 45,100 students; and Southern Methodist University, with
  nearly 11,000 students
- Texans over the age of 25 with a bachelor's degree or higher: 23.2%

A BRIEF HISTORY OF TEXAS

Texas is like the elephant the blind men examined. To the traveler who has seen its western extremes, Texas is mountainous desert. The passerby on the High Plains believes that Texas is very much like Kansas, a newly settled land of wheat fields. Pine trees, paper mills, and Confederate flags make East Texas look much like Mississippi, and on its southern boundaries, Texas seems to be a well-paved extension of northern Mexico.

The naturalist regards Texas as a diverse assemblage of desert, wetland, and plains ecosystems, separated by geological shifts and escarpments. To rock climbers, Texas is a place of desert handholds; for teenagers, it's a cluster of amusement and theme parks. For new-music lovers, Austin is the Emerald City, and to television viewers worldwide, Dallas is the home of oil barons and wives with big

Much of West Texas is arid desert.

hair. To space enthusiasts Houston is command central for the Space Shuttle; to scandalmongers it's the place that encourages economic perfidy on the scale of Enron, one of the biggest bankruptcies in history.

Hollywood depicts Texas as Cowboyland, New York writes that Texas is a redoubt of bigots and gun nuts, and Washington gives Texas the greeter's job when Congress is making overtures to Mexico. Because most Texans know only a part of our state, we shrug our shoulders and wonder what Texas really is. With so many vast regions and sometimes contradictory images, it can't be any other way. Consensus is never reached, even among those natives who are widely traveled and widely read. So we all simplify, generalize, and jump to our own conclusions, making Texas mean something a little bit different to each of us.

The task of defining Texas falls most heavily upon historians, yet many of the natural events and agricultural developments that shape Texans' lives occurred well before the arrival of Europeans here. Nobody watched Texas rise from an

West of Fort Worth on the Twin V Ranch.

The Texas oil boom started in the early 1900s.

uncharted spot of ocean floor, though that distant event was the basis of the state's role as an oil producer. Nor did anyone record the coming of the human species to the turf, nor the important centuries of agricultural experimentation that followed. Herbalists, hunters, agriculturists, and statesmen crossed and made use of this landscape. When Europeans—and recorded history—arrived, more than 50 small tribes were living in Texas, but they were rapidly decimated by the diseases introduced by explorers and colonists.

■ SPANISH COLONIAL ERA

In 1519, before the Spanish had even completed their conquest of Mexico, the explorer Alonso Alvarez de Pineda laid claim to what is now Texas. Given the eventual outcome of the interaction between the Europeans and the people they encountered here, the state's name is not without irony. Texas is a latter-day spelling of the Spanish colonial term *Tejas,* a transliteration of a word *(taysha)* used by some Indians from the East Texas Caddo civilization to mean "friend."

Spanish attempts to Christianize the native population were largely unsuccessful.

The Caddo were settled people, farmers and pottery-makers who had developed long-distance trade networks with other Indian groups. Today, however, no remnants of Texas's indigenous peoples remain inside its boundaries. Two of the three Indian tribes in Texas now recognized by the federal government—the Kickapoo and Alabama-Coushatta—immigrated to the region, as did the European population. The third tribe, the Tigua, converted to Christianity in New Mexico. They arrived in Texas with the Spanish, having been driven out of the Santa Fe area by their unconverted brethren in the Pueblo Revolt of 1680.

Spanish attempts to Christianize the Texas Indians and colonize the area were largely unsuccessful. The oldest Texas mission, at Ysleta in El Paso, was founded in 1681 for Tigua refugees. Scattered missions were begun in East, South, and Central Texas, but none achieved the goal of winning aboriginal souls for the Roman Catholic Church or creating productive, loyal Spanish citizens from the local residents. The mission inhabitants were sitting ducks for Apache and Comanche raiders; crops failed for lack of rain; and mission populations shriveled as the result of diseases. And there was little to encourage the Spaniards' efforts: in

Texas, unlike northern Mexico, explorers found no important lodes of gold or silver—nothing to inspire wholesale immigration or feverish industry.

By the end of the Spanish Colonial era there were few missions left. One that was to play a key role after Mexico achieved independence from Spain was San Antonio de Valero, established by Franciscan priests in 1718 in temporary buildings. After the mission was moved in the 1720s, the missionaries and their Indian converts built stone and adobe structures. The first permanent chapel they built collapsed in 1744. Work on another—a building later known as the Alamo—began in the 1750s, but it was never completed, and the mission's small Indian population quit the area because of repeated attacks by Apaches and allied tribes.

■ MEXICAN TEXAS

The Spanish lost what little control they had over Texas in 1821, the year their Mexican colonists liberated themselves. At the time, Mexico was too involved in its own intrigues to turn attention to its sparsely populated northern areas, including Texas. Had it not been for land hunger in the neighboring United States, the 19th century might have ended as innocuously for Texas as it began. But in 1819, in what became known as the Long Expedition—named for James Long, its leader, a doctor and merchant—American soldiers of fortune captured the Spanish settlement at Nacogdoches, in East Texas, and declared Texas independent. The uprising failed, but it heralded a movement that ultimately succeeded. Texas became a place where "Anglo" influences dominated.

Stephen Fuller Austin joined his father, Moses, in an 1821 project to bring colonists into Spanish Texas. Moses died before the project was launched, but Stephen persevered, and the first colonists arrived in December. Austin, now working with the Mexican government, successfully fulfilled his first contract to settle 300 families in Texas, then negotiated three additional contracts. These mostly American and British immigrants favored Anglo-American jurisprudence, Protestantism, decentralized government, and slavery—none of which the Spanish and Mexican leaders allowed. Some settlers were content with the Mexican government and others were opposed to extension of slavery. Because Mexico required all immigrants to be Roman Catholic, many converted to Catholicism to own land. The Mexican constitution of 1824 was in tune with the political idealism sweeping the continent—a belief that more egalitarian and democratic societies would take root to replace European corruption and authoritarianism.

Political turmoil was the only constant in Mexico City, however, and the constitutional principles were not necessarily upheld. The colonists became seriously alarmed when, in 1830, the Mexican government enacted a law that in essence banned further immigration from the United States, and made worrisome changes to the government of the state of Coahuila y Texas. Anglo colonists prepared a new constitution for Texas, which Stephen F. Austin took to Mexico City in 1833. Mexico's president, Antonio López de Santa Anna, approved it, but after treasonous words were found in one of Austin's intercepted letters, Santa Anna had him arrested. While Austin was imprisoned in Mexico City, Texans proceeded to implement their constitution, until in 1835 Santa Anna declared one-man rule, suspended the constitution of 1824, and made himself the dictator of Mexico.

■ THE TEXAS REVOLUTION

The colony rebelled, and Santa Anna set out from Mexico City to reconquer it. When he arrived in San Antonio in February 1836, he found about 150 Texas revolutionaries holed up in a former Spanish mission complex, San Antonio de Valero, the one now better known as the Alamo.

Santa Anna had doggedly driven his army—from 4,000 to 8,000 men, depending on which estimates you believe—through bitter winter weather to wipe out the nascent independence movement. In late February, he arrived in San Antonio and sent a messenger to the Alamo demanding the mission's surrender. The Texans answered with a cannon shot. Santa Anna ran up the red flag—no quarter, no surrender, no mercy—from atop San Fernando Cathedral and laid siege. As he waited and received reinforcements, couriers raced in and out of the Alamo past the Mexican forces, carrying appeals for help.

Small groups of volunteers had responded earlier to the Texans' pleas for assistance, including contingents from Mobile, Alabama, and from New Orleans. Also on the list of defenders were the Tennessean Davy Crockett; James Bowie, a former slave runner; and William Barret Travis, a South Carolinian who was lieutenant colonel of the rebels. On March 1, 32 riders from the town of Gonzales—the only reinforcements the men at the Alamo received after Santa Anna's arrival—joined the men inside.

The following day, as the Alamo defenders were desperately shoring up their makeshift fort, Texas revolutionary leaders signed the Texas Declaration of

TEXAS

FOREVER!!

The usurper of the South has failed in his efforts to enslave the freemen of Texas.

The wives and daughters of Texas will be saved from the brutality of Mexican soldiers.

Now is the time to emigrate to the Garden of America.

A free passage, and all found, is offered at New Orleans to all applicants. Every settler receives a location of

EIGHT HUNDRED ACRES OF LAND.

On the 23d of February, a force of 1000 Mexicans came in sight of San Antonio, and on the 25th Gen. St. Anna arrived at that place with 2500 more men, and demanded a surrender of the fort held by 150 Texians, and on the refusal, he attempted to storm the fort, twice, with his whole force, but was repelled with the loss of 500 men, and the Americans lost none. Many of his troops, the liberals of Zacatecas, are brought on to Texas in irons and are urged forward with the promise of the women and plunder of Texas.

The Texian forces were marching to relieve St. Antonio, March the 2d. The Government of Texas is supplied with plenty of arms, ammunition, provisions, &c. &c.

A poster in 1836 pleads for help to thwart the advance of Santa Anna's troops on San Antonio.

Independence in a convention at Washington-on-the-Brazos, creating the Republic of Texas. Three days later, Santa Anna ordered his army to attack the mission. It was beaten back. At dawn the following day, the Mexican general launched a second assault, this time reaching the walls of the mission itself. He was repulsed again. But the Mexicans had weakened the defenders and thinned their numbers. After several hours, the Mexican troops regrouped and assaulted yet again. The Texans fought from the walls and, after these were breached, fought at close quarters, hand to hand, until—as legend has it—they were all dead. (There is some indication that a half-dozen men surrendered and were immediately executed.)

Accounts of casualties vary. The most reliable estimate of the number of Mexican dead is about 600. Among the 30 or so Texan survivors—all noncombatants—were Susanna Dickinson, the wife of a killed officer, and her baby daughter; Travis's slave, Joe; and women and children from the surrounding town. Mexican troops escorted them to Gonzales.

■ BATTLE OF SAN JACINTO

After arriving at Gonzales on March 11 and hearing of the fall of the Alamo, Gen. Sam Houston realized that Santa Anna would be pursuing the remaining Texas forces. He and his citizen-soldiers, numbering fewer than 400, began retreating east toward Louisiana, urging settlers along the way to join them. The trickle swelled to a flood of panicked humanity, slogging through rain and cold and beset by disease. The retreat became known as the Runaway Scrape.

On April 16, 1836, Santa Anna crossed a bridge on Vince's Bayou with about 950 men. Three days later, Houston and his troops crept in, crossing the bayou and camping about a mile west of the bridge over which they expected their quarry to return. On April 20, they burned the bridge, cutting off any enemy retreat, and the next afternoon, with about 900 troops, they assaulted Santa Anna's camp.

Between the two camps stood a ravine whose brush screened the Texans from view until they came within 300 yards of the Mexican barricades. With cannon shot, the Texans breached the barricade—constructed of saddles, brush, and anything else that was handy—and charged into the Mexican ranks, shooting and shouting, "Remember the Alamo." In the fray that followed, Houston's horse was felled. He mounted another; it fell too. Though his ankle was shattered in the mishap, the Texas general mounted a third horse and continued his charge.

Henry Arthur McArdle's extensive historical research for his painting The Battle of San Jacinto *(1895) included interviews with participants.*

In 18 minutes, the Mexicans were defeated. Houston listed at least 650 Mexicans dead. The Texans lost nine men and 34 were wounded. Santa Anna was not to be found. The following day, however, a curly-haired Mexican prisoner in a private's uniform caught the Texans' attention because his fellow inmates treated him with deference—with some even calling him "El Presidente." The victorious Texans secured Santa Anna's signature on peace treaties. The wily general was returned to Mexico, where his colorful career included more stints as dictator punctuated by periods of exile.

■ THE RELUCTANT REPUBLIC

Modern Texans are prone to boast that their state was once a separate nation, but the Texans who achieved that distinction desired annexation to the United States, not nationhood. At the first election after independence, voters not only elected government officials, they also approved a resolution seeking admission to the Union. The U.S. Congress, loath to face Mexican retaliation, Texas's enormous debt, and the dilemma presented by acquisition of another slave-holding state, refused to approve annexation. Texas remained independent by default.

History and Culture Time Line

8000–7000 B.C. Burials from this era are the earliest so far discovered in Texas.

A.D. 1519 Spanish explorer Alonso Alvarez de Pineda is the first European to map the Texas coastline; he claims what is now Texas for Spain.

1521 Conquistador Hernán Cortés subdues the Aztec empire. Mexico, including Texas, becomes a part of the Spanish colonial empire.

1528 A crew of Spaniards is shipwrecked on the Texas coast. Led by Alvar Nuñez Cabeza de Vaca, they begin European exploration of the territory.

1681 Spaniards establish first permanent settlement at Ysleta (near El Paso).

1685 French explorer Rene-Robert Cavelier, Sieur de La Salle mistakenly lands on the Gulf Coast. The colony he sets up is abandoned by 1688 but inspires Spain to establish missions and colonies in what will become Texas.

1718 San Antonio de Valero mission—later known as the Alamo—is established.

1758 The mission of San Sabá de la Santa Cruz, near present-day Menard in West-Central Texas, is destroyed by Comanches.

1821 Mexico wins independence. Stephen F. Austin brings first Anglo-American colonists to Texas.

1830 The Mexican government passes a law stopping immigration into Texas from the United States except in special cases; relations between Anglo settlers and Mexico deteriorate rapidly.

1835 Texas Revolution begins at the Battle of Gonzales on October 2.

The Texas Rangers are formally created by Texas's provisional government.

1836 In the Battle of the Alamo, Americans hold off Gen. Antonio López de Santa Anna for 13 days before being annihilated.

Comanches kill settlers at Fort Parker and kidnap a child, Cynthia Ann Parker. She later marries a Comanche chief and gives birth to Quanah Parker, last great chief of the Comanches.

Sam Houston defeats General Santa Anna at the Battle of San Jacinto. Texas becomes a republic. Houston and Austin run for presidency; Houston wins. In the same election, voters approve a resolution to seek annexation to the United States. The U.S. Congress refuses to admit Texas.

1839 The capital is moved from Houston to Austin.

1845 Texas is admitted to the United States.

First cattle drives to northern markets begin.

1846 The Mexican War begins.

1848 Mexico cedes the American Southwest, including Texas, to the United States in the Treaty of Guadalupe Hidalgo, ending the Mexican War.

1853 Richard King buys 75,000 acres along Santa Gertrudis Creek, near present-day Kingsville, and begins to raise Texas longhorn cattle; the King Ranch eventually becomes the largest ranch in the continental United States.

1861 Texas joins the Confederate States of America.

1865 The Union reclaims Texas, and abolition of slavery is announced in Texas on June 19—two months after the Confederate surrender.

1866 The great cattle drives begin, ushering in the golden age of the Texas cowboy. The drives will continue through 1890.

1866 First producing oil well in Texas is drilled, in Nacogdoches County.

1871 The greatest number of cattle—700,000 head—is trailed to Kansas from Texas in a single year.

1874 The state government commissions Texas Rangers to patrol Texas borders.

1876 The first public institution of higher learning in the state—the Agricultural and Mechanical College, later called Texas A&M University—opens.

1881 Texas & Pacific Railway reaches Sierra Blanca in West Texas, about 90 miles east of El Paso, meeting the Southern Pacific line from the West Coast and completing a southern coast-to-coast rail route.

1885 The first Dr Pepper drink is concocted in Waco.

1894 First commercial oil field opens at Corsicana.

1900 A large hurricane destroys much of Galveston and kills 6,000 residents.

1901 Spindletop oil discovery near Beaumont launches state's first oil boom.

1910 The Mexican Revolution is declared by exiles in San Antonio. Twenty years of bloodshed ensue; refugees settle in Texas.

1929 League of United Latin American Citizens is founded in Corpus Christi.

1930 East Texas oil field begins producing, kicking off a second oil boom.

1930s Extreme drought, wind erosion, and huge dust storms plague the Panhandle and West Texas for the second half of the 1930s.

1947 An ammonium nitrate explosion devastates Texas City. Thousands are killed in the blasts, which are felt for miles.

1953 Dwight D. Eisenhower becomes the first Texas-born president of the United States.

1954 Texas women gain the right to serve on juries.

1958 Jack S. Kilby successfully tests the first integrated circuit at Texas Instruments in Dallas.

1963 Texan Vice President Lyndon B. Johnson becomes president when John F. Kennedy is assassinated in Dallas.

1969 On July 20, the first words spoken from the moon by astronaut Neil Armstrong are "Houston, Tranquility Base here. The Eagle has landed."

1973 After the Arab oil embargo is declared, a new oil boom begins.

Houston native Barbara Jordan becomes the first African-American woman from a Southern state to serve in Congress.

1988 George Herbert Walker Bush is elected 41st U.S. president.

1993 Ending a 52-day siege, federal agents storm the Branch Davidian compound near Waco, where the cult was reportedly storing assault weapons. The attack and ensuing fire kill four agents and 86 cult members.

1994 The North American Free Trade Agreement becomes effective, eliminating many commercial barriers among Canada, the United States, and Mexico.

2000 George W. Bush becomes 43rd president.

2001 The Houston energy-trading firm Enron suffers a financial collapse.

2003 Space Shuttle *Columbia* disintegrates on its return to Earth from a 16-day mission, killing all seven astronauts and raining debris across a large swath of eastern Texas and western Louisiana.

The nearly 10-year history of the Republic of Texas was marked mainly by factional fighting and escalating government debt. Most Texans were hugely relieved when, in December 1845, Texas was finally allowed to join the United States. The Republic of Texas and Mexico had never settled a boundary line, and as soon as Texas became a state, American troops put the issue to a test by crossing the Nueces River, the line Mexico honored, en route to the Rio Grande, the boundary claimed by Texas. The Mexican War ensued. Santa Anna once again led the Mexican troops, but in slightly less than two years, the United States emerged victorious. The Treaty of Guadalupe Hidalgo, signed in February 1848, secured

Antonio López de Santa Anna.

Texas's southern boundary at the Rio Grande. In that agreement, the United States also acquired a great part of the American Southwest: California, Arizona, and New Mexico, as well as portions of Utah, Nevada, and Colorado.

With the specter of Mexican invasion removed, land-hungry Americans began immigrating to Texas in droves. They were soon joined by families from Germany, Czechoslovakia, Poland, Norway, and other European countries. Between the census counts of 1850 and 1860, the population of Texas almost tripled, exploding from 212,592 to 604,215.

■ CIVIL WAR

Fewer than one in four families in the state owned slaves in 1861, when the Texas electorate voted to secede from the Union. The decision was controversial: Sam Houston—Father of the Republic and at the time the state's governor—opposed it, as did, presumably, the state's 182,000 slaves. Nonetheless, more than 77 percent of the voters approved secession.

Texas contributed about 90,000 men to the Confederate army, but two-thirds of these troops were deployed along the Texas frontier or elsewhere in the Southwest. The state experienced little fighting within its borders. Except for brief incursions into Galveston, Brownsville, and El Paso, and a blockade of Gulf ports, the Union forces were, for the most part, occupied elsewhere. Texas cotton growers evaded the blockade by transporting their crops across the Rio Grande to Mexico for export, earning money with which to import necessities and help support the Confederate cause.

Confederate forces surrendered at Appomattox on April 9, 1865, but the last battle of the Civil War was fought near Brownsville on May 13, because Texans had not yet received word that the war was over. Texas slaves had to wait even longer to learn they were free. On June 19, Union Gen. Gordon Granger, landing at Galveston, brought the first word that slaves had been emancipated, an event that is celebrated today as Juneteenth.

■ Cotton, Cattle, Railroads, and Oil

Owing to the burgeoning cotton and cattle trades, the Texas economy recovered more quickly from the Civil War than did other former Confederate states. In Northern Texas and East Texas, farmers planted more and more acres of cotton. Cattle drives to the railheads in Kansas and Missouri also began in earnest following the war, and although this era lasted only a couple of decades, the romanticized image of the cowboy—rugged and solitary, confronting natural and other obstacles—takes pride of place in the Texas mystique. Nineteenth-century cowboys are often portrayed as predominantly Anglo, but many Texas cowboys were Mexicans or African-Americans.

Railroad companies, only a minor presence in Texas before the Civil War, laid tracks all across the state after the war, lured by offers of free right of way and land bonuses. Those shining rails, coupled with quarantines instituted in some northern states against Texas cattle, which spread tick-borne "Texas fever," put the trail drivers out of business by the late 1880s. (In 21st-century Texas, cowboys constitute barely one percent of the population.) The railroads also brought Texas farmers closer to distant markets for cotton and other crops, beginning the shift from the small family farms to today's mechanized corporate megafarms.

By the time the open range had been fenced and railroads had displaced cattle drivers, Texas was entering its next major phase of development. On January 10,

1901, the Spindletop oil well came in big time—in its early days, its output gushed more than 100 feet in the air—and Texas was on its way to becoming the nation's principal supplier of oil. The discovery of "black gold," just as steam power was giving way to petroleum-based fuels, put Texas on the map, and the emergence of the automobile in the early part of the 20th century assured that oil, not ranching, would be the state's primary source of income. For the rest of the century, more ranchers remained solvent from the oil or gas wells on their properties than from the cattle running across them.

The next major Texas oil fields were discovered in the Panhandle in 1910 and in North-Central Texas in 1911, 1917, and 1919. The boom caused by one of these discoveries, the one in Burkburnett in 1919, inspired the 1940 movie *Boom Town,* starring Clark Gable, Spencer Tracy, Claudette Colbert, and Hedy Lamarr. The story of two buddies—oil wildcatters portrayed by Gable and Tracy—who stick together through the wealthy-one-day-busted-the-next cycle of an oil boom accurately portrays the atmosphere of an oil boomtown, and the problems kindled by the overnight population explosions, the feverish activity, and the risk-taking wheeler-dealers who thrived in that atmosphere.

The fever of exploration that followed these discoveries led to a succession of finds in the 1920s and 1930s. The largest field in the state, the East Texas field, was discovered in 1930. Soon, oil-drilling derricks were sprouting thick as bamboo (eventually all but 21 of Texas's 254 counties would produce some oil), resulting in overproduction and a drastic drop in the price of oil—which, in turn, prompted the Texas Legislature to enact a system of regulation.

The Mexican Civil War began in 1910, and almost immediately spilled across the border into Texas. Francisco Madero ran for president of Mexico that year, trying to unseat the 34-year dictator Porfirio Díaz, who arrested his challenger. Madero made bail and fled to exile in San Antonio. From there, he issued a call to arms to his countrymen. Other revolutionary leaders, fearing for their lives, also crossed the border. The trickle became a flood, as the leaders' supporters followed and set up communities in exile, from Brownsville to El Paso. Some of the more militant among them hatched a plan to set up a new nation for Mexican-Americans in the lands lost by Mexico as a result of the Texas Revolution and the Mexican War. Both revolutionaries and Mexican military troops came north across the border to raid for supplies, causing fear and resentment among residents in the area. Pancho Villa and his followers were prominent among the border raiders, prompting the U.S. government to send Gen. John J. Pershing to the Big Bend area, east of El Paso, to stop him. Despite Pershing's three-year efforts, using 50,000 troops, Villa remained at large. The revolution ended in 1920, but the psychological scars and ethnic enmity it created between Anglo and Mexican Texans have been slow to fade.

■ DEPRESSION AND REVIVAL

Texans tried to ignore the 1929 stock-market crash that began the Great Depression. The agrarian areas thought that stock-market problems were of concern only to those on Wall Street, and that they could get by raising their own food; Texans in the oil patch, meanwhile, were buoyed by the 1930 discovery of the huge East Texas oil field. Eventually, though, even Texans had to face bread lines, soup kitchens, and government aid programs.

The most visible legacy of the Depression was the work done by the Civilian Conservation Corps, which employed more than 2.5 million young men nationwide in improving park facilities and developing forest and soil conservation projects. Their architectural contributions can be seen in buildings in 31 state parks and several city and county parks.

In the 1930s, West Texas had to cope with not only the Great Depression, but also the Dust Bowl. In the previous decade, farmers had moved here in large numbers. They plowed up the native vegetation and planted mostly wheat; the resulting glut caused prices to drop. Unable to make a living, many abandoned their farms. When a severe drought came in the mid-1930s, the bare ground was rendered open to the winds that followed. Whipped into black blizzards, the fine, dry dirt penetrated everything, damaging eyes and lungs and ruining vehicle engines. It piled up like snowdrifts along fencerows and filled ditches. Seven times during 1935, the visibility in Amarillo declined to zero; one of the blackouts lasted 11 hours. In all, the Dust Bowl covered 100 million acres of West Texas, eastern New Mexico, the Oklahoma Panhandle, western Kansas, and eastern Colorado.

The population of Texas was largely rural until World War II. As the oil boom in East and West Texas settled down in the 1940s, factories that had made products for the war effort relocated to cities and began attracting increasing numbers of rural residents. Returning GIs saw more opportunities for jobs in cities than back home on farms and ranches. The population, which had been 55 percent rural in 1940, was almost 60 percent urban by 1950.

The signing of the Tidelands Bill by President Dwight D. Eisenhower in 1953, giving Texas the rights to its offshore oil, gave a boost to Texas's oil industry. Upon entry into the Union, Texas had won agreement from the federal government that its boundaries extended 3 marine leagues (10.35 miles) into the Gulf of Mexico from its low-tide line. There had been no disputes over these 2.4 million acres of submerged lands in the Gulf for close to a century—until oil leases hung in the balance in the mid-1940s. The resulting wrangling involved the Supreme Court, Congress, a couple of presidents, a former secretary of the interior, and a U.S. attorney general. To give you an idea of what was up for grabs: the state's portion of the receipts from oil and gas production in its tidelands through 2000 has added up to more than $3 billion.

■ INTO THE SPACE AGE

In late 1958, engineer Jack Kilby of Texas Instruments successfully tested the first integrated circuit in the company's Dallas plant, paving the way for a revolution in the electronics industry. This and subsequent research and development in electronics spurred a boom in high-tech operations, particularly in Austin and the northern Dallas suburbs. Space became the next step when the National Aeronautics and Space Administration opened the Manned Spacecraft Center, now the Lyndon B. Johnson Space Center, in Houston in 1962. This is where, since the time of the Apollo missions, astronauts have been trained and all manned space flights have been monitored.

In the mid-1960s, the Mexican government launched the Border Industrialization Program to attract foreign investment and increase job opportunities along its northern border. Private Mexican companies along the border were allowed to import parts duty-free if the parts were used to make products that were exported. Called *maquiladoras*, the factories sprang up along the border like mushrooms after a rain, using cheap Mexican labor to manufacture everything from computer disks to windshield wiper blades. By the late 1980s, Japanese companies had begun moving some of their factories to Mexico and building warehouses in Texas, New Mexico, Arizona, and California.

The entire world turned its shocked and horrified attention to Dallas on November 22, 1963, when Lee Harvey Oswald assassinated President John F. Kennedy during a motorcade. Texan Vice President Lyndon B. Johnson succeeded to the office, becoming the 36th U.S. president. Although the Warren

Commission thoroughly investigated the shooting and issued a report stating that Oswald acted alone, some people still insist that Kennedy's death was the result of a conspiracy.

The Arab oil embargo of 1973 began a period of violent ups and downs for the Texas oil industry. When oil was abundant, its price was so low that Texas producers couldn't afford to compete, depressing the oil industry. With the onset of the embargo in 1973, oil supplies were reduced. The price of a barrel of oil shot up and Texas oil producers got busy pumping. Then the federal government slapped a cap on oil prices, and drilling slacked off—until the Shah of Iran was deposed in 1979. Oil prices went up again, and all was

Jack Kilby of Texas Instruments.

rosy in the oil patch until early-1980s tax laws discouraged exploration and Arab and other producers cut their prices. In 2003, black clouds were still hanging over the oil patch.

One of the remedies sought by both Texas and Mexico for the oil bust was the adoption of the North American Free Trade Agreement, NAFTA, which went into effect in 1994. It promised to turn Mexico, not just the factory-rich border, into a giant workshop for goods to be sold in the United States and Canada. Primarily, NAFTA was crafted to chop away commercial barriers among the three countries, increasing trade, creating jobs, and raising incomes in all three. It also addressed problems of cross-border pollution, illegal immigration, and drugs. Implementing the agreement has been a slow and creaky process, however. The initial reaction in Texas was protest over jobs that might literally be "going south." A later major concern was safety, when Mexican trucks—which are not subject to the stringent inspection requirements faced by U.S. trucks—were allowed unfettered access to Texas highways.

POLITICAL PIONEERS

Texas women scored a number of political "firsts" during the 20th century. Two of the standouts were Oveta Culp Hobby and Barbara Jordan.

Barbara Jordan

One of seven children of a Texas legislator, Oveta Culp (1905–1995), a native of Killeen, Texas, became active in the Democratic Party as a young woman and married William Pettus Hobby, a newspaper publisher and former Texas governor. In the 1930s she was the president of the League of Women Voters of Texas, and by the onset of World War II, the couple owned the *Houston Post* and a radio station. During the war, Oveta Culp Hobby organized the Women's Army Air Corps, directing the training of women to take over many of the army's non-combat jobs so that more men could be released for duty in the front lines. After the war she returned to the Hobby media enterprises, which by this time included a TV station, but in 1953 she was summoned to Washington by President Dwight D. Eisenhower, who appointed her the first secretary of the Department of Health, Education, and Welfare.

Barbara Charline Jordan (1936–1996) was born in Houston. After graduating with a law degree from Boston University, she opened a law practice in Houston in 1960. She twice ran unsuccessfully for a state senate seat in the early 1960s, but in 1967 became Texas's first black state senator since 1883. In 1973, she became the first black woman from a Southern state to serve in Congress. As a member of the House Judiciary Committee, she participated in the 1974 Watergate hearings. Wrote the columnist Molly Ivins about those sessions, "Her great bass voice rolled forth. 'My faith in the Con-sti-tu-tion is whole, it is complete, it is to-tal.' She sounded like the Lord God Almighty, and her implacable legal logic caught the attention of the nation." Jordan delivered the keynote address at the 1976 Democratic National Convention, the first woman to do so. After three terms in Congress, she resigned in 1979 to accept a teaching position at the LBJ School of Public Affairs at the University of Texas at Austin.

■ CENTER OF ATTENTION

From the end of the Civil War until 1980, Texas had relied on agriculture and natural resources for survival. But since 1980, Texas, like the rest of the country, has undergone economic transformation, entering an epoch of de-industrialization. As the third millennium dawned, Texas, in concert with the rest of the United States, is reeling from the one-two punch of stock market plunges and the high-tech shakeout. Whatever happens to the economy, it is certain that Texas's population will continue to increase at a great rate: it was the second-fastest-growing state between 1990 and 2000, behind only California, with the Hispanic population growing faster than any other ethnic segment.

Texas once again became the center of world attention in 2000, when its governor, George W. Bush, became president after one of the most hotly contested elections in U.S. history. Though he received fewer popular votes than did his opponent, Albert Gore, he secured victory in the Electoral College after a debate over vote tallies in Florida that was ultimately settled by the U.S. Supreme Court. After attending Yale, Bush earned an MBA degree from Harvard Business School in 1975. He made a run at oil exploration while the bottom was falling out of the oil industry in the early 1980s, helped in his father's successful run in 1988 for the presidency, and then moved to Dallas. He bought into the Texas Rangers baseball team and became a managing general partner. Bush beat the popular incumbent, Ann Richards, to win the governorship of Texas in 1994, then handily won a second term in 1998. He stepped down in mid-1999 to run for president himself. During his presidency, Bush has headed home regularly to his ranch in Crawford, where he vacations and entertains world leaders.

In the first year of Bush's term, the financial house of cards that was the Enron energy company came tumbling down. A series of highly questionable paper transactions had made it appear for several years as though the corporation and its various holdings were reaping enormous profits. Although this was the case for some of the top officers—who sold their holdings while the stock flew high—Enron's creditors and shareholders, many of them Enron workers who had their life savings tied up in their employer's stock, were left holding the bag. Only in freewheeling Houston, wrote the business journalist Robert Bryce, could an energy scam of this magnitude have taken place.

Still more attention was focused the state in February 2003, when the space shuttle *Columbia,* 16 minutes away from a scheduled touchdown at Florida's Cape

George Herbert Walker Bush, Laura Bush, and George Walker Bush at an Austin event.

Canaveral, disintegrated in the air over North Texas, strewing debris over more than 20 Texas counties. All seven astronauts on board died. For several weeks after the disaster, Texans and volunteers from other states combed the woods on foot, horseback, and all-terrain vehicles and searched the waters of East Texas lakes looking for shuttle debris. After several months of investigation, the *Columbia* Accident Investigation Board concluded that the craft was damaged on takeoff by being hit by pieces of insulation material.

Politics, a contact sport in Texas, has thrust the state into the headlines for years and continues to do so. In the summer of 2003, Democrats in the Texas House decamped to Oklahoma for a week or so to keep the House from voting on a redistricting bill that would have favored Republican candidates. Soon thereafter, the Democratic senators took a sudden vacation to New Mexico for the same reason. Lyndon Johnson would have loved it.

THE BEGINNING OF THE END FOR ENRON

The collapse of the energy company Enron was one of the worst bankruptcies in American history. A series of shady deals made the company appear financially viable when it was anything but. Countless money managers—and their clients—were taken in by the scam, but from the start an old-line pro, Fayez Sarofim, "the king of Houston's moneymen," smelled something fishy about the dealings of Enron's chairman, Kenneth Lay, and chief executive officer, Jeffrey Skilling:

Endless possibilities.™

A billionaire himself, Sarofim hadn't become Houston's top money manager by embracing fads or the stock market flavor-of-the-week....And even though Sarofim knew Ken Lay from Houston's social scene and knew the Enron story as well as anyone, he didn't like the company....

The questions [from Sarofim's clients and staff] got particularly thick when Enron's stock was soaring during the late 1990s and early 2000. But Sarofim and his representatives always had the same answer: "We don't understand how they make money. And we don't buy anything we don't understand."

Ken Lay and Jeff Skilling may have been the princes of Houston's business community, but they hadn't passed Sarofim's smell test. And on April, 17, 2001, Sarofim's hunch was proven right.

During a conference call with analysts, Jeff Skilling, who'd been Enron's CEO for just two months, discussed the company's first quarter results. They appeared impressive....Then Richard Grubman [an analyst] got on the line....he wasn't buying Skilling's story...."You're the only financial institution that can't produce a balance sheet or a cash flow statement with their earnings" prior to conference calls, he said.

"Well, thank you very much," replied Skilling. "We appreciate that. Asshole."

Skilling's lackeys in the conference room chuckled at their boss's brazenness....a lot of Houston's old-money crowd...were shocked by the comment....They were also relieved that Sarofim hadn't invested their money in Enron....[Said] a member of one of Houston's oldest and wealthiest families... "That marked the beginning of the end."

—Robert Bryce, *Pipe Dreams: Greed, Ego, and the Death of Enron*, 2002

TEXAS MUSIC

For Texans, listening to music—be it the Tex-Mex conjunto of Santiago Jiménez's offspring, the whining honky-tonk of Lefty Frizzell, the rockabilly of lost legend Ronnie Dawson, or the metal band around the corner covering Lightnin' Hopkins— is as natural as breathing air. Genres blur, encompassing the Czech music of Frank Baca (who came to Texas from Moravia in 1860), the Western Swing of Bob Wills' Texas Playboys, the blues of Blind Lemon Jefferson, the enlightened, hip country-folk twang of Jimmie Dale Gilmore, and the techno-rap of MC 900 Foot Jesus.

So many small towns are the homes of someone you've heard of: Texarkana (Scott Joplin), Turkey (Bob Wills), Abbott (Willie Nelson), Linden (Aaron Thibeaux "T-Bone" Walker), Sherman (Buck Owens), Mansfield (Ella Mae Morse), Gilmer (Don Henley), Littlefield (Waylon Jennings), Saratoga (George Jones), Vernon (Jack Teagarden). The music might have matured in the big cities—Dallas, Houston, Fort Worth, Austin—but it was often born and suckled on the outskirts.

Though Austin is perhaps the Texas music city best known to outsiders, no one city takes all the credit—especially when you consider that Austin's best-known local heroes (Willie, Waylon, and Stevie Ray and Jimmie Vaughan) were all immigrants.

Dallas might well possess the state's richest musical heritage: it was here that Robert Johnson, considered the most influential of all 20th-century bluesmen, recorded. Blind Lemon Jefferson and T-Bone Walker, and later Freddie King and the Vaughan brothers defined at least two generations of blues artistry. Jimmie Rodgers and Bob Wills and Lefty Frizzell recorded here; rockabilly legend Gene "Be-Bop-A-Lula" Vincent set up shop. Benny Goodman's guitarist, Charlie Christian, the man who taught the world the importance of the electric guitar, was born in Dallas, and "The Big D Jamboree" lured Elvis Presley and Hank Williams to town in the 1950s. Steve Miller and Boz Scaggs had their first band here, the Marksmen, in the late 1950s; the Vaughan boys first heard the Nightcaps performing their song "Thunderbird" here.

In Dallas, 1960s rockers like the Chessmen, the Briks, the Floyd Dakil Combo, and the Five Americans ushered in Texas garage rock. Ron Chapman's *Sump'n Else* television show exposed teen audiences to Roky Erickson's psychedelia before it had a name. Marvin "Meat Loaf" Aday, Mike Nesmith of the Monkees, and Sam "The Sham" Samudio were born there; and much-heralded newcomers like New Bohemians, the Reverend Horton Heat, Bedhead, Little Jack Melody and His Young Turks, Funland, MC 900 Foot Jesus, and the Toadies honed their craft there.

There are veterans who say Dallas would have been Nashville had studio owner Jim Beck not suffocated on cleaning solution in his downtown Dallas studio in the 1950s; and perhaps it would have been a rock 'n' roll center in the 1960s had John Abdnor, who signed the Five Americans and the soul singer Bobby Patterson, not squandered his resources and efforts on his lunatic son John Jr., who scored a hit with "Do It Again—A Little Bit Slower" in the late 1960s, as part of Jon & Robin and the In Crowd, before landing in the state penitentiary a decade later for killing his girlfriend.

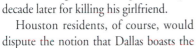

Blind Lemon Jefferson

Houston residents, of course, would dispute the notion that Dallas boasts the richest fruit of the vine, pointing to blues legends Lightnin' Hopkins and Willie Mae "Big Mama" Thornton (who wasn't born in Texas, though she began her recording career on Don Robey's Peacock label), singers Victoria Spivey (who spent time with Louis Armstrong) and Sippie Wallace, boogie-rockers ZZ Top, and modern-day country boys like Clint Black and Rodney Crowell. San Antonio folks will lay claim to Doug Sahm, and Flaco and Santiago Jiménez Jr.

Fort Worth has got country pioneer Tex Ritter, singer-songwriter T-Bone Burnett, and blue-eyed soul singer Delbert McClinton, made famous in the 1960s by the producer Maj. Bill Smith. Bobby Fuller, whose "I Fought the Law" influenced the Clash during punk's early days, was from El Paso; Janis Joplin hailed from Port Arthur.

There is no here-to-there in Texas music, no simple way to chart what sound began what style; it's all interchangeable. The Tex-Mex accordion, itself borrowed from German and Czech polka bands, creeps into the Lubbock-bred rock of Joe Ely, just as Elvis's appropriation of black R&B crept into Buddy Holly's brand of country in the early 1950s. To define the Lone Star sound is to define music itself; to chart its history, though, is to untangle knots never straightened.

—Robert Wilonsky

W E S T   T E X A S

The far western, or Trans-Pecos, region of Texas is the state's most mythical part, the place that most people think of as Texas: hot, dusty, gritty cowboy country, a region with more cattle than people, and with miles of low, rolling terrain broken by rocky outcrops and the state's highest mountains. This is the Texas of legendary trail drivers Charles Goodnight and Oliver Loving, whose true-life adventures driving cattle across western Texas and New Mexico shortly after the Civil War furnished Larry McMurtry with part of the plot of his novel *Lonesome Dove*.

Nearly all of West Texas is part of the Chihuahuan Desert, which also covers areas of southern New Mexico, a bit of southeastern Arizona, and a large swath of Mexico, extending almost to Mexico City. West Texas receives between 5 and 20 inches of rain per year—with the least amount falling on the region's far western section, and rainfall increasing to the east. Some parts of West Texas get more than that, but as an old local joke makes clear, the difference doesn't amount to much: "We had a good year last year, 22 inches of rain…but you should have been here on the day it fell!"

The dearth of rain dictates the vegetation: mainly super-sturdy creosote bush and mesquite, a scrubby survivor of a tree with a taproot that, like an iceberg, extends many times deeper under the surface than shows above. Water-hoarding prickly pear, hedgehog, and living rocks cacti keep them company, as do such succulents as lechuguilla, ocotillo, and yucca.

"Hardly anything grows higher than your waist," notes the Texas naturalist and writer Stephen Harrigan of the desert lowland. But though the terrain seems almost barren, appearances can be deceiving. More than 1,000 species of plants thrive in this arid terrain; many defend themselves from water-seeking wildlife by growing prickly thorns.

Wildlife is sparse, and a number of animals that call the desert home are creatures elsewhere unknown, like kangaroo rats, which never drink water—they eke out enough moisture from seeds—and whiptail lizards that clone themselves naturally. You'll also find poisonous snakes in West Texas, including five kinds of rattlesnakes and a copperhead.

Relief from the arid climate is only as far away as the nearby mountains, some of which reach 8,000 feet. At those elevations, the air is usually 20 degrees cooler than on the desert floor. Piñon, juniper, and oak trees grow liberally.

An ocotillo blossoms in spring near Big Bend.

This area developed as ranching country because of the lack of rain. Cotton farming, profitable in rainy East Texas, was not possible where less than 30 inches of rain fell. Only after 20th-century irrigation became available did farmers join cattle raisers in parts of West Texas.

The Trans-Pecos region is 30,000 square miles—about the size of South Carolina, or about three times the size of New Hampshire. Yet excluding the El Paso Metropolitan Area, which sits on its western edge, fewer than 56,000 people inhabit the region. While measuring the American West, the U.S. Census Bureau deemed an area "settled" when its population density exceeded six persons per square mile. By those terms, the Trans-Pecos is still frontier; indeed, four of its nine counties—Hudspeth, Culberson, Jeff Davis, and Terrell—have more square miles than people.

West Texas was settled late, in part because it was the turf of nomadic and sometimes combative Comanches and Apaches, who resisted white settlers as late as 1880. After the land was wrested from its native populations, West Texas developed as a domain of Anglos, though there was a significant Mexican minority. It was a region where economic leveling was a fact of life, because nobody with any real stake east of the 98th meridian could find much reason to brave the dust.

EARLY TEXAS IN LONESOME DOVE

Of course, real scouting skills were superfluous in a place as tame as Lonesome Dove, but Call still liked to get out at night, sniff the breeze and let the country talk. The country talked quiet; one human voice could drown it out, particularly if it was a voice as loud as Augustus McCrae's. Augustus was notorious all over Texas for the strength of his voice. On a still night he could be heard at least a mile, even if he was more or less whispering. Call did his best to get out of range of Augustus's voice so that he could relax and pay attention to other sounds. If nothing else, he might get a clue as to what weather was coming—not that there was much mystery about the weather around Lonesome Dove. If a man looked straight up at the stars he was apt to get dizzy, the night was so clear. Clouds were scarcer than cash money, and cash money was scarce enough.

—Larry McMurtry, *Lonesome Dove*, 1985

The discovery of oil in West Texas in the 1930s enabled some West Texans to acquire an education and a degree of sophistication unavailable to others. The result was an unusual cultural dichotomy, a contradiction between blue-collar roughness and white-tie elegance and erudition, sometimes within the same people. All these factors were reflected in the area's residents, who even today are considered open, egalitarian, and—because their ancestors fought hand-to-hand skirmishes with Indians—potentially fierce.

The great virtue of the Trans-Pecos is that people tired of the urban rat race can come here to get away from it all—and *really* get away. On highways other than I-10, which makes a beeline through the desert from San Antonio to El Paso, if you shut off your car engine, you hear absolutely nothing. No chirping birds, no rustling leaves, no growling motors. You almost don't need a rearview mirror. If you can't sleep in complete silence, or if you get nervous driving more than 60 miles without seeing at least a few other vehicles, this is not the place for you.

Where some might see desolation, however, others see a starkly dramatic, if not beautiful, setting. Traveling east from Presidio along FM 170 (Farm to Market Road 170), through tiny Redford to Lajitas on the western edge of Big Bend National Park, takes you along one of the prettiest drives in the state. For 50 miles, the pavement snakes, climbs, and dives. On one side of the road stand rocky canyon walls; on the other, steep banks fall down to the river.

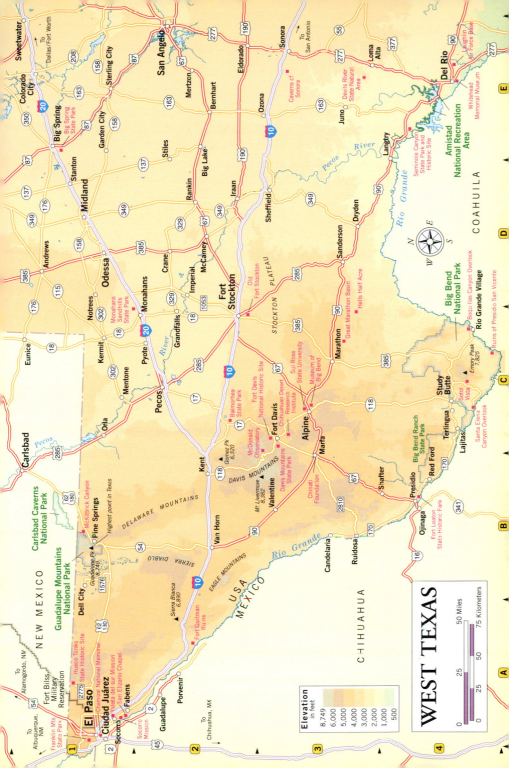

Most residents of the Trans-Pecos were born there and see no reason to leave. But a fair share of non-natives, both tourists and urban refugees, are scattered here and there, and more are arriving every week. Art galleries and crafts shops are popping up in towns like Fort Davis, Marfa, Marathon, and Alpine. Bed-and-breakfast inns, restored historic hotels, and adventure-tour outfitters have all set up shop in the Trans-Pecos.

■ EL PASO   *map page 45, A-1*

El Paso is the anchor of the Trans-Pecos and one of the more scenic cities in Texas. Nestled in a mountain range that also encloses Ciudad Juárez, its three-times-larger sibling across the border, and filled with stucco-facade homes and Santa Fe–style architecture, El Paso looks like a tourism poster for modern Mexico. In some ways, El Paso has more in common with Monterrey, Chihuahua, Hermosillo, and other Mexican cities than with U.S. towns to the north or east.

El Paso shares a certain quaintness with Mexican towns, though parts of the city reveal the impact of the border close by. El Paso's shopping malls, for instance, are

(above) Three historic Spanish-era churches can be found along El Paso's Mission Trail.
(following spread) Nestled in a beautiful mountain range, the city is one of the oldest in Texas.

gargantuan—three and four times the size they would be in a Midwestern city of the same population—because half or more of their customers come from the Mexican side of the border.

Despite its Spanish, Mexican, and borderlands influences, El Paso is in many ways thoroughly American, if not always like the rest of Texas. Much of the state, for instance, is obsessed with football, but in El Paso the emphasis is on basketball. No other town in Texas—not even Austin, home of the champion Lady Longhorns—cares for basketball as much as El Paso does. The city's economy also sets it apart from the rest of the state. El Paso is the home of mining operations, which aren't important elsewhere, and footwear and garment factories, which in earlier times tended to be located in East Texas.

El Paso lies at the intersection of I-10, which travels north-south through the city; U.S. 54, whose southern terminus is here; and U.S. 62/180, which travels west into the city from the New Mexico state line near Carlsbad. In many ways El Paso has more affinity with New Mexico than its own state. El Paso lies 324 miles south of Santa Fe, New Mexico's capital; Austin, the capital of Texas, is 573 miles east. A faction of El Pasoans has long advocated secession from Texas and attachment to New Mexico. Secession isn't popular west of the state line, though. Texans are regarded with slight contempt in New Mexico, probably because if El Paso were to join New Mexico, it would become the enlarged state's biggest city and biggest political bloc.

■ MISSION VALLEY AND THE MISSION TRAIL

El Paso is probably Texas's oldest existing settlement. Archaeological excavations have revealed the presence of a prehistoric Pueblo Indian settlement, but the first permanent community was founded in 1680, the year of the Pueblo Revolt in New Mexico. In that year, Spanish priests and Christianized native peoples, including the Tiguas (TEE-wahs) and Piros, fled to this area after being expelled by the Pueblo Indians. The Tiguas, themselves of Pueblo ancestry, came from Isleta, New Mexico, and with the Franciscans founded the Ysleta del Sur Mission in 1692. The sanctuary has known many names, the Spanish calling it Corpus Christi de la Isleta del Sur, the Tiguas naming it after their patron saint, San Antonio.

Under its several names, **Ysleta Mission** has known misfortune, including floods and fire. Although the current structure's basic size and shape resemble the original 1744 mission, Ysleta was reconstructed extensively in 1907 after fire

destroyed the nave, belfry, and transepts. The main part of the front facade is topped with a scalloped parapet, and a gleaming silver beehive dome caps the three-story tower, whose exterior is adorned with wood decorations. The entire interior, including all woodwork, was reconstructed in 1907, though the bell and a statue of Jesus were saved from the fire and placed in the rebuilt chapel. *131 South Zaragoza Road; 915-859-9848.*

Less than a mile from the mission you can learn more about the Tiguas at **Ysleta del Sur Pueblo Cultural Center,** also called the Tigua Cultural Center, which contains a tribal museum and a café that serves traditional Mexican and Tigua foods. There are crafts shops, and performances of tribal dances take place regularly. *305 Yaya Lane; 915-859-5287.*

Spanish missionaries established **Socorro Mission,** or Nuestra Señora del Socorro, 3 miles southeast of Ysleta to serve the Piros and other Indian refugees. Socorro, like Ysleta del Sur, was destroyed more than once by floods and rebuilt. The present building, erected in the early 1840s of adobe and covered with white-washed adobe plaster, turns a long, flat face to the street. A stepped parapet surmounts the central door, with the same style of parapet on the east and west ends of the wall, giving the effect of wings. The interior's outstanding feature, the ceiling, is made of saplings laid in a herringbone pattern with painted decoration. The ceiling is supported by painted beams, or vigas, salvaged from the 18th-century mission. *328 South Nevarez Road; 915-859-7718.*

The **San Elizario Chapel,** originally named Capilla de San Elceario, was the chapel for a Spanish presidio built in 1774 to protect the missions and travelers on the Camino Real—the Spanish Royal Road. The church, built 6 miles east of Socorro in 1789, became the geographical center of San Elizario, named for the same saint but spelled differently. The present building, a stucco-covered one-story adobe with a bell-tower on the front, was erected in 1877 to replace one destroyed by flood. The interior, whose noteworthy elements include the gilt-detail pillars and graceful arches, was remodeled in 1944, following a 1935 fire that destroyed the 19th-century vigas and woodwork. *1556 San Elizario Road; 915-851-2333.*

The **Mission Trail,** identified by blue signs, leads visitors to the three churches, all active parishes. The trail begins at Ysleta and extends 12 miles along the Rio Grande to Socorro and San Elizario, traversing neighborhoods that include restaurants, craft shops, and antiques stores. *Begins at Zaragoza exit off I-10, ending at FM 1110.*

Although it was reconstructed extensively in 1907 following a fire, Ysleta Mission's size and shape are roughly the same as the original 1744 mission.

■ DOWNTOWN AND NEARBY

The **Chamizal National Memorial,** a 55-acre park, commemorates the settlement of a long-running dispute. Following the Mexican War of 1848, the Rio Grande became the boundary between Mexico and Texas, but when the river flooded it often changed course, and land that had been part of one country would wind up in the other. The Ysleta and Socorro missions and San Elizario Chapel were among the sites affected. All were originally south of the river, but the shifting of the main channel put them first on one side and then the other. A 600-acre area called the Chamizal had changed nationality by 1873, and El Paso had absorbed and developed the tract as part of the city. Bickering over the Chamizal led to talks between Mexico and the United States to achieve a permanent settlement of the dispute. It was resolved in 1964, and a concrete channel was constructed to tame the river between El Paso and Juárez. The park, dedicated to fostering goodwill between the two nations, plays host to several annual events, including an international drama festival, a music concert series, and, each September 15, a Mexican Independence Day celebration. *800 South San Marcial Street; 915-532-7273.*

Magoffin Home State Historic Site is the 1875 adobe and wood-trim hacienda of Joseph Magoffin, cofounder of the first bank in El Paso and four-time mayor of the city (he was elected twice in the 1880s and twice in the 1890s). His home, on a quiet street 10 blocks east of downtown El Paso, surprises visitors who expect to see a Santa Fe–style structure with wooden vigas poking out below roof level. With its dark-green wooden shutters and handsome window and door pediments, the airy 20-room house resembles a Mediterranean villa. *1120 Magoffin Avenue; 915-533-5147.*

Downtown El Paso has other architectural treasures, including the **Camino Real El Paso.** Originally called the Hotel Paseo del Norte, this 359-room hotel was designed by the El Paso firm Trost and Trost in 1912. Lewis Comfort Tiffany created the magnificent stained-glass dome crowning the lobby bar. *101 South El Paso Street; 915-534-3000.*

Concordia Cemetery opened in 1856, and by the 1880s had become El Paso's main burial ground. The cemetery, which contains more than 65,000 graves, was originally divided into sections by ethnicity, religion, and status. One walled-off area holds the graves of 19th-century Chinese railroad workers, and "Boot Hill" was the final destination for bandits and gunslingers like the notorious John Wesley Hardin, interred here in 1895. *3800 Yandell Drive.*

To elevate your mood, visit **Franklin Mountains State Park,** whose 24,000-plus acres—including an entire Chihuahuan desert mountain range—are contained within El Paso's city limits. Among the largest urban parks in the nation, it is the habitat of mule deer, fox, an occasional cougar, hawks, golden eagles, and a variety of desert plants. It's a favorite destination for hikers, rock climbers and picnickers, though seed-grinding pits and rock paintings—some images are more than 10,000 years old—suggest that not all the park's guests came for recreational purposes. On a clear day, from certain points you can see across downtown El Paso and into Juárez. *1331 McKelligon Canyon Road (Canutillo/Trans-Mountain Exit from I-10); 915-566-6441.*

For a different perspective, head to the Franklin Mountains, where the gondolas of the **Wyler Aerial Tramway** climb to the top of 5,632-foot-high Ranger Peak. The view from the top is memorable enough, but the ride up is no less rewarding: the gondola's big windows permit unobstructed viewing of the breathtaking wilderness below. *1700 McKinley Avenue; 915-566-6622.*

■ FORT BLISS *map page 45, A-1*

Fort Bliss, east of the Franklin Mountains, gained notoriety in 1911, when Gen. John J. Pershing and 50,000 cavalry troops pursued Francisco (Pancho) Villa and his followers, who were raiding settlements on the Texas side of the Rio Grande for supplies. Pershing never caught Villa.

Today, the 1.1-million-acre fort, built in 1854, contains the U.S. Army Air Defense Artillery Center, where army personnel are put through their paces and learn how, among other tasks, to use guided missiles and anti-aircraft weapons. The center is not open to the public, but you can tour three museums near it. **Fort Bliss Replica Museum** (Pershing Road at Pleasonton Road; 915-568-4518) has exhibits of military artifacts from the 19th century in replicas of the adobe buildings that comprised an earlier military fort in the region. At the **U.S. Army Air Defense Museum** (Pleasonton Road, Building 1735; 915-568-5412), within the Fort Bliss Museum and Study Center, are indoor exhibits of civilian and military life. Outdoors, you can peruse an M-60 tank, rocket launchers, and other weapons. On display at the **Museum of the Noncommissioned Officer** (Staff Sgt. Sims Street at Barksdale Road; 915-568-8646) are uniforms and equipment dating back more than a century. To see the museums, obtain a day pass at the fort's Cassidy Gate entrance. *Off U.S. 54; 915-568-2121 or 915-568-4505.*

■ EAST AND SOUTH OF EL PASO

Two areas worth exploring east and south of El Paso are the Hueco Tanks and Guadalupe Mountains Parks, due east of the city off U.S. 62/180, and the towns, parks, and historic sites along or just off I-10 and U.S. 90. Interstate 10, the southern route out of El Paso, follows the Rio Grande southeast for about 50 miles before swinging east on its way to San Antonio and Houston. The interstate intersects with U.S. 90 at Van Horn, which can also be reached by heading south from the Guadalupe Mountains.

■ HUECO TANKS STATE HISTORIC SITE   *map page 45, A-1*

A short trip 32 miles east of El Paso along U.S. 62/180 transports you back 10,000 years in time. Hueco Tanks State Historic Site, an 860-acre park, shows evidence of having been used by nomadic tribes and cultures since humans first appeared in the region. The park's three massive granite hills, which rise about 450 feet above the desert floor, are pocked with hundreds of small hollows, or *huecos*, that collect rainwater. These water sources were important to prehistoric bison-hunters and Native American peoples such as the Apaches, Comanches, and Tiguas.

Some of the earliest visitors to the region left indelible marks behind them. More than 5,000 prehistoric drawings have been found on rock walls here, some of them depicting colorful masks. It's not exactly known when the images were drawn or by whom, but some archaeologists claim they are the work of the prehistoric Mogollon Jornada culture, which once thrived here.

Unusual among the desert-dwelling wildlife found here are tiny, translucent freshwater shrimp in rock basins; the park also is home to gray foxes, bobcats, golden eagles, and lizards. The park's interpretive center occupies a historic ranch house, and rangers lead birding trips and hiking tours. Rock climbing is an option. The best time for climbing is between October and May; in summer, rocks can become too hot to handle. *Hueco Tanks Road, off U.S. 62/180; 915-857-1135.*

■ GUADALUPE MOUNTAINS NATIONAL PARK   *map page 45, B-1*

The nearest town of any size east of Hueco Tanks is **Dell City,** 13 miles north of U.S. 62/180 on FM 1437. Spring and summer see the juxtaposition of two landscapes: cotton fields and mountains. The gold and purple backdrop is Guadalupe Mountains National Park, home to Guadalupe Peak and El Capitán.

> ## Two Takes on the West Texas Wind
>
> How could a frail, sensitive woman fight the wind? How oppose a wild, shouting voice that never let her know the peace of silence?—a resistless force that was at her all the day, a naked, unbodied wind—like a ghost more terrible because invisible—that wailed to her across waste places in the night, calling to her like a demon lover?
>
> —Dorothy Scarborough, *The Wind*, 1925
>
> ■ ■ ■
>
> ### Classic Joke:
> Out-of-state visitor to West Texan: "Does the wind always blow this way out here?"
> Texan: "Naw, sometimes it turns around and blows the other way."

At elevation 8,749 feet and 8,085 feet respectively, these are the highest and seventh-highest patches of land in Texas. Snowfall is common even in spring, and windsocks affixed to road signs alert motorists when high-wind conditions are occurring—springtime gusts can top 100 miles per hour. Camping is permitted, but there are few overnight or auto facilities. In winter, people come for the snow, in fall to see colorful foliage, and in spring and summer to glimpse the smooth red bark of the madrone tree, which grows wild nowhere else in the state.

Hikes into spectacular **McKittrick Canyon,** 7 miles east of the visitors center in Pine Springs, reveal a profusion of beautiful wildflowers from spring through fall: the brilliant oranges and reds of cardinal flower, butterflyweed, claret cup cactus, and Indian paintbrush; the bright white of Apache plume and blackfoot daisy; the pinky-purple of lion heart; and the many gold hues of prickly pear blossoms. Following the trail several miles—and up 2,000 feet—leads to McKittrick Ridge and untrammeled views of the canyon and environs. A word of advice for hikers: take water. These mountains appear green, but they stand above the driest climate in Texas. *Headquarters Visitor Center, Pine Springs, U.S. 62/180, 110 miles east of El Paso; 915-828-3251.*

■ **Van Horn and Valentine** *map page 45, B-2/3*
Fifty-three miles south of U.S. 62/180 on Route 54 lies the town of Van Horn, population 2,400—also reached via I-10 from El Paso, a distance of 120 miles. If you do travel on I-10 from El Paso, before you get to Van Horn you'll pass the

Hudspeth County seat, **Sierra Blanca,** named for the mountain range northwest of town. But most travelers heading from El Paso on I-10 don't stop until they reach Van Horn, which lies in a basin formed by the Sierra Diablo and the Van Horn and Apache Mountains. Silver and copper were mined extensively at the nearby Hazel Mine from the 1800s to the 1940s. Today's minerals run to sulfur, marble, and black gold, but Van Horn also does a booming tourist business, as it is only 55 miles from Guadalupe Mountains National Park and is the first sizable town between El Paso and Big Bend National Park.

The town's sights include the former **El Capitan Hotel** (100 East Broadway), a stellar 1930s example of Pueblo Revival architecture from Trost and Trost. The **Culberson County Historical Museum** (112 West Broadway; 915-283-8028), in the Clark Hotel, has memorabilia, antiques, and photographs belonging to the town's families, along with Indian artifacts and ranching and farming tools.

The route to Big Bend National Park leaves I-10 at Van Horn, following U.S. 90 to the southeast. U.S. 90 parallels the main historic rail route through the mountains of the Trans-Pecos. Calm reigns for most of the year in little Valentine, about 40 miles south of Van Horn on U.S. 90—the bells at the railroad crossing are the loudest thing you're likely to hear. But Valentine's postmistress has more work than she can handle the first two weeks in February, when romantics head to town seeking its postmark on their valentines.

■ **MARFA** *map page 45, B-3*

Valentine is often a pit stop for people making their way to Marfa, 35 miles southeast on U.S. 90. The wife of a railroad executive is said to have named Marfa after a heroine in Dostoevsky's *The Brothers Karamazov,* though not everybody thinks this is how the town earned its moniker. The filming of another book, Edna Ferber's *Giant,* brought Marfa its greatest notoriety. Location shooting took place here for the 1956 epic, which starred Rock Hudson, Elizabeth Taylor, and James Dean. The **Hotel Paisano** (207 North Highland Street; 866-729-3669), where the *Giant* crew and some of the cast lodged, has been a magnet for film buffs since the day the stars left town. Photos of Rock, Liz, and Jimmy adorn some of the walls, and the film plays several times a day in the *Giant* memorabilia room.

Marfa has a pop-culture connection, but it has a high-art one as well: the 340-acre **Chinati Foundation.** Occupying several buildings on the site of the former Fort D.A. Russell, Chinati was conceived in 1979 by the late sculptor Donald Judd as a repository for large-scale sculptural works. At first, the mix was limited to works by Judd, John Chamberlain, and Dan Flavin, but the collection has expanded over the years and now includes the output of art stars such as Claes Oldenburg and Coosje van Bruggen. *1 Cavalry Row, Fort D.A. Russell; 432-729-4362.*

The Chinati Foundation was established in 1979 by Donald Judd as a showcase for large-scale outdoor sculpture. Below are untitled works in concrete Judd created between 1980 and 1984.

To reach Chinati from the center of town, head south on U.S. 67 toward Presidio, turn right on Madrid Street and veer left. Go through the gates to Fort D.A. Russell and look for signs.

Dan Flavin's fluorescent-light installation may capture the eye at Chinati, but some of the light shows in Marfa have more natural—and mysterious—origins. One night in 1883, a young cowhand reported seeing flickering lights as he was driving cattle through Paisano Pass, about 14 miles east of Marfa. The **Marfa Lights** have excited curiosity and conjecture ever since. Sometimes moving around and sometimes static, sometimes appearing to split up and then come back together again, the lights, which have been observed by hundreds of people, are as eccentric as they are unexplainable. Of course many explanations have been offered. Some say it's just swamp gas, or moonlight shining on veins of mica, or atmospheric electricity. The most plausible explanation is that the lights are caused by a condition that causes light to bend so that it is seen from a distance but not up close. Whatever the cause, the lights have become something of an institution, and the Texas Department of Transportation has constructed a roadside parking area for viewers. *U.S. 90, 9 miles east of Marfa.*

■ FORT DAVIS NATIONAL HISTORIC SITE *map page 45, C-2*
North of Marfa on Route 17 is the Fort Davis National Historic Site, a former army post established in 1854 and named for Jefferson Davis, at the time President Franklin Pierce's secretary of war and later the president of the Confederate States of America. During its 37 years of operation, the fort was an outpost for troops battling Comanches and Apaches. Shortly before the onset of the Civil War, this is where Confederates experimented with substituting camels for horses. The experiments confirmed that camels were superior to horses or mules for desert duty. There was a down side, though: they smelled horrible and had the nasty habit of spitting on their handlers. Several of the fort's 25 restored buildings, furnished to the 1880s, are open for tours. *Route 118, 26 miles north of Alpine; 915-426-3224.*

In the early 20th century, the town of **Fort Davis** was a summer retreat for moneyed types looking for an escape from the muggy Gulf Coast. Breezes cooled the higher elevations, and the relative distance from the nearest large town guaranteed a get-away-from-it-all feeling. Throughout the 20th century, various entrepreneurs had attempted to turn Fort Davis into a tourist mecca, but most of the plans failed until 1961, when the Fort Davis National Historic Site was developed.

Nearly a dozen galleries and gift shops line the streets of this town of just more than 1,100 residents. Restaurant and café offerings range from pizza and barbecue to the burgundy-marinated roast beef and French silk pie served at the dining room in the historic **Limpia Hotel** (100 Main Street; 915-426-3237). Along State Street, the main drag, shops and restaurants stand alongside hotels and B&Bs. The street scene may not scream "Old West," but the **Old Texas Inn** (State Street; 915-426-3118), over the drug store and soda fountain, has the rustic look of pioneer days—though its six rooms have most of the modern conveniences travelers expect. And at least two destinations in town are sure to make you feel like you've stepped back in time.

The displays at the **Overland Trail Museum** (Fort and Third Streets; 915-426-3161)—guns, ranching and herding gear, archival photographs—illustrate the lives of people who tamed this territory. Meanwhile, at **Rattlers & Reptiles** (State Street North; 915-426-0129), just past the entrance to the fort, 20 live rattlesnakes and a dozen spiders, scorpions, and other creatures (all behind glass) give visitors a sense of just how wild these parts could be. If your historic explorations have worked up your thirst, **Blue Mountain Vineyards** (Route 166; 915-426-3763), 8 miles southwest of town off Route 17, is open for tours and tastings daily.

Nature buffs head to the **Chihuahuan Desert Research Institute,** 507 acres of desert plants and trails. Two hundred varieties of cacti can be seen in the Cactus Greenhouse, and there's an arboretum that holds 150 species of trees and shrubs indigenous to the Davis Mountain. Hikers can enjoy two developed trails that wind through the grounds, one of them a steep and rocky descent into a canyon (not for novices). Exhibits at the visitors center explain the flora and fauna of the area, and you can ask questions and pick up literature. *Route 118, 4 miles south of Fort Davis; 915-364-2499.*

A more vast display of nature unfolds at **Davis Mountains State Park.** As most of the range is at 5,000 feet and above—Mount Livermore, the highest peak and the state's fifth-tallest, tops out at 8, 378 feet—the climate is cool, and the high rainfall keeps things green almost year-round. Hiking, driving, or riding horseback are the best ways to experience the beauty and rigors of the mountains, and the 2,700-acre park provides ample opportunity for all three. Overnight accommodations are available at the 39-room Indian Lodge (Route 118; 915-426-3254), built in the 1930s by the Civilian Conservation Corps. *Park Road 3, off Route 118 North (take Route 17 north 1 mile from Fort Davis to Route 118 North); 915-426-3337.*

The importance of tradition and history to West Texas ranchers is nowhere more evident than at a site about 16 miles southwest of Fort Davis where ranching families have gathered each August for more than a century for the **Bloys Camp Meeting.** In the late 19th century, the region's ranches were so widely separated that families could not attend regular church services. Acting on a congregant's suggestion, William Benjamin Bloys, the Presbyterian minister in Fort Davis, organized a weeklong camp meeting, the first of which was held in a brush arbor and attended by 43 people. Attendance grew over the years, and facilities expanded, and today more than 3,000 fourth- and fifth-generation descendants of the original ranching families return annually. A permanent tabernacle that seats 1,885 has long since replaced the brush arbor.

■ MCDONALD OBSERVATORY *map page 45, B-2/3*
In the middle of a 30-mile highway that winds through the Davis Mountains sits the McDonald Observatory, 6,791 feet above sea level atop Mount Locke. The drive to the observatory winds through a setting dominated by pines and red-skinned madrone trees. The University of Texas, which operates the observatory, chose the site in 1939 because the night skies in the Davis Mountains area tend to be cloudless, and the high elevation keeps the telescopes above desert dust and interference from artificial lighting. On one Wednesday a month, the observatory's 107-inch telescope, which brings the moon seemingly close enough to touch, is open for public viewing. During the more frequent "Star Parties," held three nights a week, you can look through some of the observatory's other scopes—or your own—to view the heavens. *Route 118, 16 miles north of Fort Davis; 915-426-3640.*

■ ALPINE AREA *map page 45, C-3*
Most travelers breeze through Alpine—seat of Brewster, the state's largest county—and head straight south on Route 118 to Big Bend. But this town of 5,800 residents is a good place to pause: perhaps for a meal in one of the local restaurants or a stroll through the art galleries or other specialty shops. Texans and Texan wannabes are apt to linger, however, at Alpine's **Sul Ross State University** (East Highway 90, Alpine; 915-837-8011), named after Lawrence Sullivan Ross, the governor of Texas from 1891 to 1898. Despite an enrollment of only 2,000 students, the school hosts cowboy-poetry gatherings and has an agriculture program—specializing in ranching, of course—and a rodeo team.

Telescopes at McDonald Observatory have been scanning the heavens since 1939.

Rock collectors, meanwhile, seek out the 3,000-acre **Woodward Agate Ranch,** one of the few places in the world where red-plume and pom-pom agate, opal, labradorite feldspar, and other semi-precious gemstones can be dug from the earth (the ranch charges for finds by their weight). The Woodward ranch has RV sites, a campground, and a large spread filled with oak trees, a stream, and paths on which to hike, roam, or bicycle. *Route 118, 16 miles south of Alpine; 915-364-2271.*

■ BIG BEND NATIONAL PARK *map page 45, C-4*

The wild beauty within Big Bend National Park ranges from bare-rock desert mountain peaks to verdant riversides, from wide-angle dramatic vistas to the close-up splendor of delicate cactus blossoms.

Big Bend dates from 1944, when the federal government accumulated public land parcels and smaller tracts donated by Texans for the purpose of creating a national park. The name comes from its setting at the toe of a 100-mile-long dip in the Rio Grande, where it departs from its southeasterly course to run north-east. The park's nearly virgin wild land covers 801,000 acres—an area a bit larger

Big Bend may look desolate, but more than 1,100 plant species thrive here.

than the state of Rhode Island—and parts of it, like 7,825-foot-high Emory Peak, are nearly perpendicular. In the Chisos Mountains, a roughly circular mountain range contained within the park, it's not uncommon to see javelinas (ha-vay-LEE-nas)—stubby porcines with fierce tusks—coyotes, mules, whitetail deer, jackrabbits, skunks, raccoons, and even black bears.

The mountains and the valley greenery here provide rich birding country. More than 400 species of fowl are known to inhabit this region, from small desert wrens to golden eagles, from Crissal thrashers and Lucifer hummingbirds to band-tailed pigeons and Colima warblers. The bird most often seen, however, is the paisano, or roadrunner, a feisty creature that can reach land speeds of 20 miles per hour, fueled on moisture it extracts from lizards and snakes.

Botanists estimate that 1,100 plant species grow in Big Bend National Park, mostly on the desert floor, including creosote, a dozen varieties of cacti, and ceniza—a bush that grows to five feet, with gray perennial leaves and purple flowers that blossom when it rains, giving it the popular name of "barometer bush." At higher altitudes grow ponderosa pines, junipers, summer and fall wildflowers, and even aspen.

Entrances to Big Bend are in Alpine on the west and Marathon on the east. The Chisos Mountains Lodge (915-477-2291), a motel, sits in Chisos Basin, below **Casa Grande,** an imposing stack of rocks 7,325 feet high. Rooms at the motel have sunset views through a pass in the mountains, appropriately known as the Window. Chisos Basin is 10 miles from park headquarters. From there, it's 34 miles through fairly rough terrain to the Rio Grande at Boquillas Canyon Overlook—where, on the Mexican side, the river has cut the rocks into a high cliff. Across the river is the village of Boquillas del Carmen. *Big Bend National Park information: 915-477-2251.*

■ THREE TOWNS BACK FROM THE DEAD *map page 45, C-4*
Study Butte, Terlingua, and **Lajitas,** on the western edge of Big Bend National Park, are three towns that have come back from the dead. Study (pronounced STOO-dee) Butte and Terlingua were founded in the late 1800s as outposts for Mexican laborers who worked the area's mercury mines. Lajitas, a small Mexican and Indian community, was put on the map in 1916, when the troops of Gen. John J. Pershing's cavalry established a post there to protect the area from Pancho Villa's raids. By the end of World War II, however, the mines had gone bust and the communities had suddenly ceased to exist.

Two disparate events helped revive the three towns. In 1967, a group of Dallas buddies, egged on by the late *Dallas Morning News* columnist Frank X. Tolbert, invited their cronies to a chili cook-off on a remote piece of land owned by one of them. The contestants had so much fun cooking up spicy concoctions in large cast-iron pots, drinking beer, and generally being silly that they decided to turn this Texas Woodstock into an annual affair. The cook-offs received so much publicity that tourists began seeking out the nearest town, Terlingua, between contests, with the result that it and its neighbors began to sputter back to life.

An even bigger boost came in the late 1970s, when the Houston developer Walter M. Mischer began developing Lajitas, turning it into a resort community with motels, restaurants, a golf course, an RV park, a church, and an airstrip. By the mid-1980s, Lajitas had made a complete economic recovery, and its commercial success began to spill over into Terlingua and Study Butte. Terlingua is now the site for two annual chili cook-offs, and the three towns are the starting points for horseback tours, backcountry jeep excursions, and canoe and rafting tours of Rio Grande caverns.

(following pages) Lajitas was a ghost town until a developer turned it into a resort.

■ **BIG BEND RANCH STATE PARK** *map page 45, B-4*

Sprawling across more than 280,000 acres of Chihuahuan Desert wilderness to the west of Big Bend National Park is Big Bend Ranch State Park, an immense natural treasure containing defunct volcanoes, waterfalls, two mountain ranges, and rare birds, plants, and animals, including many species of bats. In general, West Texas is beloved by chiroptera for its rocky, crevice-riddled terrain, and big bats, like the Western Mastiff (with a 2-foot wing span), are not uncommon here.

Rock paintings depicting animals and human-like figures can be seen on the walls of some of the caves here, and others show unusual scribblings thought to be early attempts at written language. Vehicular access to the park is limited, and the activities here—hiking and rock climbing—are for the fit and adventurous. Access from the west is through **Fort Leaton State Historic Site** (FM 170; 915-229-3613), 4 miles east of Presidio. (Ben Leaton, the farmer who built the fort, was so wary of Indian raids that he made the walls 18 inches thick.) Access from the east is through **Barton Warnock Environmental Education Center** (1 mile east of Lajitas on FM 170; 915-424-3327), which has geological and biological exhibits. *Big Bend Ranch State Park; 915-229-3416.*

■ **MARATHON** *map page 45, C-3*

U.S. 385 leads north from Big Bend National Park through Marathon near the junction with U.S. 90. A ranching town, Marathon is the former stomping grounds of Alfred Gage, who arrived in 1878 and eventually accumulated 500,000 acres. He also accumulated a lot of money from ranching, banking, and other enterprises. By 1927, he was so wealthy he hired Trost and Trost to design the **Gage Hotel** (102 West Highway 90; 915-386-4205). Legend has it that Gage built it so he would have somewhere to stay when he visited town. He died a year after the hotel was built, so if the tale is true, he didn't get much use out of the place. The 17 period rooms bring the 1920s to life—as do the limited bathrooms: only eight of the guestrooms have them. Rooms in the luxurious 1992 addition, called Los Portales, have plumbing.

Downtown Marathon, not big but full of spirit, has crafts shops, restaurants, and a surprising number of art galleries. James Evans has been photographing the Big Bend area for two decades, and his **Evans Gallery** (21 South First Street; 915-386-4366), across the street from the Gage Hotel, is filled with beautiful images of the natural wonders to be found in Marathon and its environs.

■ **FORT STOCKTON AREA** *map page 45, C-2*

Controversy between commerce and ecology has been brewing for 40 years in **Fort Stockton,** about 60 miles southeast of Pecos on U.S. 285. Fort Stockton's pride and joy, **Comanche Springs,** has gone dry. Indians used the site for centuries before Comanches arrived, and the Spanish explorer Cabeza de Vaca probably drank from the spring in 1534. In the 19th century, this was where the San Antonio–El Paso Trail crossed the Comanche War Trail, and in 1859 the U.S. Army established the fort here to safeguard the San Antonio–San Diego mail route. Confederate troops grabbed it in 1861, but abandoned it a year later.

Old Fort Stockton, in the historic downtown section of the town, became home to the Ninth Cavalry, an African-American regiment that Indians called Buffalo Soldiers. They arrived in the summer of 1867 and set about rebuilding the fort. They marched away for good in 1886. Old Fort Stockton comprises original and reconstructed fort structures and a museum with artifacts from the period. *Williams Street between Fourth and Fifth Streets.*

Even before the fort closed, farmers had begun irrigating their crops with the gushing waters of Comanche Springs, and later a fledgling tourist industry and expanding population drew on this source. Heavy pumping of the Edwards Aquifer after 1947 gradually choked off the water supply. By 1961 the springs had dried up.

The all African-American 25th Infantry, photographed in 1883. As did the Ninth Cavalry, stationed at Fort Stockton, the 25th fought in the Indian Wars of the late-19th century.

Judge Roy Bean holds court on the porch of the "Hall of Justice," a saloon in Langtry, in this 1900 photo.

Water may be scarce in Fort Stockton, but there's plenty of it at **Balmorhea State Park,** 54 miles west of town, where recreational activities include swimming and scuba diving in a 77,000-square-foot concrete swimming pool fed by San Solomon Springs. *Route 17 off I-10; 915-375-2370.*

■ DETOUR TO IRAAN AND LANGTRY *map page 45, D-2/4*

East about 62 miles of Fort Stockton off I-10, at the junction of U.S. 190 and Route 349, is the town of Iraan, population 1,200. Iraan, where low, rolling, and mostly bare hills slope down to a green landscape along the Pecos River, was established after oil was discovered on the Ira G. Yates Ranch nearby in 1926; the town was named for the ranch owners, Ira and his wife, Ann. Iraan was the home of V.T. Hamlin, the newspaperman who created the cartoon strip *Alley Oop*—named for its title character, a time-traveling caveman who was a favorite, along with his girlfriend, Ooola, and the dinosaur Dinny, of American children in the 1930s and 1940s.

Langtry, a dot of a town on U.S. 90, 118 miles south of Iraan—take Route 349 to U.S. 90 east (from Marathon head east 105 miles on U.S. 90)—owes its existence to the colorful Judge Roy Bean (1825–1903). In 1882, Bean set up a saloon in a tent in the area to serve refreshments to workers laying railroad tracks on the

Sunset route of the Southern Pacific, on its way west to El Paso. The nearest county seat at the time was Fort Stockton, 153 miles away. A Texas Ranger suggested to Bean that he might want to be appointed justice of the peace in order to bring some semblance of law and order to the Trans-Pecos. Bean applied justice creatively. He is said to have fined a corpse $40 for carrying a concealed weapon, and while hearing the case of a man charged with killing a Chinese railway worker, reportedly released the accused on grounds that he could find no law against killing an Asian. His notoriety spread nationwide in 1896, when he staged the heavyweight championship fight between Bob Fitzsimmons and Peter Maher on a sandbar in the Rio Grande after officials in Texas, New Mexico, Arizona, and the Mexican state of Coahuila had banned the boxing match.

Records belonging to Southern Pacific Railroad state that the town was named for the railroad engineer George Langtry, but Bean claimed that he named both town and his Jersey Lilly Saloon for Lillie Langtry, known as the "Jersey Lily"—a British actress whom he admired but never met.

Bean sometimes held court in the tavern, fining defendants a round of drinks for the house. The judge, who died of natural causes, is buried at Del Rio, about 55 miles south on U.S. 90. The **Judge Roy Bean Visitor Center** provides literature about the town and its celebrity jurist, and oversees the Jersey Lilly from a building in front of the saloon. If you stop here, ask for an official map, which shows FM roads and has topographical features and population figures. *U.S. 90, West Loop 25 at Torres Avenue; 915-291-3340.*

The 2,000-plus acres of **Seminole Canyon State Park and Historic Site** reveal aspects of life in Texas past and present. Rock paintings on the walls of shelters—some of them 5,000 years old—depict what appear to be animal and human figures. Guided tours are conducted twice daily from Wednesday through Sunday in the Fate Bell Shelter. The clues to more recent Texas history include the grade leading to the original Pecos High Bridge—for many years the highest railroad bridge in North America and the third-highest in the world. Built in 1892, the bridge, whose towers suspended rail tracks 321 feet above the Rio Grande, shortened the rail distance between San Antonio and El Paso by 11 miles. A bridge nearby replaced it in 1943, but the vertiginous grade leading to the earlier span has left a permanent mark on the land, a reminder of the determination of the railroad barons to go where nature did not intend man to go. *U.S. 90, 22 miles southeast of Langtry; 915-292-4464.*

■ PECOS *map page 45, C-2*

The junction of I-10 with Route 118—the road that links the McDonald Observatory to U.S. 90—is about 10 miles west of the terminus of I-20, which leads east through Dallas to Shreveport. From the I-20 split it's about 50 miles (80 km) to the Pecos River, where the region begins.

The Pecos area, which straddles the riverbanks, is known for the succulent cantaloupe that grows there, and for being the launching pad for Billy Sol Estes, a cotton merchant who turned to crime in the 1960s (with a little help from LBJ, so it's been said). The city was established when the Texas & Pacific Railway put a stop there in 1881, back in the wild frontier days.

For a glimpse of this era, stop by the **West of the Pecos Museum** (120 East First Street; 915-445-5076) in the old Orient Hotel. The museum, on three floors, re-creates the feeling of the rugged West with period rooms and displays of saddles, guns, and clothing. Out back are horse-drawn buggies and wagons as well as the grave of gunfighter Clay Allison. If you visit in July, you can attend the **West of the Pecos Rodeo**, a century-old tradition and a fine place to see classic rodeo events and a wild cow-milking contest.

■ EAST OF THE PECOS: WEST-CENTRAL TEXAS
map page 76

West Texas east of the Pecos cannot easily be separated by geographic features from other parts of the state, but the designation seems to carry a certain authority by way of tradition. Ranching, cattle, cotton, and oil are still the mainstays of the economy in this region; were it not for deer and dove hunters, West—and especially West-Central—Texas would have little tourism. Trendy boutiques, hotels, and cafés are not as plentiful as in neighboring Central Texas, and that's probably because, to the extent that modernity allows, West-Central Texas is still frontier Texas. Throughout its vast mesquite-laden landscape, the struggle for survival here is evident everywhere. Coyotes, rattlesnakes, hawks, buzzards, deer, jackrabbits, rabbits, and a million other desperate-looking creatures compete for life in a dry terrain, as does the Texas horned lizard, better known as the horned toad.

The Pecos River courses through rough terrain that is inhospitable to all but the hardiest of plants and animals.

High Bridge soars over the Pecos River in this photograph from the late 19th century.

The first settlement along I-20 east of the Pecos that can be seen without aid of a magnifying glass is Monahans—best known in these parts for nearby **Monahans Sandhills State Park,** with 3,800 acres of Saharan-like sand dunes, some as high as 70 feet high. These dunes are a small part of a much larger chain of sand dunes stretching 200 miles into New Mexico. It's so quiet out here that the only sound you're likely to hear is the whisper of sand drifting across the dunes when the wind kicks up.

For thousands of years, this landscape was uninhabitable for all but the toughest animals—coyotes mostly—and although acorns and beans do sprout here, the overall lack of nourishing edibles meant few human souls could survive here for any length of time. All of this changed in the 1880s, when the Texas and Pacific Railroad put a stop here, and again in the 1920s, when the oil industry set up shop in Monahans, luring people and commerce.

You can still get away from it all in Sandhills State Park, though, which is rarely crowded and can be as eerily quiet as it is beautiful. Photographers love it here, especially at sunset, when the fading light plays tricks of color with the sand. *I-20, Exit 86; 915-943-2092.*

■ OIL COUNTRY *map page 45, C-1*

East of Monahans, the Permian Basin begins, a wide and low spot on the map—250 miles wide and 300 miles long—whose landscape could never be called breathtaking. Its austerity is reflected in the name of a small town a few miles west of Odessa, the aptly named **Notrees.** Locals insist that the landscape has a scenic aspect, but that's only if you like oil rigs. In this part of the state, pump jacks—those rocking horse–like contraptions that pump oil out of the ground after the derricks have drilled the wells—take the place of trees, and they are often the

OIL BOOMS AND BUSTS

In the oil industry's early days in Texas, booms were created by the discovery of oil, or even a rumor that oil might be found, in a particular location. Busts were brought on once speculators had poured too much money into too many dry holes. These days, booms and busts are triggered by different stimuli. Today, if the Middle East sneezes, Texas oilmen catch cold. If Washington changes the rules on production and pricing of oil, the domestic oil and gas industry takes to bed with a bad case of pneumonia.

Take the Arab oil embargo of 1973, for example: Oil was selling at prices below $5 a barrel before the embargo, and Texas oil cost too much to produce to bother bringing it out of the ground. The embargo pushed the price of Arabian crude up to around $17. Even with federal oil-price controls in place, Texas producers dusted off their drilling rigs and went hunting for oil. The increase in activity faltered a bit in 1976, when Washington clapped new price lids on oil, but it picked up again in 1978, when the government of the Shah of Iran fell. The price of crude went as high as $34 a barrel, and Texas oilmen scampered into the oil patch like jackrabbits. The Texas rig count—the number of rotary rigs actively drilling—blossomed from 770 in 1979 to an all-time high of 1,317 in 1981.

Then Congress passed the so-called Windfall Profits Tax in 1980 and the Economic Recovery Tax Act of 1981, and money for exploration vanished. OPEC cut its price in early 1983, and the price of domestic crude plunged to $7 by 1986. The rig count fell to 311. By May 1999, only 200 rigs were working. The number didn't go above about 350 until early 2003, when talk of war with Iraq pushed the count up to 400. And so it goes. For big-stakes gambling, Texas doesn't need casinos. From the time Spindletop spouted its first barrel, the oil business has been the biggest gamble around.

tallest things on the horizon. The Permian Basin, named for the geological formation in which oil was formed during the Permian era 240 million years ago, has for more than 60 years been the heart of the inland Texas oil industry. It has also, for obvious reasons, been the focus of higher education in Texas. Thanks to oil royalty interests from former state lands in the Permian Basin, the University of Texas is among the nation's most richly endowed educational institutions.

■ **MIDLAND AND ODESSA** *map page 45, D-1*
Midland and Odessa, the Permian Basin's oil cities, are almost the same size (populations about 90,000) and only 20 miles apart. But similarities between the two end there. Midland, the birthplace of First Lady Laura Bush, is an administrative town of skyscrapers that until the 1940s had no wells, even though 150 oil companies had headquarters there. Odessa's population quadrupled to about 10,000 between 1930 and 1940, the decade following the discovery of Permian oil in 1923, and tripled between 1940 and 1950.

A massive dust storm bears down on Midland during the drought year of 1911. The scene was repeated frequently during the Dust Bowl years of the mid-1930s.

A friendly rivalry exists between Odessa and Midland. Odessa is the site of the University of Texas, much to Midland's chagrin. The college has built a replica of Shakespeare's Globe Theatre and sponsors an annual drama festival. But if Odessa wins the prize for attractions financed by the state, Midland has the lion's share of privately financed institutions, including places like the **Petroleum Museum** (1500 I-20 West, Exit 136; 915-683-4403), which documents the history of the Permian Basin oil industry. Oil money also made possible Midland's **Museum of the Southwest** (1705 West Missouri; 915-683-2882), a small but comprehensive showcase for art and science, with a children's museum and a planetarium.

■ **BIG SPRING** *map page 45, D/E-1*
Once out of Odessa and Midland, the flat farmlands become interspersed with rocky terrain. Big Spring, 40 miles east of Midland on I-20, is an agricultural town so named because of a large watering hole that for time immemorial has quenched the thirst of bison, mustangs, antelope, and other wildlife, and provided refreshment for drivers on the Overland Trail on their way to California. Big Spring itself sits in a rocky gorge between two high foothills of the Caprock escarpment, a cliff that gradually rises in elevation as it travels for a hundred miles in a northeasterly direction.

On one of those foothills is **Big Spring State Park,** a dream destination for botanists and lovers of wildlife. Where else can you go to see 100 different types of cacti growing amid hopping jackrabbits and quickly moving roadrunners? The butterfly population, another of the park's wonders, attracts red admirals and many varieties of metalmarks. *I-20, 36 miles east of Midland; 915-263-4931.*

The northern limit of West Texas is in Borden County, whose seat, **Gail,** sits along U.S. 180 between El Paso and Dallas. Both county and city are named for Gail Borden, who moved to Texas in 1829 and became surveyor for Stephen F. Austin's colony. A many-talented man, he published a newspaper, helped lay out the city of Houston, and served in various governmental positions. In the mid-1840s, he began inventing. He lost a great deal of money developing a meat biscuit made of dehydrated meat and flour, which no one would eat. In 1856 he patented a process for condensing milk in a vacuum. Demand for the product during the Civil War assured his financial success.

■ **ABILENE AREA** *map page 76, B-1*

From Big Spring, it's at least 100 miles east along I-20 to the next big city, Abilene, population about 116,000. The largest town between Fort Worth and Midland, Abilene is a railhead and cattle-loading stop whose 19th-century denizens were known for working and playing hard. But despite its wild and woolly past, contemporary Abilene is host to three denominational colleges with a collective enrollment of about 9,000. The Church of Christ supports Abilene Christian University, the Baptists Hardin-Simmons University, and the Methodists McMurry University. The town's few attractions of note include the **Grace Museum** (102 Cypress Street; 915-673-4587), a one-stop art, historical, and children's facility. Artwork created to illustrate children's literature is the specialty of the **National Center for Children's Illustrated Literature** (102 Cedar Street; 915-673-4586).

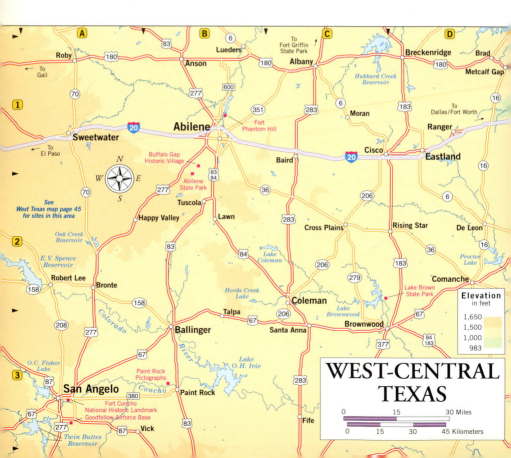

Outside Abilene, the landscape quickly gives way to gently rolling prairies. It's wide open country, of the sort that nature buffs and get-away-from-it-all types can't seem to get enough of.

About 14 miles north of Abilene on FM 600 lie the ruins of **Fort Phantom Hill,** a U.S. infantry post established in the 1850s to counter Comanche raids on white settlements. Given the woeful lack of water and absence of logs, which had to be hauled from 40 miles away to build the fort, it wasn't the best of sites. After three miserable years, the fort was abandoned, and not long thereafter burned to the ground—possibly in a blaze set by departing soldiers. The powder magazine, guardhouse, and commissary still stand, as do a number of ghostly chimneys. The ruins are on private land, but the owner welcomes respectful visitors.

History wears a different face 20 miles south at **Buffalo Gap Historic Village,** which consists of real buildings from the late 1800s and early 1900s that were moved here from elsewhere in the region. "This is a portrait of Texas life after the cattle drives ended and civilization began," says one of the curators. The village includes a doctor's office, a barbershop, a train station, and a log cabin, among other structures. The one building indigenous to the village, the first Taylor County Courthouse, opened for business in 1879. *Buffalo Gap Road (FM 89), 8 miles south of Abilene; 915-572-3365.*

■ ALBANY *map page 76, C-1*

Unassuming Albany, 35 miles northeast of Abilene on U.S. 180, has developed into a must-see for art aficionados. Another instance of oil money at work is the small town's **Old Jail Art Center,** housed in the first Shackelford County Jail, a two-story native-stone structure built in 1877. The collection holds works by Modigliani, Picasso, Renoir, Míro, and many other modern artists in addition to outdoor sculptures by Texas artists Jesús Bautista Moroles and Augusto Perez. *201 South Second Street; 915-762-2269.*

One block from the center is the **Shackelford County Courthouse** (1883), whose fanciful exterior is a riot of Victorian ideas that somehow manage to balance restraint and excess. In nearby Webb Park stands the 1874 **Ledbetter Picket House** (112 Main Street), an excellent example of frontier Texas picket-style construction, a technique in which logs were placed upright to form the walls of the building, rather than being stacked horizontally. The Ledbetter family operated a saltworks for several years in the mid-1860s on the banks of nearby Hubbard Creek.

The **Fort Griffin State Park and Historic Site,** north of Albany, is on the Clear Fork of the Brazos River; four companies of the Sixth U.S. Cavalry established it in 1867 to defend Texas settlers against attacks from Apaches and Comanches. A civilian community soon developed in the bottomland between the river and the hill where the fort was located. "The Flat," as it was called, soon gained a reputation for rowdy lawlessness, attracting such notables as Doc Holliday and Wyatt Earp. Eventually, the fort's commander declared martial law and chased a number of the more notorious residents out of town. By 1879, native tribes had all been forced into Oklahoma, and Fort Griffin was no longer necessary. The last army unit departed in 1881. The park, 15 miles north of Albany on U.S. 283, contains the partially restored ruins of the fort as well as part of the official state herd of Texas longhorn. *1701 North U.S. 283; 915-762-3592.*

■ CISCO *map page 76, C-1*
At first glance, you wouldn't associate Cisco with the hotel magnate Conrad Hilton, but this little town—46 miles east of Abilene, at the junction of I-20 and U.S. 183—is where he began collecting hotels. Legend has it that in 1919, the oil boom in the nearby town of Ranger had filled all the rentable rooms, forcing people to Cisco. When Hilton arrived in Cisco and couldn't get a place to stay, he bought the Mobley Hotel, then three years old; the rest is hotel history.

Whether the story is true or not isn't known, but we do know that the **Mobley Hotel** was the first of his many Hilton properties. Today, the building houses the chamber of commerce, a dinner theater, and a museum whose exhibits include archival photos of Cisco from the 1920s and vintage furniture from the Mobley's early days. *309 Conrad Hilton Avenue; 254-442-2537.*

■ COLEMAN *map page 76, C-2*

Coleman, seat of the same-named county, lies 52 miles southeast of Abilene on U.S. 84. In its early days, Coleman was on the Western Trail, the most important of the routes over which, between 1871 and 1883, four million Texas cattle were herded to rail and market connections in Kansas. Although Coleman sits amid dirt, dust, and rock, the surrounding area supports wondrous natural resources. Coleman isn't called "Land of Lakes" for nothing—there are several large lakes in the region, including 2,000-acre **Lake Coleman** (U.S. 84, 17 miles north of Coleman), a good spot for fishing, camping, and picnicking.

West Texas settlers struggled to defend themselves from attacks by native Apaches and Comanches. This photo is of an unidentified Comanche brave.

The Mobley Hotel, where the Hilton chain began.

The population of Coleman exceeded 15,000 in the 1940s and 1950s, when cotton farming and dairy farms were linchpins of the economy, but today Coleman County is ranching country again. And since ranching doesn't provide many jobs, fewer than 11,000 people live in Coleman County today.

Downtown Coleman has some of the small-town charms you'd expect to see— antiques shops, diners, plenty of hardware stores, and lots of churches. Stop in at the **Owl Drugstore** (312 Commercial Avenue; 915-625-2178) for a refreshment. The full-service soda fountain, in business since the early 1960s, serves sundaes, sodas, floats, sandwiches, and burgers. The proprietors are especially proud of two concoctions inspired by Elvis Presley: the "Presley Peanut Butter Sandwich" (grilled peanut butter and bananas, a Presley favorite) and, in honor of his latter-day look, "Sideburns and Shaving Cream" (bacon and mayonnaise on rye). You can gorge on these dubious delights while looking at the 40-plus pictures of the king of rock and roll splashed across the walls. A cup of coffee is only 37 cents if you get there before 11:30 in the morning.

HOW TO DRIVE LIKE A TEXAN

The official motto of Texas is "Friendship," and nowhere is that more evident than on the back roads of West Texas. On the interstates in Texas, as is true elsewhere, drivers are intent on driving as fast as they can to get to somewhere else. But in West Texas, all that changes when you turn off onto a state highway or an FM (farm-to-market) route.

Let's say you're driving down a road in West Texas, and you pass someone whom you've never met in a car on the opposite side of the road. As the other car nears, the driver may wave to you. This is not a case of mistaken identity or poor eyesight; the other driver knows he doesn't know you. And he's not trying to tell you your tire is going flat. It's just a rural Texan being friendly.

I've done an unscientific study of this phenomenon. The most likely driver to salute is male, middle-aged or older, driving a pickup truck—usually a bit the worse for wear—and probably pulling a cattle trailer or a hay wagon. The younger the driver and the sportier and newer the vehicle, the less likely you'll see a wave. Women never wave first. When saluted, they often wave back, but they never initiate the greeting.

The wave comes in many styles. There's the entire-hand-lifting-off-the-steering-wheel style. That's fairly rare. The most common style is for the hands to remain on the wheel and all four fingers of one hand to quickly unfold and extend together. The minimalist style involves the extension of only the forefinger. The polite and expected response is a casual wave in return.

The shoulder pull-off is a variant of the wave. When you approach a West Texan's car from behind, if there is room on the shoulder, the Texan pulls over and drives on the shoulder to allow you to pass—even though it is against state law to drive on the shoulder except in an emergency. He or she will pull over when the left lane is completely devoid of traffic, the view is totally unobstructed, and there is no practical reason whatsoever for doing so. You don't even have to be driving appreciably faster, or exhibiting signs of impatience and frustration. The passer should thank the passee with a friendly hand salute after the pass is completed.

Don't look for these two behaviors in South Texas, in North-Central Texas, or in urban areas, though you might see them in East Texas.

Here endeth the first lesson in driving like a Texan. Don't forget to wave.

—Mary G. Ramos

Coleman's **City Park,** a little north of town on U.S. 283, has a shady picnic area and a playground. This is where you'll find the **Coleman County Museum** (1700 North Neches Street), where displays of guns, farming tools, saddles, horse bits, and horseshoes make real the rigors of Texas frontier life.

■ SAN ANGELO *map page 76, A-3*

About midway between I-20, the northerly route through West Texas, and I-10, the southern conduit, is the city of San Angelo, a town of 90,000 that began as the civilian outgrowth of a military post, Fort Concho, a post–Civil War installation built in 1867. The 23 structures at **Fort Concho National Historic Landmark,** the town's star attraction, include a soldiers' barracks and mess hall; a hospital with beds, bone saws, and other nerve-rattling period instruments; a chapel; and an officers' quarters. *630 South Oakes; 915-657-4444.*

Concho River pearls are one of San Angelo's claims to fame. The story begins in 1650, when a Spanish expedition discovered freshwater mussels in the river but left them there because they thought the bivalves to be of no value. There they sat until 1969, when a couple of San Angelo jewelers discovered pearls in the mud of Lake O.C. Fisher, on San Angelo's northwest side. They collected the pearls for a number of months, storing them in glass jars until the market for pearls took off. Now jewelry shops in San Angelo trumpet their stock of Concho River pearl items, and the Texas Parks and Wildlife Department is so concerned about over harvesting that it requires pearl divers to carry permits.

Just down the road a piece, as we say in Texas, is one of the state's premier anthropological sites. Near the aptly named town of **Paint Rock** are 1,500 rock paintings spread out over a distance of a half-mile on a 70-foot-high limestone cliff. Different artists created the images over a long span of time, from prehistoric days to more recent times. Ceramics and rock middens found in the vicinity suggest that the earliest of these images were made at least 1,000 years ago. *FM 380, 22 miles east of San Angelo.*

■ TRAVEL BASICS

Getting Around: Interstate 10 enters Texas from New Mexico west of El Paso, parallels the Rio Grande for 85 miles, and then curves east toward San Antonio. Interstate 20 forks from I-10 180 miles east of El Paso and travels northeast

A little R&R at the Gage Hotel.

through Midland and Abilene and on east to Fort Worth and Dallas. U.S. 90 splits from I-10 at Van Horn, 140 miles east of El Paso, and travels southeast through Marfa, Alpine, and Marathon, on its way to San Antonio and points east. Route 118 heads south from I-10 at Kent, 37 miles east of Van Horn, going through Fort Davis and Alpine before reaching the western edge of Big Bend National Park. U.S. 285 enters Texas from New Mexico 140 miles east of El Paso and heads southeast through Pecos and Fort Stockton to connect with U.S. 90 54 miles east of Marathon. U.S. 385 zips into Odessa from the north, travels south for 50 miles, jogs west at I-10 to Fort Stockton and continues south to Big Bend National Park.

Climate: Much of West Texas is hot and dry in the summer, mild and wet in the winter. Average highs in summer range from 95 to 98 degrees in El Paso, and are slightly milder in West-Central Texas. Temperatures can soar to 110 degrees Fahrenheit or higher throughout the region. Average summer lows are 61 to 72. In winter, highs average 55 to 67, with lows between 28 and 35 degrees. El Paso has the lowest average annual precipitation in the entire state, but rainfall averages increase east of the region, reaching about 24 inches in the Abilene area. Most precipitation occurs in late spring and early fall.

DALLAS AND FORT WORTH

At night from the air, Dallas and Fort Worth form a vast expanse of light in the otherwise black sea of North-Central Texas. By day, the two cities appear strung together by freeways, high-rises, and suburbs. Yet, despite these appearances of unity, this is an odd couple. Psychically and physically, Dallas, a high-energy, all-business city fueled by banking, trade, insurance, and high-tech industry, belongs to wet, fertile East Texas. Fort Worth is the Old West—an overgrown cowboy town with raw edges and a reputation for rambunctiousness.

The legendary rivalry between the two prairie cities is mostly history now, but the bitterness was palpable for years. Dallas natives referred to Fort Worth scornfully as "Cowtown," while Fort Worth's boosters replied that "Fort Worth is where the West begins; Dallas is where the East peters out." The mutual sneering became a nuisance about the time the two cities realized that they needed to cooperate to build a regional airport capable of handling the increased air traffic and larger jets that were on the way. Discussions about a joint facility had begun as early as the 1940s, but kept getting hung up on such decisions as which direction the terminal building should face. Differences were finally shoved aside, and what is currently the nation's second-largest such facility—Dallas–Fort Worth International Airport (DFW)—was unveiled in 1974.

In recent years, the sniping between the two cities has subsided. Both have cooperated in efforts to market the region to international big business, in particular to Latin American oil interests. City leaders have also worked together on a commuter rail line—the Dallas Area Rapid Transit (DART) Trinity Railway Express—connecting downtown Dallas to its next-door suburb, Irving. The line, extended west a little at a time, now provides a link between downtown Dallas and downtown Fort Worth, with several stops along the way, including DFW.

■ **DALLAS** *map page 87*

Dallas looms large in the American consciousness as the home of the Cowboys football team, the place where President John F. Kennedy was killed, and the site of J.R. Ewing's ranch, Southfork, in the 1980s TV series *Dallas*. Only the assassination site, however, is actually within city limits. The ranch is outside the town of Parker, 24 miles northeast of downtown Dallas, and Texas Stadium, where the

Dallasites know how to mix business with pleasure, but don't expect a three-martini lunch.

Dallas Cowboys play their home games, is in Irving, 12 miles west of downtown. While we're at it, the University of Dallas is also in Irving, and the University of Texas at Dallas is in Richardson, 15 miles northeast of town. Within the city itself, though, is an increasingly important cultural scene that includes the Dallas Museum of Art, the Meadows Museum, and the Dallas Symphony Orchestra.

Technically, "Big D," as some Texans have called Dallas, encompasses 378 square miles and supports 1.2 million residents. But Dallas and a number of large suburbs are indelibly fused into a sprawling whole that takes up all of Dallas County—a 908-square-mile area with a population of 2.2 million—and slops over into Denton and Collin Counties as well. In the last quarter of the 20th century, the suburbs of Dallas began sprouting high-tech campuses and high-rise headquarters for national corporations, and now have their own suburbs. This larger Dallas is, like its nucleus city, largely focused on white-collar pursuits and is known for formality, especially in business circles. This is a buttoned-down metropolis: no open collars, gold chains, or blue jeans, please. And Dallas exhibits a puritanical side. Liquor isn't sold in many sections of the city, and "power breakfasts"—beginning about 6:30 A.M.—are more common than three-martini lunches.

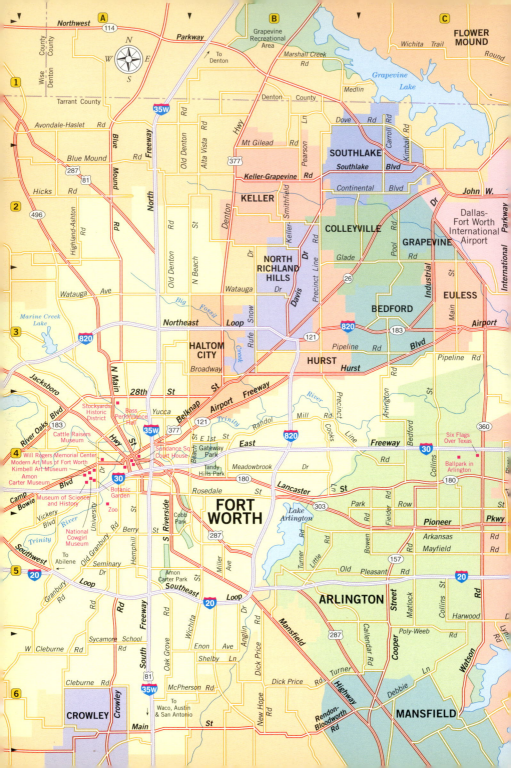

DALLAS-FORT WORTH

0   3   6 Miles

0   3   6   9 Kilometers

Dallas was founded on ambition. In 1841, when John Neely Bryan, Dallas's first white settler, founded the city, there wasn't really any need for its existence, as natives proudly note: the Trinity River wasn't commercially navigable, and no railroad lines had been laid. But Dallas was promoted from its earliest days with tales of a great river connected to the sea (false) and of fertile black farmland (true). When John B. Billingsley and four brothers came here with their families in 1842, he recorded in his journal that:

> We had heard a great deal about the three forks of the Trinity River and the town of Dallas. This was the center of attraction. It sounded big in far-off states. We had heard of it often, yes, the place, but the town, where was it? Two small log cabins, the logs just as nature formed them…chimneys made of sticks and mud and old mother earth serving as floors. . . .This was the town of Dallas, and two families, ten or twelve souls, was its population. . . .

The city's businessmen attracted the north-south Houston and Texas Central Railroad in 1872 and the east-west Texas & Pacific Railway in 1873, giving Dallas a good start on becoming a transportation and distribution hub. Early on, Dallas's business leaders developed a tradition of close involvement in civic affairs and cooperated to promote the city. Dallas rode into prosperity on a cloud of cotton in the 20th century, as the 1940 *WPA Guide to Texas* noted:

> Set in the midst of vast cotton fields. . .Dallas is the foremost inland spot cotton market in the United States. . . .It leads the world in the manufacture of cotton gin machinery, due to the inventions in the 1880s of Robert S. Munger, a Dallas man, who made many improvements on the earlier inventions of Eli Whitney.

Dallas acquired manufacturing industries during and after World War II, eventually becoming the largest wholesale trade complex in the world. Texas Instruments began in Dallas in 1930 as Geophysical Service Inc. (GSI), concentrating on developing seismographic processes used in oil exploration. The company experienced tremendous growth during World War II as a result of its experiments with transistors. In 1951, GSI became Texas Instruments, and TI became world famous in 1954 when it developed the world's first transistor radio. In 1958, the company introduced the first integrated circuit, and in 1971 it was again the envy of the technological world when it unveiled the first portable hand-held calculator.

DALLAS FIRSTS

Because Dallas has found itself at the hub of so many diverse interests—commercial, social, intellectual, and artistic—it is the home of many American firsts. Among them:

▶ The nation's first 7-Eleven convenience store, which opened at Edgefield and 12th Streets on July 11, 1927—or 7/11/27. The 7-Eleven Store No. 1 still occupies the site, but the original building was razed.

▶ The country's first large-scale shopping center, Highland Park Village. The upscale shopping venue was built in 1931.

▶ The original "white out" product, Liquid Paper, invented by Bette Nesmith Graham, the mother of Monkees guitarist Michael Nesmith. A secretary in Dallas in the mid-1950s, she experimented in her kitchen, developing a formula that could be dabbed over typos with a small brush to cover them up.

▶ The first monolithic integrated circuit (microchip), invented in 1958 by engineer Jack Kilby of Texas Instruments. Kilby's discovery ushered in the semiconductor and electronics age. He later was the co-inventor of the hand-held calculator.

▶ The first Mary Kay "house party" for cosmetic sales. Mary Kay Ash started her famous company in 1963, an operation that today has 900,000 consultants in 33 countries. In 1969, Ash began rewarding her best sales people with pink Cadillacs.

The first 7-Eleven store was established in Dallas in 1927.

So many high-tech firms, including Nortel Networks and Electronic Data Systems (the latter-day political gadfly H. Ross Perot founded EDS), made their headquarters in Dallas's northern suburbs of Richardson and Plano that in the 1990s they earned the sobriquet "Silicon Prairie." The high-tech fallout at the turn of the 21st century delivered a rabbit punch to the area, however. Cost-cutting measures and pink slips have become the order of the day at some companies, where CEOs young and old have gone back to the drawing board to develop more sensible business plans than those concocted at the height of Internet fever.

A business-oriented city with boundless self-confidence and a zest for life, high-energy Dallas is home to cowboys and internationalists, high-culture mavens and aficionados of the lowbrow. A combination of savoir faire and brass tacks sustains Dallas, a truth perhaps nowhere more evident than in the robust restaurant scene, whose chefs whip up everything from fussy French and nouveau Cajun to down-home specialties like barbecue and broiled alligator. In surprising and at times contradictory Dallas, the surface rarely tells the whole story. The city parks along Turtle Creek and White Rock Lake, for instance, are great retreats to soothe the soul—but, as with much of Texas, their complicated underlying geography required appreciable taming to make them hospitable. In a short visit to this city you may not comprehend the complexities, physical and psychological, that lie underneath its apparently plain facade. Immerse yourself in its art, architecture, and history, though, and you'll begin to get an inkling.

■ CENTRAL CITY

West End Historic District   *map page 87, E-4*

The West End Historic District is where folks went a century ago to buy farming equipment, tools, ice, candy makers, and other items. After decades of deterioration, the area was designated a historic district in the 1980s, and today the neighborhood's handsome brick warehouses contain restaurants, offices, and some of Dallas's best-loved shopping destinations. Also in this area are Dealey Plaza and the Texas School Book Depository, the two key locales in the assassination of President John F. Kennedy. Dallas's link to Kennedy's murder has always been to the city's chagrin, but more than four decades after the event, scores of visitors continue to descend on the West End to view the area where the president was shot.

The **Sixth Floor Museum,** in the former Texas School Book Depository—from whose sixth floor Lee Harvey Oswald pointed his rifle at Kennedy—contains some

This photo of John F. Kennedy riding in his motorcade with Jacqueline Kennedy and Gov. John B. Connally and his wife, Nellie, was taken moments before the president was shot.

fascinating documents, photographs, films, and other artifacts. Also on display here are dozens of photographs of the Kennedy motorcade taken by Dallas residents, along with the FBI model of Dealey Plaza used by the Warren Commission, which concluded that Oswald had acted alone. Assassination buffs also seek out more obscure locales, among them the Texas Theater (231 West Jefferson Boulevard), where Oswald was arrested, and his former home, both in Dallas's Oak Cliff neighborhood. Oswald is buried in Rose Hill Memorial Park in Fort Worth. *411 Elm Street, at Houston Street; 214-747-6660.*

Dallas County Historical Plaza, a cluster of important structures and public spaces, incorporates Founder's Plaza, which contains a replica of the type of log cabin that Dallas founder John Neely Bryan lived in, and Dealey Plaza, named for George Bannerman Dealey, the founder of the *Dallas Morning News* and a major civic planner. *Bordered by Market, Elm, Commerce, and Houston Streets.*

A statue of George Dealey stands on a pedestal of dark-red granite near the **John F. Kennedy Memorial,** a stark cenotaph designed by Philip Johnson, the New York City–based architect and friend of the Kennedy family. *At Main and Market Streets.*

Overshadowing the log cabin is the former **Dallas County Courthouse,** often called "Old Red." Built in the early 1890s in the Richardsonian Romanesque style—turrets, massive arches, marble pillars, and all—it now houses the city's Tourist Information Center. If the building, designed by M. A. Orlopp, strikes you as oddly proportioned, there's a good reason: the clock tower and 4,500-pound bell were removed in 1919 following structural failure. Much of the interior detail is original, including the cast-iron staircases and marble wainscoting. The graceful stained-glass lunettes above the entranceways are reproductions of the originals. *100 South Houston Street, between Main and Commerce Streets.*

West End Marketplace, in the former Brown Cracker & Candy building, houses some fun shops. **Wild Bill's Western Store** sells just about every type of belt, boot, and hat imaginable. **Antique Angle** is where Dallasites go to find old editions of magazines like *Colliers* and *Life,* along with memorabilia plugging everything from

(above) The Dallas County Courthouse—"Old Red"—was built in the early 1890s.
(previous pages) A cattle drive re-created in bronze recalls the cattle roots of Dallas.

Elvis to *Batman* to *I Love Lucy.* The marketplace is also a magnet for foodies. **Little Taste of Texas** stocks chilies, hot sauces, and peppers, while next door at **The Fudgery** singing and dancing staffers whip up 10 flavors of the gooey confection. *Elm Street to McKinney Avenue, between Record and Lamar Streets; 214-748-4801.*

Convention Center Area *map page 87, E-3*
Pioneer Plaza, a 4-acre former parking lot adjacent to the Dallas Convention Center, celebrates a part of the city's early history. The artfully landscaped plaza has as its centerpiece sculptor Robert Summers's larger-than-life bronze interpretation of a cattle drive: three cowboys on horseback herding 70 longhorn steers. Some detractors of this 1995 artwork have argued that cattle drives were not part of the city's past, and that the piece projects a false image of Dallas history. But herds did pass through town from the early 1840s to the early 1850s on the Shawnee Trail, the easternmost cattle-driving route. The cattle gathered in southern and central Texas, were driven north through Austin and Waco, crossed the Trinity River near the site of Pioneer Plaza, headed up what is now Preston Road to the Red River, and then went on to Missouri. Cattle may not have been as important as cotton to Dallas's development, but don't tell visitors that: many of them are crazy about the bronze bovines. *South Griffin and Young Streets.*

The Arts District *map page 87, E-3*
In 1979, Dallas voters approved a ballot measure that led to the creation of the Arts District, a 17-block, 62 acre area, from Ross Avenue to McKinney Avenue, between Akard and Routh Streets. Over the years, many Dallas arts institutions have moved or established themselves here, including the Dallas Museum of Art and the Dallas Symphony Orchestra. The Nasher Sculpture Center opened to great fanfare in late 2003.

Dallas has specialty museums to suit a variety of audiences and interests—the Meadows for Spanish art, the Trammell Crow for Asian art, and the Nasher for sculpture. The **Dallas Museum of Art** is unique for being unapologetically populist, appealing to every sensibility. Its comprehensive permanent collection covers the arts of Africa, Asia, ancient Greece, and the Near East, and the painting collection includes works by artists from John Singleton Copley to Gerhard Richter. The most popular draw is an installation that recreates rooms in the Mediterranean villa belonging to Texas swells Wendy and Emery Reves. Here, lavish furniture and other accoutrements of gracious living set off masterpieces by Cézanne and van Gogh. *1717 North Harwood Street; 214-922-1200.*

ARCHITECTURAL STATEMENTS

Dallasites are proud of their city's eclectic architecture, which includes grand and unusual statements like the 1978 **Reunion Tower** (300 Reunion Boulevard), whose architects, Welton Becket & Associates, designed the 50-story structure as four concrete cylinders topped by a geodesic dome (with a popular observation deck), and more conventionally intriguing ones like I. M. Pei's **Morton H. Meyerson Symphony Center** (2301 Flora Street), which opened in 1989. Pei also designed the Brutalist **Dallas City Hall** (1500 Marilla Street), in the shape of an inverted pyramid. The building, which has seven floors above ground and two below, was completed in 1978. Across the street, the stepped-back face of the **J. Erik Jonsson Central Library** (1515 Young Street), designed by the local firm of Fisher & Spillman and completed in 1982, appears to have been broken off from the front of City Hall.

Amid the skyscrapers and frenetic activity of downtown is Philip Johnson's tranquil **Thanks-Giving Square** (Pacific, Bryan, and Ervay Streets), an extraordinary garden and chapel set in a triangular plaza. Johnson's white spiral chapel, inspired by the minaret of the Great Mosque in Samarra, Iraq, draws the eye to the north end of the square, where its alabaster whorls are reflected in the mirrored panes of a nearby office tower. Interfaith services are held in the 80-seat chapel, whose ceiling spaces are adorned with stained-glass windows designed by the French artist Gabriel Loire.

A green-glass skyscraper with a triangular top, **Fountain Place** (1455 Ross Avenue), formerly Allied Bank Tower, is visible from just about anywhere in town. The brash strength of Harry Cobb and I. M. Pei's 62-story giant is mitigated at street level by a 3-acre plaza shaded by bald cypress trees and filled with waterfalls and bubbling, squirting fountains.

One of Frank Lloyd Wright's last projects was the 479-seat **Kalita Humphreys Theater** (3636 Turtle Creek Boulevard), in William B. Dean Park. The building, completed in 1959, bears many of the celebrated architect's signature elements: gold tapered columns, a profusion of windows, and his characteristic avoidance of right angles.

The brick and gray-granite **Adolphus Hotel** (1321 Commerce Street), with its richly ornamented facade and two-story variegated-slate mansard roof, is arguably Texas's premier example of Beaux Arts architecture. Tom P. Barnett of St. Louis designed the 1912 structure after Dallas businessmen asked the brewery magnate Adolphus Busch to help them build a first-class hotel. The building is replete with French Renaissance and Baroque statuary and bronze details.

The 1921 **Majestic Theater** (1925 Elm Street; 214-691-7200) is the last of a gaggle of movie theaters that once lined a section of Elm Street known as Theater Row.

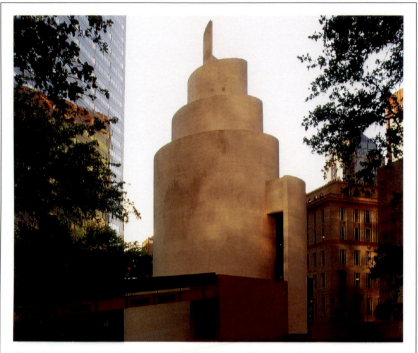

(previous page) Reunion Tower. (above) The design of the spiral chapel in Thanks-Giving Square was a tribute to the minaret of the Great Mosque in Samarra, Iraq.

John Eberson, the architect of many early-20th-century movie palaces, designed this Renaissance Revival beauty with an exterior rich in applied ornamentation and elaborate window moldings. A highlight of the equally ornate interior is the massive proscenium arch, whose decoration is echoed throughout the auditorium, even on the undersides of the balconies.

The architect-statesman Sir Alfred Charles Bossom designed another Renaissance Revival icon, the 1922 Magnolia Building, today the **Magnolia Hotel** (1401 Commerce Street; 214-915-6500), as the headquarters of Magnolia Petroleum. At the time—and for two decades thereafter—the structure was Dallas's tallest. The 40-foot-long, 30-foot-high neon Pegasus perched atop the building was the logo of Magnolia Petroleum—and later Mobil, whose predecessor purchased Magnolia in the 1920s. Though partially obscured today by taller buildings, the horse was an instantly recognizable beacon for decades, visible as much as 75 miles in any direction.

The Dallas developer Raymond D. Nasher and his late wife, Patsy, assembled what many art critics claim is one of the most important collections of modern sculpture ever—more than 300 works by Rodin, Giacometti, Miró, Calder, Serra, and other stars of the medium. Their collection's new home, the **Nasher Sculpture Center,** opened in late 2003. The Italian architect Renzo Piano, most famous for designing the Pompidou Center in Paris but also responsible for the main Menil Collection building in Houston, created sandstone-colored gallery pavilions; and Peter Walker, a landscape architect based in Berkeley, California, designed the adjacent 2 acres of gardens. *2001 Flora Street, between Harwood and Olive Streets; 214-242-5100.*

Trammell Crow, another Dallas-based developer, and his wife, Margaret, assembled the **Crow Collection of Asian Art,** which focuses on works from China, Japan, India, and Southeast Asia. The highlights include displays of Chinese jade, Japanese scrolls, and some medieval stone sculptures from India.

Art appreciation takes many forms at the Dallas Museum of Art.

Also in the collection is the sandstone facade of an 18th-century Indian residence, and a tree-shaded garden on the museum building's Ross Avenue side contains sculptures by Auguste Rodin, Emile Antoine Bourdelle, and Aristide Maillol. *Trammell Crow Center, 2010 Flora Street; 214-979-6430.*

The performing arts are also represented in the Arts District, most notably at the **Morton H. Meyerson Symphony Center,** informally called "The Mort." The center has been the home of the Dallas Symphony Orchestra since 1989. An acoustical dream of a concert hall, the auditorium has an adjustable canopy that allows fine-tuning of the room's sound to suit the pieces performers are playing on a given day. Outside the building are sculptures by Eduardo Chillida, Henri Laurens, and Jacques Lipchitz. *2301 Flora Street; 214-670-3600.*

Art is everywhere in Dallas, even in the stations of the **DART light-rail line.** The subjects of the murals, sculptures, and designs generally reflect life in the stations' neighborhoods, with many of the images whimsical ones, like the giant bird footprints embedded in the floor of the Mockingbird Lane Station elevator and the giant clocks sprouting at four downtown stations. The clock in the Pearl Station (Bryan Street, east of Pearl Street) is an enormous sunflower with five blossoms, the center of each a working clock face.

■ OUTSIDE CENTRAL CITY

Deep Ellum *map page 87, D-3*
Several freedmen's towns formed on the outskirts of Dallas after the Civil War. One of them, centered on east Elm Street, evolved during the 1920s and 1930s into Deep Ellum, a mecca for jazz and blues musicians such as Blind Lemon Jefferson, Huddie "Leadbelly" Ledbetter, and Sam "Lightnin' " Hopkins. The scene fell apart in the 1940s and 1950s, and by the early 1980s little or nothing was left of this once-lively turf. Following a cooperative private-government effort in the mid-1980s, Deep Ellum ("Deep" for its original location on the far end of Elm Street and "Ellum," for the local pronunciation of elm) evolved into a funky entertainment, dining, and shopping district. *Elm and Main Streets, between the Good-Latimer Expressway and Hall Street.*

The late-night club scene attracts a mostly young crowd that patronizes hot spots like **Trees** (2709 Elm Street), the **Gypsy Tea Room** (2548 Elm Street), and **Club Dada** (2720 Elm Street).

Huddie "Leadbelly" Ledbetter

Music lovers in the know head to **Sons of Hermann Hall** to hear the sounds of well-known and up-and-coming performers—mostly country, folk, and blues artists, with occasional rockers. Arlo Guthrie, Sara Hickman, the Light Crust Doughboys, Marcia Ball, Hank Thompson, the Barn Stompers, the Brownstones, and Four Mile Mule have all cut loose at this great venue. Sons of Hermann is a German fraternal insurance benefit society that started in New York in 1840. Dallas's first lodge was founded in 1890, and a couple of lodgers built Ellum's Sons of Hermann Hall in 1911. *3414 Elm Street; 214-747-4422.*

Fair Park *map page 87, F-4*
Less than a mile from downtown and a few blocks east of Deep Ellum is Fair Park, 277 acres of landscaped greens, open spaces, gardens, and trails. Also here are some fine museums and perhaps the largest collection of art deco structures in the world, most of them constructed or renovated for the Texas Centennial Exposition in 1936. *1300 Robert B. Cullum Boulevard; 214-421-9600.*

Fair Park's standout deco specimen is the exuberant **Hall of State** (3939 Grand Avenue; 214-421-4500), credited to the Houston-based architect Donald Barthelme, the father of the famous author of the same name. Inside the building's massive doors, in the semicircular Hall of Heroes—one of Dallas's most impressive interior spaces—statues of the founders of the Republic of Texas, among them Stephen F. Austin and Sam Houston, stare down at visitors. Looming over the Great Hall is an enormous gold emblem bearing the five-pointed star, the heraldic stamp of Texas; nearby murals by Eugene Savage depict key moments of Texas history.

Three other Centennial buildings are still in use. **Science Place I** (1318 Second Avenue; 214-428-5555), originally built as the Dallas Museum of Fine Arts, houses a museum with interactive exhibits and a newer wing that contains an IMAX theater. A statue of a mammoth guards the entrance to the **Dallas Museum of Natural History** (3535 Grand Avenue; 214-421-3466), whose team of architects included Mark Lemmon and Clyde Griesenbeck, and whose exhibits survey Texas's natural environment. The Spanish Romanesque **Fair Park Music Hall,** designed by a leading local architectural firm, Lang and Witchell, is home to the **Dallas Summer Musicals** (214-421-5678), a Broadway show series, and plays host to other stage productions. Most of the other vintage buildings in the park are in use only in October during the **State Fair of Texas** (214-565-9931).

Also in the park are the **African-American Museum** (3536 Grand Avenue; 214-565-9026), whose permanent holdings include African art and African-American art and folk art; and the **Age of Steam Railroad Museum** (1105 Washington Street; 214-428-0101), an outdoor collection of rolling stock whose highlight is the Union Pacific's *Big Boy,* one of the longest and most powerful steam locomotives ever built. Football fans head to Fair Park each New Year's Day to the **Cotton Bowl** (3750 Midway Plaza; 214-638-2695), which hosts one of college football's oldest post-season events (it started in 1937).

Old City Park *map page 87, E-4*

Old City Park, just across a maze of freeways south of downtown, is a 13-acre village of 38 historical structures brought together from around Dallas County to reflect the period between 1840 and 1910. The park includes a working farm, Victorian homes, a school, a general store, a small-town hotel, a church, and early-20th-century commercial buildings. *1717 Gano Street; 214-421-5141.*

The semicircular Hall of Heroes, within the Hall of State building, holds statues of Stephen F. Austin and Sam Houston, among other Texas notables.

DALLAS SPORTS

The National Football League's **Dallas Cowboys** won two Super Bowls under their first and much-admired coach, Tom Landry, in 1972 and 1978, and three more in the 1990s—two under Jimmy Johnson and the last under Barry Switzer. After the team hit a dry patch, the 'Boys' mercurial owner, Jerry Jones, hired fabled coach Bill Parcells in 2003 to turn things around. The Cowboys can be seen during the season behind the revolving door at **Texas Stadium.** *Off Route 183, Irving; 972-785-5000.*

The area's National Basketball Association team, the **Mavericks**—whose logo for some unknown reason is a mustang (wild horse), not a maverick (unbranded calf)— plays its home games in the massive **American Airlines Center,** near the West End Historic District. The Mavs have played well in recent years under coach Don Nelson. The **Dallas Stars** of the National Hockey League, who play at the same arena, are playoff regulars; in 1999 they won the Stanley Cup with a gut-wrenching seventh-game triple-overtime victory over Buffalo. *2500 Victory Avenue; 214-747-6287 (Mavericks); 214-467-8277 (Stars).*

President George W. Bush was, for a spell, a part-owner of the **Texas Rangers,** who have had few ups and many downs in recent years. In 1994, the American League baseball team, based in the suburb of Arlington, christened a new open-air stadium, the **Ballpark in Arlington,** which has a red-brick facade, natural grass, and a vaguely Ivy League ambience. *1000 Ballpark Way, Arlington; 817-273-5222.*

Baseball is not the only summer pro sport in Dallas. The **Mesquite Championship Rodeo** stages professional competitions—bull riding, steer wrestling, roping, and chuck-wagon and barrel racing—every Friday and Saturday night from early April through early October. Yee-haw! *Resistol Arena, 1818 Rodeo Drive, Mesquite (I-635, Exit 4); 972-285-8777.*

Swiss Avenue Historic District *map page 87, E-4*
The architectural styles of the Swiss Avenue Historic District's stunning early-20th-century homes range from Italian Renaissance and Tudor to Craftsman and Prairie. Following its heyday, the grand neighborhood gradually declined, and by the 1970s some of the huge homes had been subdivided into apartments and at least one had been converted into a house of ill-repute. A group of residents persuaded City Hall to designate the area a historic district, which has led to a renaissance. *Swiss Avenue, from La Vista Drive to Fitzhugh Avenue; 214-826-1967 for info about the district and the annual Mother's Day tour of homes and gardens.*

Adjacent to the Swiss Avenue district is the **Munger Place Historic District,** developed in the early 1900s by Robert S. Munger, who made his fortune improving cotton-gin technology. His son, Collett Munger (Collett and Munger Streets in the district are named for him) managed the district after the elder Munger died, apparently reinforcing most of his father's strict ideas about uniform house styles, setbacks, and lot sizes. The predominant design style of two-story houses with expansive porches and wide eave projections reflects the influence of Frank Lloyd Wright's Prairie architecture, but a few Craftsman, Colonial Revival, and Mission-style residences can also be spotted. *From Junius Street to Reiger Street, between Henderson Avenue and Prairie Avenue.*

The nearby 22-acre **Wilson Historic District** contains many well-restored homes, though only one sits on the lot on which it was originally built; the others were moved to the enclave from elsewhere in Dallas. *Swiss Avenue at Liberty Street.*

Southern Methodist University *map page 87, E-3*
Dallas was selected as the site for Southern Methodist University (SMU) because of the growth and development of North Texas in the early 1900s. Although the campus has expanded from its simple beginnings in domed Dallas Hall, at the head of Bishop Boulevard, subsequent buildings have retained the unified red-brick Georgian theme. The university's Cox School of Business is well regarded, as is its Meadows School of the Arts, whose outstanding alumni include the actress Kathy Bates and the playwright Beth Henley.

The Dallas oil tycoon and philanthropist Algur H. Meadows loved Spanish art. While in Spain hunting for oil in the 1950s, he spent his off hours in Madrid's Prado, where he fell in love with the works of Goya, Murillo, Velázquez, and Ribera. He was so transfixed that in 1965 he founded the **Meadows Museum of Art** and began filling it with his favorite art. The museum has one of the largest collections of Spanish art in the world outside of Spain—a sensational stockpile of 670 paintings, sculpture, and works on paper, among other treasures—along with works from the Middle Ages, art of the Renaissance, and contemporary paintings and sculpture. Meadows died in 1978, but his museum continues to make important acquisitions, including its late-1990s purchase of El Greco's *Saint Francis Kneeling in Meditation.* In 2001, the Meadows moved from cramped quarters into a 66,000-square-foot red-brick Georgian structure designed by the Chicago architects Hammond Beeby Rupert Ainge. *On the SMU campus, 5900 Bishop Boulevard; 214-768-2516.*

NorthPark Center *map page 87, E-3*

Dallas is a shopper's paradise, with as much or more retail space than New York City or Los Angeles, and one of its best malls is **NorthPark Center.** Home to many upscale and midrange chains, it also has a day spa, **Origins,** that caters to the weary shopper in need of a different kind of retail therapy. More impressive than NorthPark's retail operations, though, is its sculpture—the center serves as an informal gallery for works from Raymond D. Nasher's collection that aren't displayed at the Nasher Sculpture Center. Pieces by Jim Dine, Anthony Caro, Frank Stella, and others are stationed throughout the mall. *Bounded by Northwest Highway, Boedecker, Park Lane, and North Central Expressway; 214-363-7441.*

The **Biblical Arts Center,** near NorthPark Center, exhibits art and artifacts with religious themes. The highlight is Torger Thompson's 124-foot-wide and 20-foot-tall mural *Miracle at Pentecost,* which depicts more than 200 Biblical characters, some of them larger than life. On the half-hour, the mural is unveiled to the accompaniment of a sound and light show. *7500 Park Lane; 214-691-4661.*

Dallas Arboretum and Botanical Garden *map page 87, F-3*

The **Dallas Arboretum and Botanical Garden,** a short distance east of downtown, fills 66 acres with towering trees, flower gardens, gushing fountains, meandering trails, and rolling lawns. The eight garden settings include the Palmer Fern Dell, where trails lead through dozens of varieties of ferns, and the Woman's Garden, complete with reflecting pool and sculptures. The main walkway through the grounds, the Lyda Hunt Paseo de Flores, blooms with color throughout the year. *Entrance is on the 8300 block of Garland Road; 214-327-8263.*

A showstopper amid the arboretum's greenery is the 1939 **DeGolyer House,** a hacienda designed in the Spanish Mission style by the Beverly Hills architects Denman Scott and Burton Schutt for Everette DeGolyer, a geophysicist and oil entrepreneur. The 13-room house is a showcase for 17th- and 18th-century furnishings, paintings, and antiques, most of them collected by DeGolyer and his wife, Nell Goodrich DeGolyer, on their many voyages abroad. Nearby is the 1938 Camp House, which the Houston-based architect John Staub designed in a style that tastefully combines Tudor, art deco, and colonial motifs. The headquarters of the Dallas Arboretum and Botanical Society, the house is not open to the public. *8525 Garland Road; 214-327-8263.*

(opposite) Dallas Arboretum and Botanical Garden (above) and the 109-acre Fort Worth Botanic Garden (below) are among the many verdant settings in the two cities.

■ BEYOND DALLAS

Southfork Ranch *map page 87, F-3*

Southfork Ranch won worldwide fame when its exterior was used as J. R. Ewing's luxury ranch home for 356 episodes of *Dallas*. Now a museum devoted to the television show, the ranch house is filled with such memorabilia as the gun that was used to shoot J.R. on a season-ending cliffhanger and saddles used by stars. The tour guides usually dispense a juicy anecdote or two. A tram ride covers most of the 300-acre property, offering views along the way of the quarter horses that are still bred and trained here (not to mention the silver-and-blue Lincoln driven by Jock, J.R.'s formidable daddy). *Hogge Road (FM 2551), Parker; head east 5.5 miles from U.S. 75's Parker Road exit and turn right; 972-442-7800.*

Denton *map page 273, E-4*

A highway sign on the northbound I-35 approach to Denton, 35 miles north of Dallas, reads "Denton and all that jazz!" Much of that jazz emanates from the bands of the University of North Texas's College of Music, which have garnered acclaim in festivals far and wide, including the Montreux, Antibes, and Spoleto jazz festivals. The One O'Clock Lab Band (lab bands are identified by the hour at which they rehearse), whose members are the department's most accomplished student musicians, tours extensively, and has, over the years, issued 35 albums, two of them Grammy winners.

Polka lovers know Denton as the home base of Brave Combo, a quintet described as "merry pranksters" by one California reviewer who didn't know how else to describe their mix of polkas, Latin American dance tunes, zydeco, acid rock, elevator music, and other styles. The five musicians, who have been playing since 1979, can be heard just about anywhere: on national TV, on movie soundtracks, and at rock clubs, outdoor festivals, and weddings.

Denton, population 90,000, is a government and university town set in pleasant countryside of rolling hills and open fields. Downtown Denton's architectural sensation, the **Denton County Courthouse on the Square,** was designed by W. C. Dodson in an eclectic mix of the Victorian, French Second Empire, and Romanesque Revival styles. With turrets at all four corners and capped by a domed clock tower, the three-story sandstone and pink-granite structure houses county offices as well as the Denton County Courthouse-on-the-Square Museum, which has photographs, artifacts, and Denton memorabilia. *110 West Hickory Street; 940-349-2850 (museum).*

HEAVEN HAVE TO GO SOME TO BEAT THIS

Lee Martin's novel Quakertown *is based on a true story about an African-American neighborhood in Denton that was razed to make way for a city park. The passage below describes Quakertown in its prime:*

When Little got back to Quakertown that evening, he saw the janitors and maids and cooks coming down the long hill from the college. They were laughing among themselves, throwing up their hands, relieved to be rid of work for the day, thankful to be away from the college where they had learned to move about with their eyes cast down to the floor, to mumble, "Yes, miss," when need be, or "No, miss," or "Sorry, miss."

Now they were back in Quakertown, the neighborhood of homes and businesses their ancestors had managed to build in the years following Reconstruction, subscribing to Booker T. Washington's philosophy of self-help rather than returning to the plantations.

In the evenings, someone out for a stroll might hear the clack of dominoes slapped down on a kitchen table . . . or the voices of the AME Church Choir going to work on "Couldn't Hear Nobody Pray." Or, if it was Saturday night, a blues singer at the Buffalo Bayou Café—Mabel Moon, maybe, or Big Mama Annie, Hocey Simms or Choo Choo LaDeau. Third Sundays, the Heroines of Jericho put out a feed. They laid plywood sheets over sawhorses the length of Frame Street, and everyone came toting kitchen chairs, sat down, elbow to elbow, and packed away catfish gumbo, garlic grits, Cajun cabbage, sweet potato pudding, red beans and rice, pork chops, barbecued chicken, baked ham, hot rolls with peach peel jelly, apple pie, sugar pie, black walnut pound cake. "Lord," someone would say. "Heaven have to go some to beat this."

—Lee Martin, *Quakertown,* 2001

At 90 feet long and 42 feet wide, the **Little Chapel in the Woods,** on the campus of Texas Woman's University, is as petite as the courthouse is massive. The chapel, dedicated in 1939 by Eleanor Roosevelt, was designed for this serene and densely wooded setting by the Texas architect O'Neil Ford and his partner Arch Swank. Soaring parabolic masonry arches create a feeling of spaciousness, and light filtering through stained-glass windows made by 300 university students renders a dark, enigmatic glow. The architects had meditation in mind, but in recent years this has become a popular wedding venue. *Near the southwest corner of Bell Avenue and East University Drive; 940-898-3644.*

■ FORT WORTH *map page 86*

Fort Worth, formed at the confluence of the Trinity River's West Fork and Clear Fork, began humbly in 1849 as a military post set up to protect settlers in East Texas from Indian raids. Named for Gen. William Jenkins Worth, a hero of the Mexican War, the city became a supply station for the Butterfield Overland Mail and the Southern Pacific Stage Line on their routes to California. After the Civil War, Fort Worth became a major hub for cattle drivers moving Texas cattle north toward the famed Chisholm Trail, and northern cattle buyers made the city their southern headquarters.

In the early 1870s, a cluster of saloons opened on the lower end of Rusk Street to quench the thirst of the many traveling cowboys. This boozy ward soon became the nucleus for "Hell's Half Acre," a sprawling, brawling area eight city blocks long and four blocks wide, jammed with bars, dance halls, brothels, and gambling dens. Although officials made sporadic efforts to clean up the Acre, it became a notorious hideout for outlaws like the Sam Bass gang, Butch Cassidy and his sidekick the Sundance Kid, and others. With the end of the cattle-driving era, the Acre lost most of its primary customers, and by 1900 Hell's Half Acre was history.

After railroads arrived, starting with the Texas & Pacific in 1876, cattle pens and loading facilities were built near the tracks north of downtown. Several home-grown beef-processing plants were established there, and by 1903, local business-men had enticed the packing-house giants Swift and Armour to establish branch plants in the stockyards area. Nearby, the Fort Worth Stock Yards Company built the Fort Worth Livestock Exchange, a still-extant Spanish Mission–style building that became the focus of activity.

Although Fort Worth has historically been associated with oil and cattle, follow-ing the outbreak of World War II the area's suburbs attracted defense contractors like Consolidated Vultee Aircraft, Chance-Vought, and Bell Helicopter Company. The aircraft and auto plants that encircle the region have made Fort Worth a labor union town and sometimes a liberal stronghold, at least by West Texas standards. Fort Worth is refreshingly unpretentious, and though it trades on its cowtown image for tourism purposes, it supports outstanding fine-arts organizations and its cultural district is walkable and attractive. The city has also preserved a great deal of its architectural heritage, especially downtown.

An Old West feel prevails along the Exchange Avenue entrance to the Fort Worth Stock Yards.

■ **FORT WORTH CULTURAL DISTRICT**   *map page 86, A-4*

Oil wealth has endowed Fort Worth with attractions one wouldn't normally associate with a city whose nickname is "Cowtown." Most of them are conveniently clustered together in the Fort Worth Cultural District, southwest of downtown.

At the time of his death in 1955, Amon G. Carter, a newspaperman, oil mogul, and philanthropist, left provisions in his will for the creation of the **Amon Carter Museum.** Originally called the Amon Carter Museum of Western Art, the facility opened in 1961 with Carter's collection of paintings by Frederic Remington and Charles M. Russell. By 1967, the museum had undergone a name change and had begun to incorporate works by American artists of the 19th and early 20th centuries. The photographic collection, among the country's largest, spans the history of the medium, from 19th-century daguerreotypes to 21st-century digital prints. *3501 Camp Bowie Boulevard; 817-738-1933.*

Downhill from the Amon Carter Museum is the **Kimbell Art Museum,** the legacy of industrialist Kay Kimbell and his wife, Velma Fuller Kimbell. The building, by the great modernist architect Louis I. Kahn, is an impressive feat of imagination and engineering, consisting of six long concrete galleries with barrel-vaulted ceilings and skylights running the length of each. Baffles underneath the skylights diffuse the harsh Texas sun, creating an even luminosity throughout the building. For Kahn, the vaults and baffles realized one of his great architectural ambitions, to "define spaces through unification of light and structure." The Kimbell collection, though, can hardly be upstaged by a building, even one as singular as Kahn's. Works by Tiepolo, El Greco, Caravaggio, Goya, Velázquez, and Corot share space with old masters paintings, neoclassical and postwar sculpture, and 20th-century paintings. The 52,000-square-foot museum also exhibits Greek and Roman antiquities, African and Pre-Columbian art, and one of the largest collections of Asian art in North America. *3333 Camp Bowie Boulevard; 817-332-8451.*

The Japanese architect Tadao Ando's design for the **Modern Art Museum of Fort Worth** comes dangerously close to outdazzling the art. The building, which opened in 2002, consists of five glass pavilions built on a shimmering lagoon. The idyllic mood sets the right tone for contemplating one of the country's strongest collections of post–World War II painting and sculpture. The 53,000-square-foot exhibition space holds works by icons of modernism and later movements, from Picasso and Jackson Pollock to Carrie Mae Weems, Andy Warhol, and Cindy Sherman. *3200 Darnell Street; 817-738-9215.*

The **Will Rogers Memorial Center,** the site of the midwinter Southwestern Exposition and Livestock Show, is an enormous complex that sprawls over 85 acres, 45 of them under one roof. The art deco Coliseum, Will Rogers Auditorium, and the Landmark Pioneer Tower in front of it were built in 1936, the year of the Texas Centennial. In subsequent years came the Amon G. Carter Jr. Exhibits Hall and the Will Rogers Equestrian Center, plus additional arenas and numerous barns. Electra Waggoner Biggs's statue of Will Rogers, one of the early 20th century's most popular performers, stands near the tower at the main entrance to the complex. *3401 West Lancaster Avenue; 817-871-8150.*

When rancher Connie Douglas Reeves of Fredericksburg, Texas, was inducted into the **National Cowgirl Museum & Hall of Fame** in 1997, at age 95, her advice to cowgirls was "Always saddle your own horse"—great advice for women in any field. Exhibits at the museum, near the Will Rogers Memorial Center, honor more than 160 women like Connie—from pioneers to rodeo performers to entertainers—who "exemplify the pioneering spirit of the American West."

Patrons size up a cubist masterwork at Fort Worth's Kimbell Art Museum.

The museum's interactive exhibits, photographs and artifacts—costumes, saddles, photographs, programs, memorabilia—explain the contributions of Indian guide Sacajawea, sharpshooter Annie Oakley, performer Dale Evans, Supreme Court Justice Sandra Day O'Connor, painter Georgia O'Keeffe, and many others. *1720 Gendy Street; 817-336-4475.*

SOUTHWESTERN EXPOSITION AND LIVESTOCK SHOW AND RODEO

A place called Cowtown *has* to have a stock show, and the one held in Fort Worth every year since 1896 is a doozy. Its formal name is Southwestern Exposition and Livestock Show and Rodeo, but since that's way too long for comfort, most people just call it the Fort Worth Stock Show. The first shows were held in the Northside stockyards district, but the Will Rogers Memorial Center and Coliseum, in the Fort Worth Cultural District, has been the event's home since 1944.

The first one ran two days; today the show, attended by more than 900,000 visitors, spans 23 days from mid-January to early February, and it's chock full of livestock competitions, stock auctions, ranch and professional rodeos, carnival rides, and entertainment. More than 200 vendors peddle everything from belt buckles to ranching equipment, and—as we say in Texas, "Now you ain't gonna b'lieve this"—pig-grooming supplies: one vendor will sell you everything you need to prepare your porker for competition.

The rodeo is arguably the most popular part of the Stock Show—or, rather, the rodeos. First, there's a one-day ranch rodeo, with working cowhands competing in real-life cattle-handling skills. Instead of riding bulls—not a talent you need on a ranch—they demonstrate ranch doctoring, calf branding, stock sorting, bronc riding, and wild-cow milking. The two-day *Exhibición Charra Mexicana* includes a traditional Mexican rodeo and entertainment—mariachi bands, *folklorico* dancing, and more. Then there's the 17-day, 30-performance professional rodeo staged by 900 cowboys and cowgirls, with competitions in calf roping, steer wrestling, bull riding, bronc riding, and barrel racing. Chuck-wagon races and fireworks provide extra excitement.

Ranch families bring more than 20,000 animals: cattle, horses, donkeys, and mules, but also llamas, goats, pigs, chickens, rabbits, and pigeons—to compete in the shows. Some visitors enjoy wandering through the livestock barns, watching young competitors preparing their animals for show: where else can you watch a goat getting a shampoo and blow-dry, followed by a spritz of hair spray?

(above) The Modern Art Museum. (following pages) Longhorns at the Fort Worth Stock Yards.

The **Cattle Raisers Museum,** in the Texas and Southwestern Cattle Raisers Association headquarters, outlines the history of Texas's cattle industry with audio-visual displays, historic photographs, and artifacts. Exhibits also honor ranching pioneers such as Charles Goodnight—who with Oliver Loving blazed the Goodnight-Loving Trail, which opened up cattle driving west to New Mexico and Colorado's market—as well as the lesser known but well-represented black cowboys: nearly 8,000 black ex-slaves and free men who joined the cattle industry after the Civil War. *1301 West Seventh Street; 817-332-8551.*

■ **GARDENS**   *map page 86, A-4*

The 109-acre **Fort Worth Botanic Garden,** a major Depression-era public-works project, continues to pay annual aesthetic dividends. Among the 21 gardens here are the Lower Rose Garden, whose classical design was inspired by the Villa Lante gardens in Bagnaia, Italy, and the Oval Rose Garden, where many Texas roses grow. (The peak blooming times for the roses are April and October.) The Japanese Garden is achingly beautiful in fall, when the leaves on the maples begin to turn, and spring, when cherry and other blossoms burst forth. *3220 Botanic Garden Drive, at University Drive; 817-871-7686.*

Going with the flow at the Fort Worth Water Gardens.

Although it's called **Fort Worth Water Gardens,** this popular attraction, designed by Philip Johnson and John Burgee in the 1970s, is actually four blocks of concrete, waterfalls, and water sculptures imaginatively shaped to look like an impromptu canyon. Dropping below street level by almost 100 feet, this urban gorge is filled with plants and trees around which water rushes, spills, swirls, and cascades into a series of pools. Some locals think of the gardens as a giant drain, but on a hot summer day there's no mistaking it for anything but a cooling oasis. *Between Houston and Commerce Streets, south of the Convention Center.*

■ SUNDANCE SQUARE *map page 86, A-4*
Sundance Square, named for Butch Cassidy's pal the Sundance Kid, who hid from the law in downtown Fort Worth, is an entertainment and shopping district of new buildings and renovated early-20th-century ones. Among the latter is the medieval-style **Knights of Pythias Hall** (Third and Main Streets), the square's oldest building and the world's first Pythian Temple—both points of distinction for this fraternal order established in Washington, D.C., in 1864. A 7-foot-tall knight created in 1882 from galvanized iron stands in a niche above the third floor. *Houston, Commerce, Second, and Third Streets.*

The **Sid Richardson Collection of Western Art** is the legacy of a wealthy wild-catter who lived in Fort Worth until his death in 1959. Since 1982, the museum has displayed Richardson's collection of paintings by Frederic Remington and Charles M. Russell. It is no coincidence that his museum is in Sundance Square. The square was developed by Richardson's grandnephews, collectively known as the Bass family. Perry Richardson Bass, Sid Richardson Bass, Edward Perry Bass, Robert Muse Bass, and Lee Marshall Bass are among the wealthiest individuals in Texas, their cumulative assets totaling several billion dollars. Because they pour many millions into renovating vast areas of the city, one writer has referred to the Bass clan as the Medicis of Fort Worth. *309 Main Street; 817-332-6554.*

The 2,000-seat **Bass Performance Hall**, another product of the Bass family's largesse, is the home of the Fort Worth Symphony Orchestra, the Fort Worth Opera, Texas Ballet Theater, and, once every four years, the Van Cliburn International Piano Competition. The building has almost the exact same dimensions as New York's Carnegie Hall. Behind the creamy limestone facade, stacked lobbies are linked by marble staircases and decorated with silvery columns and arches trimmed with art glass. The 2,000-seat horseshoe-shaped auditorium's elaborate balcony fronts are detailed with wood trim and gold sconces, the overall effect recalling the opulence of opera houses of the 1800s. You can't miss the hall: two enormous bas-relief trumpeting angels are mounted on the facade. *Fourth and Calhoun Streets; 817-212-4325.*

■ FORT WORTH STOCKYARDS NATIONAL HISTORIC DISTRICT
map page 86, A-4

Western-theme establishments line Exchange Avenue, the main artery of the Fort Worth Stockyards National Historic District, occupying buildings that once housed meat-packing and other concerns. The past bleeds through here and there—you'll most certainly catch a whiff of it during the daily (weather permitting) longhorn cattle drives. The drives start from the **Fort Worth Livestock Exchange** (131 East Exchange Avenue). Inside the exchange, the **Stockyards Museum** (817-625-5087) has exhibits about the stockyards and the men who worked them. Western-style nightlife is celebrated in nearly two dozen Historic District clubs. On weekends, **Billy Bob's Texas** (2520 Rodeo Plaza; 817-624-7117) presents stars and rising stars in country, pop, and rock music. *From North Main Street to Decatur Avenue, between NE 23rd and NE 28th Streets.*

■ TRAVEL BASICS

Getting Around: Interstate 20 enters Fort Worth from the west, jogs a little south, crosses the Dallas–Fort Worth boundary, and continues east through the southern reaches of Dallas. U.S. 80 parallels it east of Dallas, a few miles to the north. Interstate 30 splits off from I-20 west of Fort Worth, cuts directly through the two cities, turns northeast and continues toward the northeast corner of the state. U.S. 75 comes south into Dallas from Oklahoma, becoming the North Central Expressway in town. Interstate 45 appears to be a continuation of U.S. 75 going south to Houston and Galveston. Interstate 35 comes south from Oklahoma toward Fort Worth; 35 miles north of Fort Worth, it splits: I-35W goes through Fort Worth, I-35E goes through Dallas. About 65 miles south of Dallas, the two legs rejoin; I-35 then proceeds south through Waco, Austin, and San Antonio to Laredo on the Mexican border.

Dallas Area Rapid Transit (DART; 214-979-1111) operates bus service within the city of Dallas; DART's electric-powered light-rail trains run from downtown Dallas to Richardson and Plano on the north, Garland on the northeast and two areas of Oak Cliff to the south. In cooperation with the Fort Worth bus system,

The Fort Worth Livestock Exchange, photographed shortly after it opened for business in 1902.

known as **"The T,"** DART also operates the commuter diesel trains of the **Trinity Railway Express**, from downtown Dallas's Union Station (Houston and Young Streets) to downtown Fort Worth's Intermodal Transportation Center (1000 Jones Street, at Ninth Street; 817-215-8600). The line's several stops include DFW International Airport.

Climate: Temperatures in the Dallas–Fort Worth area are hot in summer, with highs usually reaching the high 90s Fahrenheit, with occasional spikes up to 105 or more. In the hottest months, July and August, lows average in the 70s and sometimes don't dip below the mid-80s.

Winters here are often mild, with highs in the 50s and lows in the 30s. Cold snaps can occur for a few days at a time when Arctic fronts move through, but snow and ice are rare. Rain averages 36 inches annually, with the heaviest precipitation coming in May and October and the lightest in January and February. Expect high winds, at times gusting from 30 to 40 miles per hour, at any time between early February and late April.

E A S T   T E X A S

Texas east of I-35 and north of I-10 stands out from the rest of the state as a color: it is definitively, gloriously *green*. The region's lushness is unmistakable, even in winter. Of 207 species of trees native to Texas, 142 grow in the acidic soils of East Texas; 79 of them, including the Southern sugar maple and the pignut hickory, can be found only in that part of the state. East Texas is verdant largely because it receives 30 or more inches of rain a year, with the eastern edge receiving nearly twice that amount. Pine trees—longleaf, shortleaf, and loblolly—provide the ever-green background throughout the year, and in summer, magnolia, oak, elm, hick-ory, tupelo, sweet gum, and black gum trees add subtly varying shades. Creamy white magnolia and dogwood blooms and pink azalea blossoms create springtime accents, and the brilliant oranges and reds of sweet gum leaves against the pine trees render autumn dramatically beautiful.

East Texas is the state's most densely populated sector. Its approximately 50,000 square miles account for only 19 percent of the state's land area, but are home to more than 40 percent of its people, most of whom live in Dallas and Houston. Drivers in West Texas can easily go 90 miles to get from one town to another; in East Texas, most towns lie within 10 or 12 miles of their neighbors.

The people who originally settled East Texas had, for the most part, moved west into Texas from the Deep South, and the region still bears their influence. They were small landholders and farmers, raising crops along with a few head of live-stock. Since the land was fertile and well-watered, they could grow all they could handle on a few acres; they had no need of the vast acreage essential to survival in West Texas and the Panhandle.

Rural East Texans tend to stay close to home. Even when they take jobs in cities, many prefer to commute from their piece of land in the country. Cafés and restau-rants in smaller towns throughout the region serve mostly Southern-style foods: the chicken is fried, and the fish of the day is usually catfish, also fried, and served with (fried) hush puppies and french fries. Cream gravy is generously ladled over entrées, mashed potatoes, and biscuits at breakfast; and many otherwise healthful vegetables are seasoned with smoked pork: fatback, bacon, or hog jowl. Overt racial discrimination is a thing of the past, but you'll still see the occasional pickup truck displaying a Confederate battle-flag bumper sticker.

In East Texas, sometimes even the water—in this case, Caddo Lake—is green.

■ COTTON, CATTLE, LUMBER, AND OIL

When the journalist John Gunther drove through Texas in 1946, he noted that the "east is, by and large, cotton country, with tenant farming, a Mississippi Delta culture, mushrooming industries, big towns, poor whites, most of the state's Negroes, and, of course, oil." The key words in his description were "cotton," "industry," and "oil." In all these pursuits, East Texas was the state's pioneer.

Though the Spanish had established several outposts in Texas prior to the 19th century, nowhere was it thickly populated until Anglo settlers came to East Texas following the Mexican War of Independence in 1821. For the most part, the settlers came from the Old South in search of new lands to seed in cotton. Since the crop couldn't thrive west of the 30-inch rainfall line without deep-well irrigation, East Texas became the site of the state's first big cotton plantations, and the birthplace of commercial agriculture in Texas.

Cotton cultivation began in East Texas during the slavery era. By the dawn of the 20th century, about three-quarters of the state's acreage lay east of today's I-35, and two-thirds of those who cultivated it were tenant farmers. The tractors and harvesting machines that became available to American farmers after World War II made it possible for a single family to cultivate a large plot—up to a half-mile square, or 320 acres, sometimes more. But the cost of machinery made big farms almost necessary: volume had to be sufficiently high to justify the large expense. Because land was cheaper in West and North Texas and the drier climate meant fewer insect infestations, cotton growing in East Texas began to decline. After deep-well irrigation became common in the west and north at the end of World War II, the East Texas cotton economy slipped even more. By the early 1960s, most Texas cotton farming had shifted west of I-35, where most of today's crop is grown. Since 1880, Texas has been the United States's leading cotton producer; Texas today harvests approximately one-fourth of total U.S. production each year.

After the Civil War and the emancipation of slaves, two less labor-intensive agricultural activities began taking the place of the old crop in East Texas. According to Texas myth, ranching was conducted on huge spreads of South and West Texas, but East Texas has long been the industry's literal birthplace: cattle were born here so that mother cows and their calves could feast on East Texas grasses until the latter could forage for themselves. As yearlings, the calves were shipped to larger spreads in the western part of the state, where the bacteria and insects that flourish in humid climes couldn't harm them as much.

Texas harvests close to one-fourth of the total U.S. production of cotton each year.

Before the late 1960s, cattle populations were fairly well dispersed across Texas, with the exception of a few desert counties in the sheep-and-goat country of the Trans-Pecos. Today, the highest concentrations are in East Texas, where the cattle are born, and the Panhandle, where they are fattened and slaughtered. But unless you leave the highways and drive down one of the many dirt roads in rural East Texas, you might never guess the cattle are here. Like so much else in the life of the region, cattle ranches are screened from view by a curtain of pine trees along the highways. And the numbers aren't great in any one pasture, because the mostly small-time farmers here only keep between 10 and 100 cattle on their home places.

The influx of settlers after the Texas Revolution created a demand for lumber, and the sawmills that had been operating for the previous two decades in East Texas, the only naturally wooded part of the state, became the nucleus of a growing industry. By 1860, at least 200 were in operation. Toward the end of the 1870s, railroads proliferated, and lumbermen began building larger mills. Many of the operators were of the "cut it all and get out" school of lumbering; within 50 years, 18 million acres of virgin pine forests had been felled for lumber. Virgin pine can now only be found in natural preserves, though plantation pines have since returned to some of the clear-cut acreage.

The Waco citizenry prepares for the Waco Texas Cotton Palace Pageant in this 1927 photo.

With its ample supplies of water and trees, East Texas became an ideal location for paper manufacturers; more paper than lumber comes from the plantation pines here. Clear-cutting is the rule, to the chagrin of the state's ecologists, whose concerns sometimes clash with those of both owners and workers; the sawmills and paper plants that dominate parts of the region are major sources of employment.

East Texas is also where the oil boom began. The first commercially significant strike in the state's history came at Corsicana, 55 miles southeast of Dallas, shortly before the turn of the 20th century. Workers drilling a water well for the city in 1894 found oil instead. By the following year, a company had been formed to exploit the find; the wells around Corsicana produced about a half-million barrels of oil per year, leading to construction of the state's first refinery.

Texas moved into oil big-time on January 10, 1901, when the Spindletop gusher blew its stack near Beaumont. First, six tons of 4-inch drilling pipe shot up out of the drill hole, followed by a geyser of oil 100 feet high. After it was capped, the well put out an estimated 100,000 barrels a day. During its first year the

Spindletop well produced more than three million barrels of oil. For months it produced more oil than anybody could handle; until storage facilities could be built, the surplus had to be stored in holes, or tanks, dug out of the earth.

The oil companies Texaco, Mobil, and Gulf arose from the Corsicana and Spindletop discoveries, and refineries sprang up at Port Arthur, Beaumont, and Houston to process Spindletop's output alone. But even the Corsicana and Spindletop booms didn't make Texas the leader in national petroleum production. The discovery of the gigantic East Texas field did that. In 1930, a well near Kilgore started to produce oil, initially 300 barrels per day. Not long after, 1,000 wells sprouted, all in a 40-by-5-mile patch. With no regulation of well numbers or spacing, oil-hungry operators drilled wells on every available piece of land. In some cases, the legs of drilling derricks touched each other. Within seven months, the glut of "Texas tea" pouring out of northeast Texas had driven the price of oil from 99 cents per barrel to 13 cents. The feverish overproduction had reduced the reservoir pressure in the field by 130 pounds per square inch, making the remaining oil extremely difficult to extract. The Texas Legislature passed regulations restricting production, and Texas Rangers were sent into the field to maintain order. Oil smuggling became as common as cattle rustling had been in a previous era. The East Texas field had produced more than five billion barrels of oil by the early 1990s.

SON OF SPINDLETOP

One of the sons of Spindletop was the legendary billionaire Howard Robard Hughes Jr., born in Humble, Texas, the only child of an Eastern man attracted to the state by the excitement surrounding the Spindletop discovery. Hughes Sr., the founder of the Hughes Tool Company, made his fortune developing specialized drilling tools for oil exploration. His son inherited his father's love for things mechanical and his mother's health phobias. He had a fling at making movies and founded Hughes Aircraft to develop planes for the military. One of those, an experimental flying boat made of laminated wood—and the largest plane ever built—was nicknamed the Spruce Goose. Its maiden (and only) flight took place in 1947. Hughes built an empire that at various times included Hughes Tool, the RKO movie studio, many Las Vegas properties, Air West, and Trans-World Airlines. By the early 1970s, Hughes's health was deteriorating, and he had become increasingly reclusive. He died in April 1976, while en route to a Houston hospital.

The three big oil companies expanded over the years, eventually merging with competitors to form still larger corporations. Texaco began as the Texas Company, sired in Beaumont by Joseph S. Cullinan and the New York investor Arnold Schlaet in 1902. The name was changed to Texaco Inc. in 1959, and following a merger completed in 2001 became known as ChevronTexaco. (The conglomerate is now a California-based company.) ExxonMobil began as Magnolia Petroleum Company in 1911, a consolidation of several earlier companies: the J. S. Cullinan Company, which began operating a refinery at Corsicana in 1898; the Corsicana Petroleum Company, organized in 1899; and the Security Oil company, which had been the George A. Burts Refining Company, which itself had begun in 1901 in the wake of the Spindletop discovery. (Lots of wheelin' and dealin' and tradin' goes on in the Texas "awl bidness," as some locals pronounce it.) Mobil Oil Company was formed in 1959 as an operating division of Socony Mobil; Magnolia Petroleum merged with Socony Mobil later in 1959, and Mobil merged with Exxon Corporation in 1999. Gulf Oil Corporation was an expansion of the J. M. Guffey Petroleum Company, which was organized in May 1901 to exploit the Spindletop discovery. Guffey organized the Gulf Refining Company to be the refining and marketing arm of the company. Gulf Oil was formed in 1907. It's now based in Chelsea, Massachusetts, but at least it's still called Gulf Oil.

■ FROM DALLAS TO WACO

To travel south from Dallas to Waco along I-35 is to cross 90 miles of rolling prairie, most of it empty, save for the occasional cedar tree or clutch of grazing cows. Make a short detour into Waxahachie, however, 30 miles south of Dallas on I-35, and you'll be treated to an over-the-top piece of Victorian architecture that evokes the grandeur of a previous era.

■ WAXAHACHIE *map page 129, A-2*
The red sandstone and granite **Ellis County Courthouse,** which opened in 1897, is perhaps the grandest of several Texas courthouses designed by James Riely Gordon. The detailing of this exuberant Richardsonian Romanesque edifice includes multiple pairs of faces, one attractive, and the other grotesque. Waxahachie lore claims that one of the stonemasons became enamored of a local girl who did not return his interest, so he recorded his love and his anguish in stone for all eternity. The carvings, so sophisticated in their level of detail, could not have been done

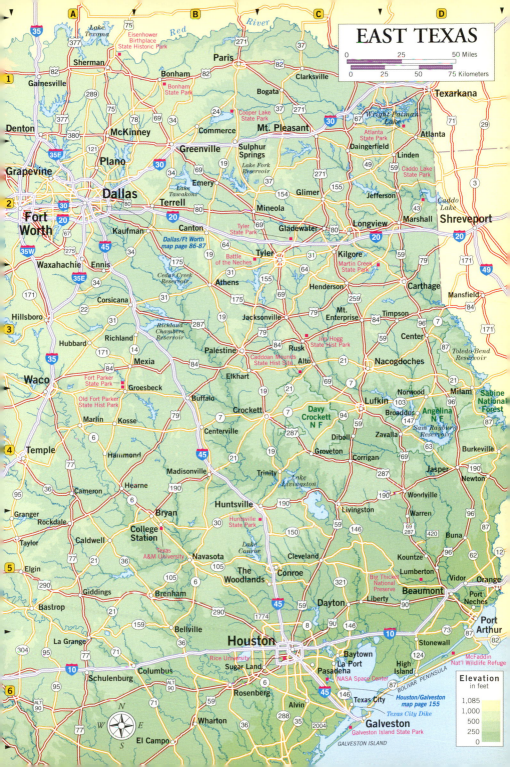

EAST TEXAS

0   25   50 Miles

0   25   50   75 Kilometers

Elevation in feet

| 1,085 |
| 1,000 |
| 500 |
| 250 |
| 0 |

by one person, however, and are thought to be the work of several German stone-masons who traveled throughout the Midwest and South. *115 West Franklin Street.*

The 2,500-seat **Chautauqua Auditorium** is a visible reminder of the days when traveling Chautauqua programs brought education, culture, morality, and enter-tainment to rural towns across the country. The organization was created in Chautauqua Lake, New York, in 1874 by Methodist minister John Vincent and businessman Lewis Miller. Chautauqua started as a summertime school activity for people living outside the city, but over the course of several years it developed into full-time classes and eventually a correspondence course for hungry minds and souls stuck in far-flung climes.

The edifice of the Ellis County Courthouse features the handiwork of German stonemasons.

Chautauqua Auditorium.

By the turn of the 20th century, the Chautauqua concept had become so popular that the organization decided to take its show on the road, first to the northernmost regions of the country and then to the southern states. Bible lessons, speeches on morality and civics, music, and storytelling enchanted thousands of people who by design or just bad luck found themselves marooned in the middle of nowhere. Waxahachie's Chautauqua Auditorium, one of only a handful of such places in the Southwest, was built in 1902 and remained a popular gathering place until the late 1920s, when radio, movies, and the automobile made Chautauqua programs obsolete. The auditorium was extensively renovated in 1976 and is used today for music and theater productions. *Getzendaner Park, South Grand Avenue off West Main Street.*

■ CORSICANA *map page 129, A-3*
Antebellum houses, buildings, and monuments of the state's first oil boom provide a rich historical backdrop to Corsicana, 55 miles southeast of Dallas on I-45. Oil was accidentally discovered here in 1894—the drillers were actually looking for water—and within a dozen years nearly 300 wells were operating in a 5-by-2-mile strip east of town. In 1897, the state's first refinery was built here.

The Collin Street Bakery has been selling its celebrated fruitcakes since 1896.

Production has gone down, up, and back down since the heady rush of Corsicana's first oil boom, but owing to refinements in methodology, production has recently been between 200,000 and 300,000 barrels of oil per year. Today, Corsicana is best known for the Original Deluxe Fruitcake, which has been produced by the **Collin Street Bakery** (401 West Seventh Avenue; 903-872-8111) since 1896. The bakery ships fruitcakes all over the world and sells them year-round in Corsicana.

■ WACO   *map page 129, A-3/4*

Waco straddles the borders of East, West, and Central Texas, but the town's history ties it most strongly to the eastern part of the state. Like Dallas, Waco was established on the Brazos River early in the 1840s, during the era of the Republic of Texas. An ancient agricultural village of native Americans had occupied the area nearest the river. By the onset of the Civil War, Waco's commerce was largely dependent on the cotton plantations of the Brazos Valley. A cotton mill in town produced cloth for the Confederacy, but the local economy was devastated when manpower was drained by the demands of the Confederate military. The area recovered rapidly, however, when cattle drives from Texas to the Midwest began after the war; a major trail bringing cattle up from the south crossed the Brazos River at Waco. The introduction of railroads here in the 1870s and 1880s turned the city into a shipping hub for cotton, wool, and hides.

Many people come to Waco to see **Baylor University,** which consolidated with Waco University in 1887. The Baptist university's 450-acre campus is as sprawling as it is attractive, with many open green spaces, pleasant walks organized around distinctive buildings, and restaurants and cafés. There's even a golf course.

Academics, poetry aficionados, and lovers of the decorative arts seek out the **Armstrong Browning Library,** which houses one of the largest collections of documents relating to Robert and Elizabeth Barrett Browning. The two starry-eyed Victorian poet-lovers never visited Texas, but Andrew Joseph Armstrong, a long-time Baylor English professor, admired their poetry; starting in 1906, he began collecting the poems and all things relating to them. The archive owns many precious first editions, unpublished manuscripts, critical analyses, biographies, and letters written by the poets.

A grand Renaissance-style manse designed in the mid-1940s by the Fort Worth architect Wyatt C. Frederick, the library brims with handcrafted furniture and

The crime-fighting feats of the mighty Texas Rangers are celebrated at their hall of fame.

sculpture from the late 1800s. The Elizabeth Barrett Browning Salon showcases a stunning collection of porcelain figurines and antiques, and there are many fine paintings and drawings, most of them portraits of the two poets by various artists. One painting, an oil portrait by Pen Browning of Robert, his father, rests in a gold-leaf wood frame bearing elaborate carvings of bells and pomegranates. It's a motif seen throughout the house—on the molded plaster ceiling, at the tops of pilasters, around doors and windows, and on the border of the terrazzo floor. The motif refers to a collection of essays Browning penned called *Bells and Pomegranates*, a name he used to symbolize the "music and meaning" of poetry. Many of the library's 56 stained-glass windows depict themes from the Brownings' poems. *Eighth Street at Speight Avenue; 254-710-3566.*

The soft drink Dr Pepper—no period in the name, if you please—was invented at Waco's Old Corner Drug Store in 1885, one year before Coca-Cola. The bottler has established a shrine to the company's history, the **Dr Pepper Museum,** inside the 1906 bottling plant where the soda was first commercially produced, and the 18,000-square-foot facility is a hoot. Vintage photographs reveal the people behind the drink, including its inventor, Dr. Charles Alderton, a pharmacist who liked to

Texans honor their athletic heroes at the Texas Sports Hall of Fame.

play with fizzy fruit juices. An audio-animatronic double of the good doctor explains the history of Waco and the drink. You can watch 40 years of Dr Pepper TV commercials on DVD, pick up Dr Pepper memorabilia at the gift shop, and visit the fully stocked soda fountain to sample refreshments, most of them made using this famous drink. *300 South Fifth Street; 254-757-1025.*

To revel in the Wild West, head over to the **Texas Ranger Hall of Fame & Museum** (Fort Fisher Park, I-35 Exit 335-B; 254-750-8631), known for its collection of 19th-century pistols and its photos of the Rangers' biggest criminal catches (and a few they didn't nab). Exhibits at the nearby **Texas Sports Hall of Fame** (Fort Fisher Park, 1108 South University Parks Drive; 254-756-1633) chronicle Texas tennis and high school football and basketball.

■ **WACO TRAGEDIES**

Two follies a hundred years apart—one bizarre, the other plainly tragic—bracket Waco's modern history. The first, called the Crash at Crush, was a publicity stunt staged near Waco. On September 16, 1896, more than two dozen trains delivered between 35,000 and 40,000 passengers to witness the Great Train Wreck. The

The Crash at Crush was a staged event that centered on the deliberate collision of two speeding locomotives. Three spectators were killed by flying debris.

temporary village of Crush, complete with saloons, eateries, and politicians on the stump, was created solely for the spectacle. Two Baldwin steam locomotives, both pulling six freight cars, met in the center of the village. Their engineers then backed them up a mile in opposite directions before hurtling them down the track at each other at an estimated 45 miles per hour. The engineers jumped to the ground just in time, but on impact both trains' boilers unexpectedly exploded, sending iron and steel shrapnel into the crowd. Two young men and a young woman were killed, and a photographer lost an eye.

The death toll from Waco's second tragedy, which unfolded in early 1993, was far greater. The Branch Davidians, a radical sect of Seventh-Day Adventists, had lived here for years in obscurity, but under the leadership of David Koresh they had begun storing arms at their Mount Carmel compound, about 10 miles northeast of the city. When the U.S. Bureau of Alcohol, Tobacco, and Firearms got wind of this development, 100 ATF agents were called in to raid the place. Four agents and five Davidians died in the ensuing gunfight, and the Federal Bureau of Investigation began a 51-day siege. On April 19, FBI agents attempted to end the standoff by ramming the Davidian compound with tanks and injecting tear gas inside. A building erupted in flames, killing more than 70 of those inside.

■ TEXAS A&M *map page 129, A/B-5*

The educational center of East Texas lies about 90 miles southeast of Waco along Route 6. College Station (usually mentioned along with the town next door as Bryan–College Station) is best known for Texas A&M University, which was originally called Agricultural and Mechanical College of Texas.

Even though most Texans prefer the country-boy stereotype of the honest, self-effacing "Aggie," some Texans—especially University of Texas "Longhorns"—tell Aggie jokes that paint A&M students and alums as dumb hicks. "Did you hear about the fire at the Aggie library?" they might ask. "It burned both books." Teasing quips make A&M a part of everyday conversation across the state, but Aggies insist that Texans too rarely discuss the school's virtues. One of those is undeniable: during World War II, Texas A&M provided 14,000 officers, including 29 generals, to the American military, more than any other college in the nation.

A&M, which numbers about 45,000 students, is the oldest of the state colleges in Texas. It was founded in 1876, five years before the University of Texas. Because the federal Morrill Act of 1862 provided grants to state colleges that emphasized agricultural and mechanical arts, A&M began life as an agro-tech college, known for producing farmers and engineers. Later, its curriculum was expanded to include military science (the Corps of Cadets is a revered Aggie tradition). Women were admitted to the institution on a limited basis starting in 1963, and on an equal basis with men since 1971.

In 1997, the **George Bush Presidential Library and Museum** opened on a plaza adjacent to the Presidential Conference Center and the Texas A&M Academic Center. The library's location on the campus is a source of confusion; many mistakenly think George Herbert Walker Bush—the 41st president—attended the school. Rather, the site was selected because of its proximity to Houston, Bush's adopted home. Photographs, videotapes, memorabilia, and changing exhibits tell Bush's story, from his early years at Yale to life at 1600 Pennsylvania Avenue. Thousands of objects are on display, many of them gifts given by heads of state, as well as personal effects from Bush's Camp David and White House offices. *1000 George Bush Drive West; 979-691-4000.*

One of the most fervent college rivalries in the country is that between A&M and the University of Texas at Austin. Tensions reach a head each Thanksgiving Day, when teams from the two schools meet on the gridiron. Despite their athletic and other competition, the two universities share one of the largest endowments in the nation, the Permanent University Fund, composed in large part of 2.4 million acres of land. The Congress of the Republic of Texas began the process in 1839 by setting aside 220,000 acres of prime agricultural land to support a university—but years passed and no university was built. The state legislature added even more land to the endowment in 1858. Still no university appeared. In 1876, with settlers pouring into the new state and demanding good land for farming, the university lands were switched to arid West Texas, giving the university an immense plot of land of dubious value. But when oil was discovered in the Permian Basin in 1923, things changed overnight; today the fund's book value is about $3 billion. At first, UT received all the income, but in 1931 the state divided the profits between UT, which receives two-thirds of the fund's income, and A&M, which gets the remaining third. This has given the UT Longhorns, as they call themselves, the basis for what they recite as the original Aggie joke: "Do you know why UT gets two-thirds and A&M gets one-third? . . . Because the Aggies got first choice!"

■ HUNTSVILLE *map page 129, B/C-4*

Texans and historians know Huntsville as the town where Sam Houston lived and died. A city filled with many old and beautiful trees, among them ancient live oaks, Huntsville lies 47 miles east of College Station on Route 30 and about an hour's drive north of Houston on I-45. The **Sam Houston National Forest,** 255 square miles of pine trees and hardwoods, starts on Huntsville's southeastern edge. **Houston Memorial Museum and Park** (1402 19th Street; 936-294-1832) contains Sam Houston's first and longtime home, as well as the more elaborate Steamboat House, where the onetime general, Texas president, governor, and U.S. senator died in 1863. Both dwellings are furnished with period furniture, as is Houston's former law office. Houston and his family are buried in **Oakwood Cemetery** (Avenue I and Ninth Street), near downtown.

People outside Texas are more likely to associate Huntsville with **Sam Houston State University** than with the institution's namesake. The school, with 13,000 students, numbers among its alumni the CBS news anchor Dan Rather and is nationally known for its penology program. The students of the prison-studies program needn't travel far to intern: Huntsville is the headquarters of the Institutional Division of the Texas Criminal Justice Department—the state's far-flung penal system, the second-largest in the United States—and seven prison units ring the city. To most Texans, Huntsville is synonymous with "the Big House."

Sam Houston: first president of Texas and the "wounded Achilles of San Jacinto." The politician is buried near downtown Huntsville.

SAM HOUSTON

And life in the new town [of Houston] was sure to be gay. President Houston never lost sight of his position as the most eligible bachelor in the republic, and the removal of the seat of government to Houston city at the end of April 1837 picked up the pace of his social whirl. It also doubtless increased the frequency with which he was seen in public wearing the wonderful clothes to which he had always been so partial.... Not everyone was impressed. Vice President Mirabeau Lamar was temporarily out of Houston's hair, vacationing back in Georgia, but one Lamar partisan (William D. Redd, 23 May 1837) wrote derisively to his principal:

I find the President extreamly courteaous when he out for general inspection, this seldom oftener than once in sunshine, between eleven & two, he... dresses himself gaudily in self peculiar taste viz. black silk velvet gold lace crimson vest and silver spurs.

By taking a stiff drink, Houston... makes himself again *Hector* upon his feet and no longe the wounded Achilise of San Jacinto ... and with a tread of dominion in his aroganic step strides ... across his own nominated metropolis... to the barkeeper.

—James L. Haley, *Sam Houston,* 2001

Downtown at the **Texas Prison Museum** are guns used in notorious crimes and more than a century's worth of incarceration tools, including balls-and-chains and "Old Sparky," the state's electric chair from 1924 to 1964. *491 Route 75 North, at I-45 Exit 118; 936-295-2155.*

■ PINEY WOODS *map page 129, C-6 to D-2*

Cities mark the boundaries of East Texas on I-35 to the west and I-10 to the south, but small towns and farms are the wellspring of the region's life. Out-of-state tourists rarely visit these towns and their surrounding woods, but East Texas's beautiful national forests and preserves, remnants of the once-vast Piney Woods region, are worth an excursion. The Piney Woods runs roughly in a straight line from Baytown, on I-10, north to the Arkansas line, following several routes, and east to Louisiana. The forested region was once much bigger, about 5,500 square miles of virgin forest.

The region wasn't settled during the era of the Republic of Texas and had few plantations or slaves. But the arrival of railroads in the 1880s introduced large-scale exploitation of the area's timber, and lumbering soon supplanted livestock as the primary source of income. At that time, the forest was mostly virgin longleaf pines, the oldest of which were 4 feet in diameter and on average 150 feet tall, three times as tall as today's commercial pines at harvesting. The ancient pines produced lumber nearly as dense as hardwood and so rich in resin that boards made from them could withstand weathering for generations without paint or protective coverings. The longleaf's tight grain and the relative absence of knotholes made it ideal for furniture and cabinets.

On a drive through the Piney Woods, from as far south as Beaumont to as far north as Texarkana, the evergreens give the landscape a steady dominant hue year-round, with little seasonal change. Your neighbors on the road are likely to be either guys in pickup trucks pulling cattle trailers or two-ton trucks heading for a sawmill or paper mill, hauling log trailers that leave a wake of bark and dirt.

■ **BIG THICKET NATIONAL PRESERVE** *map page 129, D-5*
The Piney Woods region survives in its most lush natural state at Big Thicket National Preserve—nine land units and six water corridors in scattered sites, totaling 152 square miles of virgin pines, underbrush, and marshland. The diversity of the Big Thicket is the result of a convergence of ecosystems that took place during the last Ice Age, bringing together hardwood forests from the east, the Gulf coastal plains, and the Midwest prairies in one geographical area.

The chief tourism office for Big Thicket operations is at its Turkey Creek unit in Kountze. Trails here cross primeval terrain that supports virgin longleaf and more than 85 other tree species, as well as 60 shrub species and 1,000 varieties of flowering plants. Nearly 300 species of birds are known to inhabit the thicket, including red-cockaded woodpeckers, brown-headed nuthatches, and the Bachman's sparrow. Coyotes, bobcats, and armadillos are common in this region, and you're likely to see one or all on a hiking trail here. This is desolation wilderness, and one hears no swish of auto traffic and sees no sign of telephone wires. Only the occasional sound of an airplane passing overhead interrupts the serene chirp and rustle of the forest. *6102 FM 420, off U.S. 69/287, Kountze; 409-246-2337.*

The **Great Texas Coastal Birding Trail,** running for 500 miles from the Louisiana border all the way to Mexico, is essentially a series of wildlife-viewing

sites—310 in all—near major roads and highways. The upper end of the trail crosses the southern end of East Texas and includes sites from Buffalo Bayou in the Houston area to Beaumont, Port Arthur, and the Big Thicket. Maps, which have information about the birds likely to be found at each site and the best season to visit, can be obtained from Texas Parks and Wildlife (888-892-4737).

■ WOODVILLE *map page 129, D-4*

Woodville, about 40 miles north of Beaumont on U.S. 69, is to bass fishing what Las Vegas is to gambling. The nearby Sam Rayburn Reservoir—about 15 miles northeast of Woodville on Route 190/96—is one of the largest inland bodies of water in Texas. Containing 115,000 surface acres of water, the reservoir typically teems with black, white, striped, spotted, largemouth, and Florida bass. Fishing in East Texas is a big deal. At least 1.5 million Texans buy fishing licenses each year, about 75 percent of them for lakes in this region. Boat rigs—cars or pickups with a trailer and a sturdy, showy fiberglass boat in tow—throng the streets of Woodville and Jasper, and coffee-shop conversations are sprinkled with references to "a pumpkinseed Berkley Power lizard," "a tequila sunrise," or a "fliptail lizard," with "buzzbait" thrown in for good measure. Only a bass angler knows for sure what it all means.

■ NACOGDOCHES *map page 129, C-3*

Nacogdoches, 150 miles north of Houston on U.S. 59, is the historical center of the Piney Woods. Caddo Indians were clearing and farming this area at least 500 years before 1716, when one of the five original Spanish missions in Texas was established. Tantalizing glimpses of Caddo Indian culture can be gleaned about 25 miles west of Nacogdoches at **Caddoan Mounds State Historic Site** (Route 21; 936-858-3218). One was clearly a burial site; the skeletal remains of bodies have been unearthed here. The others appear to have been temple mounds. Dating from A.D. 1250, and perhaps even earlier, the earthen structures—between 18 and 26 feet high—are the subject of ongoing archaeological study.

Evidence from the Caddo burial grounds found in Nacogdoches has led archaeologists to conclude that the tribe inhabited the area between A.D. 1250 and 1450.

(previous pages) The Great Texas Coastal Birding Trail runs for 500 miles, from the border of Louisiana all the way to Mexico.

A few hundred years later, Nacogdoches was Mexico's major gateway to the east and a favorite stop for Spanish and American travelers and traders, and by the early 19th century the area had become a focus of revolutionary fervor. In 1819, a group of Mississippians invaded Texas. Under the leadership of Dr. James Long they set up a provisional government at Nacogdoches and declared themselves independent of Spain, calling their rebel state the Republic of Texas and promising men 10 sections of land each to join their ragtag army. The Long Expedition, as historians call it today, fell apart within a year, a victim of poor financing, poor supply lines, and a Mexican government counter-offensive.

Nacogdoches became the camp of a more notable insurgency from 1825 to 1827. Haden Edwards, the head of a settlement company, ran afoul of the Mexican government over land titles held by the American colonists he had brought in. With 200 followers, he and his brother Ben declared a revolt. They set up the State of Fredonia and named Nacogdoches its capital. Newspapers across the country ran stories about "200 Men Against a Nation." The affair brought diplomats from the United States and Mexico into negotiations, but was settled, as the Long Expedition had been, when Mexican troops quelled the rebels.

In 1832, the Mexican commander of the Nacogdoches area demanded that the East Texans surrender their guns. The settlers refused, formed their own militia, and defeated the Mexican garrison at the Battle of Nacogdoches. Although the land remained in Mexican control, never again were Mexican troops stationed there.

The **Old Stone Fort,** on the campus of Stephen F. Austin State University, is a replica of the 1779 structure that witnessed these turbulent events, though not at this location. Erected as a mercantile building called La Casa Piedra (The Stone House), it was constructed of local iron-rich stone, with interior walls of 10- by 14-inch adobe bricks and with sills and casements of hand-hewn black walnut.

At its original location, today's Main and Fredonia Streets, the building stood under nine different flags, including those of three aborted revolutions. It was here that both Long and Edwards set up their governments, and here also that the first newspaper in Texas was for a time published. The "Fort" designation came from La Casa Piedra's incarnation as the Old Stone Fort Saloon in the late 19th century. The building was razed in 1902, but preservationists bought the old stones and in 1936—the year of the Texas Centennial—they reconstructed the historic building where it stands. The fort's museum contains memorabilia of pioneer and Indian life. *Clark and Griffith Boulevards; 936-468-2408.*

In its original incarnation the Old Stone Fort was the scene of many historic moments; nine national flags flew over it, including those of three failed revolutions.

Two miles south of the fort is the **Sterne-Hoya Home,** built in 1828 by Adolphus Sterne for his wife, Ava. A German immigrant who had landed in Nacogdoches in 1824, Sterne worked in various trades and held strong political views. That may be why he ended up playing a part in the Fredonian Rebellion, for which he was later tried for treason but saved from the gallows by influential friends. Prior to independence, Sterne welcomed many colorful rebels into his house, including Sam Houston, who lived with the Sternes for a spell, and Davy Crockett, who stayed there for two weeks in 1835. Sterne sold the house to Joseph von der Hoya in 1869. The humble two-level dwelling, now a museum, contains furniture from both the Sterne and Hoya families, as well as portraits of Sterne and his wife, Sam Houston, and Davy Crockett. Portions of Sterne's diary, kept while he lived here, are on view. *211 South Lanana Street; 936-560-5426.*

The Nacogdoches area made international headlines more recently when the Space Shuttle *Columbia* broke up on reentry into the atmosphere on February 1, 2003, and debris rained down on the city and the surrounding woodlands of East Texas and Louisiana.

■ JACKSONVILLE AND HENDERSON *map page 129, C-3*

Love's Lookout in Jacksonville, roughly 26 miles northwest of Nacogdoches on U.S. 69, serves up what East Texans say is, hands down, the region's most spectacular view, a 35-mile panorama of pine and dogwood trees from a 720-foot-high ridge. The lookout was named for a former owner, Wesley Love, who planted a 600-acre peach orchard in the vicinity in the early 1900s.

Henderson, 35 miles northeast of Jacksonville on U.S. 259, was the center of the boom surrounding the East Texas Oil Field between 1930 and 1940, but these days is more widely known for its **Syrup Festival,** held each November. Syrup lovers from all over Texas come to Heritage to learn the old-fashioned method of making ribbon cane syrup, produced by cooking down the juice squeezed from sugar cane. The smart little **Depot Museum** (514 North High Street; 903-657-4303) has the lowdown on the festival and everything you might want to know about locally made syrups, as well as exhibits on area history.

■ TYLER *map page 129, C-2*

Thirty miles north of Jacksonville on U.S. 69 is Tyler, whose airport serves most of the region. As late as 1940, about half the roses grown commercially in the United States came from the Tyler area. Though competition has reduced the city's share of the industry, it is still celebrated in the 14-acre **Municipal Rose Garden** (1900 West Front Street; 903-531-1212), where 400 rose varieties are cultivated, along with many varieties of camellias and daylilies. The city also salutes its horticultural industry with an annual festival on the adjoining fairgrounds.

About 10 miles northwest of Tyler, off Route 64, is the site of the **Battle of the Neches.** Around 1820, a group of Cherokees settled in the area. Their relations with the Mexican government were generally friendly, and they aided it in combating the 1826 Fredonian Rebellion at Nacogdoches. At the outbreak of the Texas Revolution in 1836, Sam Houston, the republic's first president, negotiated a treaty with Cherokee leader Chief Duwali, also known as Chief Bowles, guaranteeing the tribe neutrality in the conflict and promising it lands along the Angelina River. But the republic's senate refused to ratify the agreement, and Mirabeau B. Lamar, the republic's second president, appointed a commission to expel Cherokees from Texas. Chief Duwali refused to comply, and on July 15 and 16, 1839, Texas soldiers attacked his people, along with Delawares and Shawnees. At least 800 Indians were slaughtered, including Chief Duwali.

Until 1940, half the roses grown commercially in the United States came from Tyler.

■ CANTON, KILGORE, AND MARSHALL *map page 129, B/D-2*

Canton, a small town about 36 miles northwest of Tyler on Route 64, and 59 miles southeast of Dallas on I-20, bills itself as the home of the nation's largest flea market, **First Monday Trade Days,** held the weekend before the first Monday of each month. The outdoor market covers more than 100 acres and accommodates 3,000 vendors, so if you attend, wear comfortable shoes.

Kilgore, about 50 miles north of Nacogdoches on U.S. 259, was the urban center of the 1930s East Texas oil boom, which brought 24,000 wells to a 40-by-6-mile patch of the Piney Woods. At one point, 1,100 oil derricks stood within the city limits of Kilgore, two dozen of them occupying one block alone, known as "the World's Richest Acre." One of the derricks is preserved today as a monument to the era. Entrepreneurs became so frenzied during the boom that a few of them drilled a well through the terrazzo floor of the Kilgore National Bank.

Transportation has always been a key to the success of the Harrison County seat, Marshall, which lies 35 miles east of Kilgore on I-20. In the 19th century the city was a regional railroad hub, and in the 20th century the interstate arrived. The county's famous natives include Lady Bird Johnson, the civil rights leader James L. Farmer Jr., the boxer George Foreman, and the journalist Bill Moyers.

The accomplishments of these and other locals are duly honored at the **Harrison County Historical Museum** (903-938-2680), whose other exhibits include Caddo Indian artifacts and Civil War memorabilia.

■ JEFFERSON AND CADDO LAKE *map page 129, D-2*

The restored commercial buildings of downtown Jefferson lend this town, located 45 miles northeast of Nacogdoches on U.S. 59, the look and feel of a small Old South river-port town. Established during the era of the Republic of Texas, the town sits a few miles west of Caddo Lake, which vacationers ply in rented canoes, taking in views of cypress trees dripping with Spanish moss.

According to an Indian legend, the lake was formed one night when a Caddo chieftain enraged some powerful shaking spirits. The less romantic truth is that Caddo Lake was formed when an ancient 170-mile logjam in the Red River backed up the waters of Big Cypress Bayou, an arm of Cypress Creek, like a dam.

The river port's population was 7,300 in 1872, making it one of Texas's largest cities, second only to Galveston in volume of waterborne commerce. In those days, steamboats working Big Cypress Bayou ran on the Mississippi River from Jefferson to St. Louis and New Orleans, by way of the Red River's dip into Louisiana. Furniture came to Jefferson from Europe via New Orleans, and cotton and produce were shipped out. The town had the state's first icehouse and was the first to use gas for lighting.

Local folklore has it that Jefferson's decline began when, confident of the continuation of the riverboat trade, its leaders refused to make deals with the railroad tycoon Jay Gould. Stung by the town's rebuff, he supposedly refused to run his Texas & Pacific Railway through Jefferson and sent it through the town of Marshall, 16 miles to the south. Locals point to a curse Gould allegedly inscribed in the guest register of Jefferson's venerable Excelsior House hotel. Said guest register is on display in a glass case in the hotel's lobby, and there it is: the date, January 2, 1882, with Jay Gould's purported signature and, alongside it, "The end of Jefferson, Texas." Whoever signed the register, it wasn't Gould. He didn't visit Jefferson until many years later, and the Texas & Pacific laid tracks through the area in the early 1870s, long before Gould acquired the T&P in 1879.

The cause of Jefferson's decline was not Jay Gould but the U.S. Army Corps of Engineers, which in 1873 dynamited the Red River logjam. Water levels in Caddo Lake and the bayou dropped so low that riverboat travel became impossible.

Caddo Lake and **Cypress Creek** have been the subject of controversy ever since. In 1914, Cypress Creek, mostly a muddy bayou after the clearing, was dammed, creating Caddo Lake anew, and making barge traffic possible where automobiles couldn't pass because of bayou mud. This success was followed in 1968 by federal approval of a measure to create deep-water channels linking East Texas to the Red River.

The channels haven't been dug yet, but the business community has geared up to revive the project. East Texas environmentalists, meanwhile, are opposing any step forward. In the meantime, campers can pitch tents or spend a day canoeing at **Caddo Lake State Park** (245 Park Road, Karnack; 903-679-3351), a remote setting with campsites, cabins, and boat ramps. The narrow-gauge **Jefferson & Cypress Bayou Railway** (400 East Austin Street; 903-665-6400), operates steam engines that tour the banks of Big Cypress Bayou on one-hour, 5-mile excursions.

■ TRAVEL BASICS

Getting Around: Interstate 10 hugs the southern border of East Texas, coming in from San Antonio and going through Houston, Beaumont, and Orange on the way to Louisiana. Interstate 20 comes in from Fort Worth and Dallas, passing near Tyler on its way to Shreveport. Interstate 30 starts west of Fort Worth, goes through Dallas, and progresses to the northeast corner of Texas to exit into Arkansas. Interstate 35 marks the western border of East Texas, running from San Antonio in the south to the Oklahoma border in the north, hitting Dallas and Waco along the way. Interstate 45 begins in downtown Dallas, passing Huntsville on its way to Houston and Galveston, and U.S. 59 travels from northeast Texas south through Nacogdoches to Houston. Route 21, sometimes signed as OSR—for Old San Antonio Road—originates in San Antonio and wanders through rural areas of East Texas, from Bryan to Nacogdoches and on to Louisiana.

Climate: Winter highs in the northern part of East Texas average about 60 degrees Fahrenheit but the temperature can get as high as the mid-80s. Lows average in the upper 30s, though a record low of 5 degrees has been recorded. In summer, highs average in the low 90s, but the temperature can rise as high as 110. Summer lows are usually in the low 70s, though lows of 50 degrees are possible. Precipitation averages 43 inches annually, with most of it occurring in May, June, and November.

A butterfly alights upon a coreopsis blossom at an East Texas flower emporium.

H O U S T O N
A N D   G A L V E S T O N

The biggest city in the state—and the nation's fourth-largest—is sprawling Houston, population 1.9 million. If you've just wandered in from the countryside, you'll need to speed up—especially on the highways. Getting downtown, or anywhere in 540-square-mile Houston, is a challenge. The city seems to be one giant freeway system. Interstate 45 drops in from the north—from Dallas—and continues another 45 miles south to Galveston. In addition to its interstates, Houston has a dozen other highway routes, including a loop more than 40 miles in circumference that circles the city. But drive you must: although a light-rail system, the first portion of which debuts in 2004, will eventually stretch from downtown to Reliant Stadium, "Houston public transportation" remains something of an oxymoron.

Given Houston's reputation for economic swashbuckling, from before the oil days to Enron, it is perhaps fitting that two speculators gave the town its start. New York brothers John Kirby Allen and Augustus Chapman Allen promised a grand future for Houston in 1836, touting a vision of ships from New York and New Orleans, crammed with riches and sailing up Buffalo Bayou.

Gail Borden surveyed and mapped Houston, and the Allen brothers successfully lobbied the fledgling Texas Congress to name it the temporary capital of the new republic—a distinction it held only from 1837 to 1839. Houston's settlers were chiefly immigrants from the Deep South who endorsed the slave-plantation system, and the town developed a segregated social structure as a result. The city's housing patterns still reflect that way of life to some degree. Until civil rights laws affecting housing began to be enforced in the 1960s, African-American residents were by and large segregated into areas like Houston's Fifth Ward, which started as a freedmen's town after the Civil War, when newly freed slaves left East Texas plantations and moved into cities seeking work.

Shortly after Houston's founding, cargo ships filled with commercial products landed at Galveston and transferred their loads to river steamships, and thence to Houston for distribution. But the second part of the Allens' plan—getting great ships up Buffalo Bayou, which was usually choked with branches and debris—

The skyscraping Transco Tower is a bold statement of Houston's industrial aspirations.

took a little longer. A rudimentary channel was dug in 1881 through Galveston Bay and Buffalo Bayou to a turning basin just below Houston. This was deepened, widened, and lengthened in 1914 into the Houston Ship Channel, now one of the largest in the country. The Port of Houston (713-670-2416) conducts tours of the Houston Ship Channel.

The discovery of Spindletop Oil Field in nearby Beaumont in 1901 dramatically changed Houston's economy to one of petroleum shipper and processor. During World War II, shipbuilding was added to the mix. Throughout a century of development, Houston has remained the largest unzoned city in the United States, with officials here placing their trust in the free enterprise system rather than the heavy hand of regulation.

Houston's most explosive growth occurred during the oil boom of the 1970s and early 1980s, when a thousand people moved here each week. The Sunday help-wanted ads of Houston's two dailies, the *Houston Chronicle* and *Houston Post,* were being read by thousands of people in the East and Midwest, and rental trailers stacked up in Houston from all over the country as people moved in. By the mid-1980s, a quarter of Houston's residents had been born outside the state. Then came the oil bust, which devastated the economy. Houston's population thinned, and across its suburbs houses were abandoned, their notes unpaid. Oil remains a vital part of the economy, however, and Houston retains its role as an office town for the petroleum industry. The suburbs—Pasadena being the most notorious example—are refinery and petrochemical plant towns.

Oil may reign supreme in Houston, but this is also a hospital town, as well as a center for biotechnology. Texas Medical Center became famous for heart transplants by Drs. Denton Cooley and Michael DeBakey in the late 1960s, and the M. D. Anderson Center is known for its pioneering cancer work. Houston is also home to **Rice University,** sometimes called the Harvard of the South. The institution was named for William Marsh Rice, who became wealthy in the early days of the republic as the co-owner of a grocery store and, later, as the founder of the Houston and Galveston Navigation Company. He moved to Mexico during the Civil War and then to New York in 1896, where he was murdered four years later by his butler and lawyer in a scheme to share his estate. His will called for the establishment of a university. By 1912, when it finally opened, the endowment stood at more than $9 million—enough money at the time to allow students to attend without paying tuition, a privilege that continued until 1965.

HOUSTON

0   3   6 Miles
0   3   6   8 Kilometers

6 Veterans Memorial Dr

To Dallas-Fort Worth

45

North

Hardy

Parkway

Terminal

George Bush International Airport

59

8 Sam Houston Toll

Sam Houston Rd

Tomball Pkwy

8

Rd

Windfern

Fairbanks-N Houston Rd

N Houston-Rosslyn Rd

Aldine-Westfield Rd

Aldine-Mail Rd

Eastex Freeway

Greens Bayou

Mt Houston Rd

Garrett Rd

Sheldon Res

1

2 Northwest Freeway

Hempstead Rd

Clay Rd

Campbell Rd

Bingle Rd

Long Point Rd

Katy

290

610

Pinemont

White Oak Bayou

Wheatly

Airline

E Little York Rd

E 43rd

Dr Tidwell

Road

Rd

Homestead Rd

Halls Bayou

Ley Rd

E Houston Rd

Wayside

Bayou

Beaumont Rd

Ralston Rd

Rd

BR 90

Rd

8

3 To San Antonio

10 Katy Freeway

HOUSTON

Memorial Park

Bayou Bend

Memorial Dr

San Felipe

E 11th

Hardy Dr

Jensen Dr

Liberty Rd

10 East Freeway

Wallisville Rd

GALENA PARK

610

Port of Houston

To Beaumont

10 Freeway

8

Houston Arena

Navigation

Harrisburg

Clinton Dr

Buffalo Bayou

To San Jacinto Monument San Jacinto Museum of History & La Porte

Menil Collection

Rienzi

Cy Twombly Gallery

Richmond Hall

Rothko Chapel

Westheimer Rd

Westpark Frwy

59

BELLAIRE

Bellaire Blvd

Southwest

Bissonnet

Gessner Rd

Hillcroft

S Post Oak Rd

Blue Ridge

Contemporary Arts Museum

Museum of Fine Arts

Zoo

Rice University

Hermann Park

Byzantine Fresco Chapel

Houston Museum of Natural Science

Orange Show

45

Wayside Blvd

Clinton Dr

Griggs Rd

Allen-Genoa

Shaver St

Spencer

Preston

Pasadena Frw

PASADENA

Red Bluff Ave

Beltway

Rd

225

8

610

Main

ALT 90

Reliant Stadium

610

Mykawa St

Bellfort

45 SOUTH HOUSTON

Fairmont Pkwy

East

Genoa-Red Bluff Rd

4

8 Main St

ALT 90

Six Flags & Waterworld

Holmes Rd

Reed Rd

Freeway

Sims Bayou

South Acres Dr

Rd

Rd

Rd

William P Hobby Airport

Almeda-Genoa

Hall

Galveston Road

45 Freeway

Almeda

Genoa

Schurmier Rd

COUNTY

288

8

5 McHard Rd

MISSOURI CITY

HARRIS CO FORT BEND CO

Toll

HARRIS CO BRAZORIA CO

Airline

South

Cullen

Brookside Rd

Airline Rd

Telephone Rd

E Broadway

S Main St

Clear Creek

Dixie Farm Rd

Standolind

To Galveston, Space Center Houston & Armand Bayou Nature Center

Pearland-Sites

BRAZORIA CO GALVESTON CO

35

E Parkwood Ave

HARRIS CO

6

GALVESTON

45

To Houston

0   1   2   3 Miles

Scholes Airport

Moody Gardens

Stewart

342

51st

Seawolf

Broadway

Ave A

Ave F

Moody Mansion

Seawall

25th

28th

Blvd

PELICAN ISLAND

Waterway

Ferry

Railroad Museum

Elissa & Texas Seaport Museum

Historical Museum

Ashton Villa

87

Bishop's Palace

Gulf of Mexico

Houston's Main Street, photographed in the late 19th century.

Despite the oil bust and the more recent fallout from the Enron scandal, Houston continues to show promise, thanks in no small part to the cultural diversity generated by immigration in the 1980s. More than 100 ethnic groups live here, including many Mexicans, Central Americans, and Asians, along with large communities of American Indians, East Indians, and Vietnamese. Many Houstonians of Iranian descent arrived to work in oil- and energy-related industries in the late 1970s. Today the population of this once-typical white/black Southern town is split almost equally into thirds: Hispanics, Anglos, and all other groups, many of them Asian. The city's diversity is also reflected in its gay community, the largest in Texas, which is centered in the Montrose district, southwest of downtown.

Houston remains a significant port, handling chiefly petroleum products and grains. It ranks first in the United States in foreign waterborne commerce, second in total tonnage. Labor unions have always been stronger here than in Dallas, because workers in heavy blue-collar trades—in this case oil refining, petrochemical production, and shipping—tend to organize more than do their counterparts in white-collar and service industries. As a result, lawyers across the state petition judges to try claims lawsuits in the working-class towns of suburban Houston.

The weather in Houston is sometimes so overpowering it becomes the thing you remember most about the place. This may not be the hottest city in Texas, but it can be the most miserable, because its humidity is always high. People visiting Houston on business might not notice this as much as the average tourist, however, because most of the buildings in downtown Houston are connected by an extensive network of underground tunnels. July, August, and September are nearly unbearable: rainfall in these months is frequently torrential, and the lightning accompanying it can be dangerous. It's no wonder that three huge sports-and-entertainment spaces here have retractable roofs.

■ VISITING HOUSTON

Houston's attractions are scattered throughout the city. Most of the art museums and galleries are in the Museum District, near downtown, or in surrounding neighborhoods, but the city's most popular venue, the National Aeronautics and Space Administration's Lyndon B. Johnson Space Center, is 25 miles south of downtown off I-45. The San Jacinto Monument, a massive spire commemorating the success of the Texas Revolution, is about the same distance to the east of downtown, off Route 134.

■ MUSEUM DISTRICT *map page 155, B-3/4*

The two main buildings of the **Museum of Fine Arts,** or MFA, are such bold statements of modern architecture that most people assume the MFA itself is new, but it was established in 1900 and is one of the oldest museums in the Southwest. From 1924 until the early 1950s, the MFA lived on its current site in a cramped white neoclassical facility designed by William Ward Watkin, but in the early 1950s the museum commissioned the great architect Mies van der Rohe to design an expansion. Cullinan Hall was completed in 1958, and the Brown Pavilion followed in 1974, several years after Mies van der Rohe died. Together, these halls, exemplars of the architect's spare International Style, make up the Caroline Wiess Law Building, which contains the bulk of the museum's collection. In 2000, the MFA expanded again, opening an elegant multilevel structure with 28 spacious galleries designed to accumulate light from the building's central skylit atrium. The building can be entered either at street level or through a tunnel—splashed with the colorful light of James Turrell's neon sculpture *The Light Inside*—from the Law building's lower level.

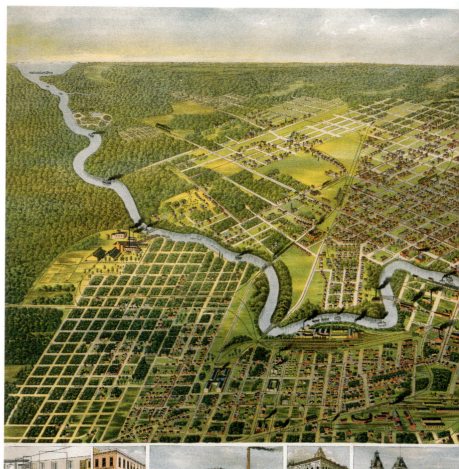

LAND & TRUST COMPANY'S BANK and SAFETY DEPOSIT VAULTS.

ELECTRIC POWER STATION OF THE HOUSTON CITY STREET RAILWAY CO.

A. NAMPE, DRY GOODS AND MILLINERY,
77 & 79 MAIN ST., HOUSTON, TEXAS.

CITY HALL AND TOWN MARKET.

DIRECTORY OF PUBLIC BUILDINGS, HOTELS, RAILROADS and SOME OF THE LEADING MANUFACTORIES.

HOUSTON

A cartographer drew this map of Houston, looking south, in 1891.

The MFA's permanent collection is as deep as it is fresh. The Law building houses masterworks of the Renaissance and baroque periods, 19th-century European art, and an ample survey of Asian, Pre-Columbian, Oceanic, and African art. The museum's particular strength is modern art: the holdings include many pivotal works from the mid-20th century, as well as paintings, prints, and sculpture from the later minimalist and pop movements. On a stroll through the Lillie and Hugh Roy Cullen Sculpture Garden, you can mingle with great works by Rodin, Giacometti, Louise Bourgeois, and Henri Matisse in an attractive natural setting designed by Isamu Noguchi. *1001 Bissonnet Street; 713-639-7300.*

The MFA maintains two excellent house museums within a few miles of the facility, and they're both worth a look. **Bayou Bend,** just outside downtown Houston, is the former estate of philanthropist Ima Hogg, the daughter of James Stephen Hogg, Texas's first native-born governor. The two-story pink stucco mansion, designed by the Houston architect John F. Staub in the late 1920s, is famous for its collection of 19th-century American furniture and paintings. Fourteen acres of gardens, filled with camellias, roses, gardenias, azaleas, and other wonderfully scented flowers and shrubbery, surround the 28-room house, which Hogg donated to the museum in the 1950s. *1 Westcott Street; 713-639-7750.*

Meanwhile, the single-story villa **Rienzi,** set on 4 acres of gardens, is filled with the furniture, paintings, and decorative arts collected by the philanthropists Carroll and Harris Masterson III. Carroll Masterson was the daughter of a founder of the Humble Oil Company, now part of Exxon; Harris was the son of a Houston businessman. *1406 Kirby Drive; 713-639-7800.*

John and Dominique de Menil were French émigrés who landed in Houston after World War II. He was an aristocrat of Napoleonic lineage, she the heiress to the Schlumberger Ltd. oil fortune. Together, they amassed one of the most important private art collections in the world, most of which can be seen at the **Menil Collection,** in a sublime white-steel and gray-cypress building constructed in 1987 by Renzo Piano. Though not encyclopedic, the collection spans three millennia, from Greek and Roman antiquities to a Warhol *Elvis.* From the intervening eras are rare books and illuminated manuscripts, the arts of many tribal cultures, prints and drawings, Byzantine icons, and contemporary paintings, drawings, and sculpture. Dominique de Menil's first love in art was surrealism, and the collection reflects this passion with myriad works by René Magritte and more than 120 sculptures, paintings, and drawings by Max Ernst. *1515 Sul Ross Street; 713-525-9400.*

The Menil Collection is housed in a serene structure designed by architect Renzo Piano.

Within walking distance of the Menil Collection are four additional spaces created by Dominique de Menil. The most enigmatic of these is the **Rothko Chapel** (3900 Yupon Street; 713-524-9839), which was conceived by the artist Mark Rothko and de Menil as a meditative "environment" in which to appreciate 14 color field paintings Rothko completed between 1965 and 1966. Philip Johnson worked with the painter on the design of the octagonal chapel, but a dispute caused Johnson to leave the project, which was finished by the Texas architects Howard Barnstone and Eugene Aubry in 1971. Critics claim the paintings have faded over the years, but this doesn't seem to matter to the thousands who visit annually to reflect on Rothko's ethereal art. Barnett Newman's 26-foot-tall *Broken Obelisk,* dedicated in 1967 to the memory of Rev. Martin Luther King Jr., sits amid the reflecting pool outside the chapel.

The **Byzantine Fresco Chapel** (4011 Yupon Street; 713-521-3990), built in 1997 to a design by the de Menils' son, Francois, contains precious 13th-century frescoes filched by thieves from a chapel in Cyprus in the 1980s. The Menil Foundation recovered the shards in the late 1980s, secured approval from officials

A passion for oranges inspired this work of folk art.

of the Church of Cyprus for a long-term loan, and then had them restored. Francois de Menil's architecture of warm woods and glass both complements and offsets the ancient, crumbling dome and apse on which the frescoes appear. Renzo Piano designed the spare spaces of the **Cy Twombly Gallery** (1501 Branard Street; 713-525-9450), which exhibits 30-plus paintings, drawings, and sculptures by this devotee of abstract expressionism. The glow at **Richmond Hall** (1500 Richmond Avenue) emanates from the evanescent light sculptures of the minimalist installation artist Dan Flavin.

Although not in the Museum District, the **Orange Show,** in East Houston, is a must-see if you want to experience the full spectrum of Houston's arts scene. A 3,000-square-foot, handmade structure built between the mid-1950s and 1979 by retired postal worker Jeff McKissack, the Orange Show is devoted to the healing powers of the orange. The structure itself is a series of mazes made of cinderblock and covered with brick, steel, and all sorts of found objects: railroad ties, tractor seats, mannequins, whirligigs, wagon wheels, and many waving Texas flags. Colorful tiles cover just about everything, some of them spelling out words and phrases dear to McKissack's heart, like "I Love Oranges" and "Eat Oranges And Live." The Orange Show's simple message: Eat oranges and be healthy. McKissack even wrote a book on the subject, *How to Live One Hundred Years and Still Be Spry.* Alas, McKissack himself didn't live to be 100. He died at age 77, shortly after the site opened, unaware that Houston's art community had recognized his creation as a folk-art environment worthy of preservation. The Orange Show is open from March through December. *2401 Munger Street, off I-45 (Telephone Road Exit from the north, Tellepsen Exit from the south); 713-926-6368.*

The **Contemporary Arts Museum** began in 1948 when a group of Houston art lovers, including John and Dominique de Menil, decided they wanted to see more art of their own time. Early shows combined stars like Max Ernst and Alexander Calder with lesser-known regional artists. The formula hasn't changed much over the years, though many of yesterday's up-and-comers, like James Turrell, are now the big draws. The building, a two-level aluminum number constructed in 1972 by Gunnar Birkerts, is as spacious as it is eye-catching. Opening-night parties are magnets for the local art-scenesters. *5216 Montrose Boulevard; 713-284-8250.*

Exhibits at the **Houston Museum of Natural Science** survey everything from space sciences to gemology to the zoology of Africa's Serengeti Plain. There's also a planetarium, an IMAX theater, and exhibit halls containing some of the scariest dinosaur skeletons imaginable. At the popular Cockrell Butterfly Center, hundreds of butterflies, mostly from Central and South America, fly free in a rainforest-like environment filled with tropical flora and fauna. (Butterflies are attracted to bright colors, so wear lots of orange, yellow, and red if you want to be covered by the flickering creatures.) *Hermann Park, 1 Hermann Circle Drive; 713-639-4629.*

Survey shows of work by regional artists are popular draws at the Contemporary Arts Museum.

Thoughts of Houston generally revolve around images of oil derricks and sky-scrapers. This is understandable, given the oil money that has poured into the area and the number of high-rise office towers that have sprouted up over the years, but the city also contains many places to enjoy nature, among them **Memorial Park,** a 2-square-mile swath of greenery west of downtown. Sycamore, ash, and palmetto trees populate the park's botanical garden, in groves and stands best appreciated while coursing the bayou in a rental canoe. Long-distance joggers often like to start downtown at Wortham Theatre Center, on Texas and Smith Streets, and trot west along Allen Parkway and the bayou to the park, nearly 6 miles away. The route rewards runners with excellent views of downtown sky-scrapers and redbuds, azaleas, and blooming pear trees. The hiking-jogging trail along the bayou is lined with contemporary sculpture; the park also has a golf course, tennis courts, and hiking, running, roller-blading, and bicycling paths. *Interstate 10 and Loop 610 West; 713-845-1000.*

■ SOUTH HOUSTON   *map page 155, D-6*

The very words "science museum" can be coma-inducing, but **Space Center Houston** upends most expectations. Essentially the official visitors center for NASA's Lyndon B. Johnson Space Center, this highly entertaining facility provides a solid overview of what goes on at Johnson, from crew preparation to lift-offs, space travel, and landings.

A full-size model of the crew compartment of a space shuttle rests in Space Center Plaza, and non-claustrophobic types are welcome to hop aboard. Films in the Starship Gallery document the history of manned space flight, and nearby are two space capsules that have orbited the Earth: *Faith 7* from the Mercury mission, and the *Apollo 17* module that landed on the moon. A tram tour stops off at the Johnson Space Center's historic Mission Control Center, from which NASA staffers navigated *Apollo 11* back to Earth after an equipment malfunction. Through the wonders of computer simulation, would-be astronauts can land a space shuttle in the *Feel of Space* gallery. The center also holds moon rocks, thousands of pho-tographs, memorabilia, and an exhibit of space helmets. *1601 NASA Road 1, 25 miles south of downtown, I-45 Exit 25; 281-244-2100.*

Mother Nature offers up American alligators and other reptiles at the 4,900-acre **Brazos Bend State Park,** 28 miles south of Houston. Set amid the Brazos River floodplains, the park's riverbanks are lined with a rich variety of trees,

President John F. Kennedy honors John Glenn at the Manned Spacecraft Center (now Johnson Space Center) after the astronaut's historic February 1962 flight. Glenn, inside a Mercury spacecraft, became the first American to orbit the Earth.

including enormous sycamores, moss-draped oaks, and willows. Patient observers will be rewarded with views of rare birds and animals such as raccoons, white-tail deer, and bobcats. Several challenging trails wind through the property, and there's a paved, wheelchair-accessible nature trail with signs written in Braille. The George Observatory here has exhibits on space exploration and meteors. *From Houston, take Route 288 to Rosharon and travel west on FM 1462; 979-553-5101.*

Trails at 2,500-acre **Armand Bayou Nature Center** wind through hardwood forests, coastal tallgrass prairie, and coastal salt marsh. This is a terrific place, especially for birders, to get away from it all. Because of the center's position on the Central Flyway, the largest migratory bird route in North America, ornithologists come here to see blue jays, doves, finches, and dozens of other species. A 600-foot-long boardwalk also leads through the forest. The boardwalk's route is less circuitous than those of the trails, but a walk along it still provides glimpses of

Houston Sports

Fans in Houston tend not to be as effusive as their counterparts in Dallas, but listen to the chatter on any of the myriad sports talk-radio shows here and you'll realize that passions in this town run pretty deep. New facilities for the pro baseball, basketball, and football teams have made attending games a pleasure.

Major League Baseball's **Houston Astros** (713-627-8767) play home games at—and no jokes about juiced balls—**Minute Maid Park** (501 Crawford Street, west of U.S. 59). The 41,000-seat venue has a retractable roof—an absolute necessity if you expect fans to attend games from April through November in this hot, humid city. The ballpark was called Enron Field when it opened in 2000, named for the energy-trading company with the creative accounting practices. When Enron filed for bankruptcy, Minute Maid, another Houston-based corporation, stepped up to bat.

The **Houston Rockets** (713-627-3865) are banking on their ebullient Chinese superstar, the 7-foot, 5-inch Yao Ming, to help them to return to the glory days of the mid-1990s, when the team won back-to-back National Basketball Association championships. The Rockets play their home games at the **Houston Arena** (1465 Polk Street; 713-571-1022), which opened in 2003. And, yes, it too has a retractable roof. If the early-21st century economic slump abates, the arena may yet bear the name of a local corporate sponsor.

The **Houston Texans** (832-667-2000), who debuted in 2002, play in the world's first retractable-roof National Football League stadium: **Reliant Stadium** (north of I-610 between Route 288 and U.S. 90), complete with removable grass. Honestly. The 70,000-seat park sits next to the 1965-vintage wonder of the world, the Astrodome, now renamed the Reliant Astrodome. The much-maligned Astrodome was the world's first air-conditioned sports arena, and is the first place where artificial grass, or Astroturf, was used in professional play, largely because natural grass couldn't survive in the artificial climate.

wild deer, squirrels, raccoons, and countless birds in their natural habitats. Also on the grounds are a bird blind, a bison-viewing platform, a raptor exhibit, a small observatory, an interpretive center—the exhibits include ones on snakes and turtles—and an 1895 farmhouse containing vintage farming equipment. Boating and canoe trips down the bayou take place on Saturdays. *8500 Bay Area Boulevard (I-45, Exit 26 south), Pasadena; 281-474-2551.*

■ **EAST HOUSTON** *map page 155*
Alfred Finn, a local architect, designed the
San Jacinto Monument, which rises 570
feet over the site where Sam Houston tri-
umphed over General Antonio López de
Santa Anna in the final battle of the Texas
Revolution on April 21, 1836. Built
between 1936 and 1939, the cenotaph is
made of concrete and 100-million-year-old
Cordova shellstone quarried north of
Austin. At its top rests a nine-pointed, 35-
foot-tall star weighing 220 tons. Symbolic
of the independent spirit of Texas, the monument—when measured from its base to
the top of its star—stands taller than the
Washington Monument in Washington,
D.C. From the observation deck at the
489-foot-level, you can see the historic battleground, the Houston Ship Channel,
Buffalo Bayou, and beyond.

At the base of the monument, behind
two impressive 15-foot-tall bronze doors
bearing reliefs of the six flags that have
waved over Texas, is the **San Jacinto
Museum of History,** whose exhibits
include rare maps, military gear, and
weapons used in battle. The 35-minute film
Texas Forever revisits the conflict and the
events leading up to it. The 573-foot-long
Battleship *Texas,* the only surviving naval
vessel to have participated in both world
wars, is moored at the park. *All three sites:
3523 Battleground Road (Route 134), in La
Porte, a 25-minute drive east from downtown Houston; 281-479-2431.*

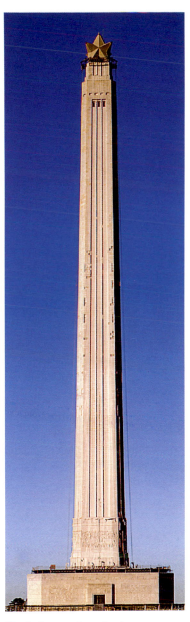

San Jacinto, a spire to inspire.

■ GALVESTON *map page 155, and page 129, C-6*

Galveston is the New Orleans of Texas, with its own Mardi Gras celebration, trolley cars, antebellum mansions, grand hotels, strip bars, and gambling. The town sits at the southern end of I-45 on sandy, flat Galveston Island, which is 27 miles long and less than 3 miles wide at its broadest point. A key southern port since its inception, Galveston has in recent times become an important tourist destination because of its location along the Gulf of Mexico.

Galveston Island has the best natural harbor in the Gulf of Mexico between New Orleans and Veracruz—a fact not lost on the pirate Jean Lafitte, who maintained headquarters in Galveston from the early 1800s until the United States government chased him out in 1821. During the Civil War, the port of Galveston was blockaded—and, for a few days, captured—by Union naval forces. It was there that the conquering Union army disembarked, on June 19, 1865, to give Texans their first notice that slaves had been emancipated. The date became known as Juneteenth and since then has been a holiday in Texas and cities across America.

Following the Civil War, Galveston became the Ellis Island of the Gulf, the point through which European immigrants to the Southwest passed, and sometimes settled. As a consequence, the population of Galveston includes many more people of Greek, Italian, and Russian-Jewish descent than any other city in the state. Another vestige is unusual civic pride. Even native Galvestonians who have moved elsewhere distinguish themselves as BOI, or "born on the island."

By 1870, Galveston was the most populous city in Texas. It received the state's first electric lights and telegraph, as well as its first medical college, a branch of the University of Texas. But the port was the basis for Galveston's prosperity, and the recurring threat of hurricanes, the difficulty of maintaining a sufficient depth of water on the approach to the port, and the rudimentary ship channel that Houston dug in 1881 led to a decline of both the shipping business and the population before the end of the 19th century.

Much of the fuel for Allied forces was shipped out of Galveston during World War II, and for years the city's beaches were dirty with oil spilled from ships sunk a few miles out by German U-boats. More recently, chemicals from nearby refineries and spills from Gulf oil rigs so polluted Galveston Bay that former U.S. Sen. Lloyd Bentsen called it "the only bay in the country with an octane rating." Cleanups have been effective, however, and Galveston Island is sometimes cited as an environmental victory. Between the two world wars, Galveston became notorious for

Texas Rangers destroy contraband liquor during the early 1930s.

gambling and the free flow of liquor. Prostitution had also flourished here since the Civil War, earning Galveston its reputation as the Sin City of the Gulf. But the Texas attorney general shut down much of the illegal activity in the late 1950s.

■ STRAND NATIONAL HISTORIC LANDMARK DISTRICT
map page 155, B-6
In the 19th century, the neighborhood that now carries the label the Strand National Historic Landmark District was a vibrant commercial center known as "Wall Street of the Southwest." Banks, cotton concerns, lumber companies, and other businesses set up shop here, and a budding tourism industry brought in restaurants and hotels. You can dip into the Strand's colorful history by picking up a walking-tour leaflet at the Strand Visitors Center; the tour passes well-preserved buildings from the 1800s and early 1900s, many of them now housing restaurants, shops, and lofts. Each December, about 75,000 visitors pour into town for Dickens on the Strand, two days during which locals wrap themselves in Victorian-era fashions to promenade and carouse. *From 20th Street to 25th Street between Water and Mechanic Streets. Visitors Center, 2215 Strand Street; 888-425-4753.*

This player enjoying the Strand's outdoor chess board puts a little English on her move—though by the look of things she'll need more than that to salvage this game.

The **Railroad Museum** has amassed one of the state's largest collections of retired railroad cars—35 in all, some dating from the early 1900s. Near the tracks is the art deco Santa Fe terminal, restored to its 1932 appearance. In 1982, the New York artists Ivan and Elliot Schwartz created life-size, stark-white sculptures of passengers, dressed in fashions of the 1930s, sitting in the waiting room like ghost travelers. The extensive audiovisual displays here relate the history of Texas rail. *25th and Strand Streets; 409-765-5700.*

A stately neoclassical bank building has been transformed into the **Galveston County Historical Museum.** On exhibit here are artifacts—bottles, buttons, glassware—from an archaeological dig believed to be Jean Lafitte's Galveston head-quarters, "Maison Rouge," as well as maps and documents used to navigate the region. The original lens of the South Jetty Lighthouse is on display, and text panels and archival photographs reveal the sense of panic that engulfed Galveston after the 1900 hurricane leveled the city. Maps on hand reveal areas hardest hit by the tempest, and a primitive film made a day after the hurricane shows panoramic shots of the devastation. The 1921 museum building itself is a dazzler; designed by the Chicago architects Weary and Alford, it features a barrel-vaulted ceiling, elabo-rate friezes, and Italian-marble pilasters. *2219 Market Street; 409-766-2340.*

Galveston Island Trolley cars run from the Strand to the Seawall and Pier 21 (and also to downtown). Another view of Galveston can be had by taking a ride aboard the stern-wheeler the *Colonel* (409-740-7797), which tours Galveston Bay.

Speaking of colonels, the jam-packed **Colonel Bubbie's Strand Surplus Senter** is an odd duck: a military-surplus store that actually stocks military surplus. Hanging from rods, piled into boxes and barrels, and stacked on the floor are leftovers from more than 60 countries' armed forces, everything from German sunglasses to British bosun's pipes to Danish navy T-shirts. Colonel Bubbie (pronounced "Booby") sells all these items, but also maintains an enormous rental warehouse full of authentic military gear for use in movies, TV shows, and theater productions. Many of the uniforms worn by the actors in *Saving Private Ryan,* for instance, came from here. *2202 Strand Street; 409-762-7397.*

■ THE SEAWALL   *map page 155, B-6*
Seawall Boulevard, better known as the Seawall, was built after what residents still call "The Hurricane," a 1900 storm that killed 6,000 people on the island and between 4,000 and 6,000 on the mainland. All but the stoutest structures were destroyed by winds that gusted up to 120 mph, and even the buildings that withstood the wind were heavily damaged.

The Seawall is a magnet for tourists and those who depend upon them.

Seventeen feet above the mean low tide, the Seawall stretches west for more than 10 miles from near the island's eastern edge. (Three miles of the wall were constructed between 1902 and 1904, and subsequent additions were made throughout the last century, most recently in the 1960s.) A local hangout for walkers, joggers, and tourists, some of them on rented bicycle carts, the Seawall is a low-key version of Atlantic City's Boardwalk or Los Angeles's Venice Beach. Piled between the Seawall and the shoreline are massive chunks of pink Texas granite—the same rock used to build the State Capitol in Austin, but used here to mitigate the damaging effects of ferocious hurricane tides.

Despite the weather dangers, the Seawall area has evolved into hot beachfront property, and hotels, restaurants, gift shops, sports-equipment rental operations, and beach condos line the boulevard's inland side.

The National Oceanic and Atmospheric Administration (NOAA) operates the **Kemp's Ridley Sea Turtle Research Center,** established here in 1978 to save the endangered loggerhead and Kemp's Ridley sea turtles. You can tour the center for free on Tuesdays, Thursdays, and Saturdays; reservations are recommended. *4700 Avenue U; 409-766-3670.*

The Galveston Hurricane of 1900 was America's deadliest natural disaster, killing more than 6,000 of the city's 30,000 residents.

TEXAS-SIZE DISASTERS: THE HURRICANE

Galveston had experienced many hurricanes by 1900, when the city's most devastating storm took place. The book Isaac's Storm *recounts the story of the hurricane through the life of Isaac Cline, the U.S. Weather Bureau's Galveston chief, who was later faulted for not warning the citizenry sooner of the gale's enormity.*

Downtown no one paid much attention to the storm. As the lunch hour approached, men set out as usual for their favorite restaurants. One of the most popular was Ritter's Café and Saloon on Mechanic Street... in the ground floor of a building that also housed a second-floor printing shop with several heavy presses.

Now and then a powerful gust of wind shook the front windows with enough force to draw the attention of the diners. . . . Between gusts, the diners continued talking business with a nonchalance that had to be contrived. They were aware of the storm, and knew it was getting stronger.

Moments later a powerful gust of wind tore off the building's roof. The "blast effect" caused by the wind's sudden entry into the enclosed space of the second floor apparently bowed the walls to the point where the beams supporting the ceiling of Ritter's slipped from their moorings. The ceiling collapsed into the dining room, amid a cascade from the second floor of desks, chairs, and the brutally heavy printing presses.

There must have been warning. A shriek of steel, perhaps, or the pistol-crack of a beam. Some men had time to dive under the big oak bar along one wall of the room.

Spencer and Lord died instantly. Three others died with them—Kellner, Dreckschmidt, and young Dailey. Five other men were badly hurt. Ritter dispatched a waiter to find a doctor.

The waiter drowned.

—Erik Larson, *Isaac's Storm*, 1999

■ EAST END HISTORICAL DISTRICT *map page 155, B-6*

By the late 1800s, Galveston had accumulated a fair number of tycoons—cotton merchants, bankers, grain exporters, jewelers, physicians, developers, and the just plain filthy rich. Most of the well-heeled, like the lumber entrepreneur Frederick Beissner, lived in grand style in the 40-block enclave now known as the East End Historical District. A reflection of Galveston's gilded age, the neighborhood is listed on the National Register of Historic Places and is well worth a guided tour or

Galveston's Bathing Girl Revue, photographed along the Seawall in 1926.

even an unguided stroll. Many of the mansions were built between 1875 and 1905, and the styles range from Greek Revival to Tudor to Victorian, and sometimes a mix of all three. You can learn about tours at the Heritage Visitor's Center (409-762-3933). *From 11th to 19th Streets, between Mechanic Street and Broadway.*

The original owners of **Ashton Villa**—James Moreau Brown and his wife, the former Rebecca Ashton Stoddart—were admired members of the Victorian social set. Brown, a successful businessman, became the president of the Galveston, Houston and Henderson Railroad in 1859, the year this Mediterranean-style, pink stucco house was completed. Others soon followed Brown's lead, and today this trendsetting East End manse, based largely on an idea by the Philadelphia architect Samuel Sloan that Brown saw in a magazine, is a house museum displaying furniture, heirlooms, and knickknacks. It is also a repository for just about everything ever owned by Brown's daughter, Bettie Brown, a much-admired and colorful figure from Galveston history.

Bettie lived in the house all her life, from 1859 until her death in 1920. A world traveler and bon vivant, Bettie filled Ashton Villa with souvenirs, furniture, and art she picked up from her travels to China, India, Japan, and Egypt. She was also a painter, and the house today is a showcase for many of her paintings, some of which were considered quite naughty because they showed women doing slightly off-color things such as revealing an ankle or a petticoat. The Brown family is said to have weathered the great 1900 hurricane in the house; maybe that's why the museum's audiovisual programs on the hurricane have such impact. *2328 Broadway; 409-762-3933.*

Another great East End house that withstood the hurricane was the **Moody Mansion,** a 42-room Richardsonian Romanesque traffic-stopper built in 1893 for Mrs. Richard Willis, the wife of a grocery store magnate. The mansion, designed by William Tyndall, was sold in 1900 to W. L. Moody Jr., who had amassed a fortune in cotton, banking, hotels, and insurance. Moody lived in the house until his death in 1954, whereupon his daughter, Mary Moody Northen, inherited the property and began an extensive renovation. The house is now a museum for Moody family heirlooms and the many things that Mary Northen—also a world traveler—acquired along the way. Her exquisite taste is reflected throughout the house, from the eclectic furniture, tapestries, and paintings to the fine jewelry and vintage clothing. The Lalique and Christmas plate collections are remarkable. Moody Mansion itself is deceptively fey: underneath all the copious architectural flourishes are walls of 12-inch-thick brick. *2618 Broadway; 409-762-7668.*

Not to be outdone is the **Bishop's Palace,** a multi-turreted mansion of limestone, pink and gray granite, and red sandstone that took six years to build. The fanciful house was erected in the 1880s for Walter Gresham, a Galveston lawyer for whom money was no object. That this was the case is apparent when you observe the level of detail lavished on the many rooms; the handcrafted grand staircase; the window casings, moldings, and door lintels; and the ornate fireplaces and mantles. The house, designed by Nicholas Clayton, derives its name from the Catholic bishop of Galveston, the Reverend Christopher Byrne, who lived here from 1923 until his death in 1950. Still owned by the local archdiocese, the mansion is open to the public but accommodates the current bishop when he is in town. *1402 Broadway; 409-762-2475.*

TEXAS-SIZE DISASTERS: THE EXPLOSION

In 1947, two freighters carrying about 3,000 tons of ammonium nitrate exploded, killing 700 people, wounding nearly 5,000, and destroying Texas City, 10 miles north of Galveston. Out of the ensuing legal battle came the first ruling by U.S. courts that held the federal government accountable for its actions. The passage below describes the impact of one of the explosions.

As the *Grandcamp* disintegrates, molten chunks of the 14-million-pound ship rage up and across the city and Galveston Bay. The tons of sisal twine in its cargo ignite into fiery coils that are rocket-launched into the sky before raining down. The forty-thousand-pound deck is shot one-half mile away. Pieces of the hull are thudding into the wakes of shrimp boats in Galveston Bay, almost capsizing some of the vessels. Others are plunging onto the collapsed roofs of the shacks in El Barrio and The Bottom, immediately setting the interiors of those homes ablaze.

As the ship explodes, the entire basin is scooped out, and a twenty-foot-high tidal wave rises up in the north slip, as if every drop of scalding water has been knocked into one giant sheet and is crashing 150 feet onshore, in the immediate direction of Frank's Café. Plowing over the docks and toward the people stretched along the waterfront, the tidal wave is filled with diesel fuel, hydrochloric acid, ammonium nitrate, and styrene. Cresting at the top of the wave is a 150-foot-long, thirty-ton hydrochloric acid barge named The *Longhorn II*. When the wave thunders down, it slaps the block-long barge 250 feet inland, on top of a no parking sign and on top of the twisted, smoking skeleton of Chief Henry Baumgartner's fire truck.

—Bill Minutaglio, *City on Fire*, 2003

■ **ON THE PIERS** *map page 155, B-6*

From the county museum it's a mere 15-minute walk on 21st Street to Pier 21 and the **Texas Seaport Museum** and, berthed just outside the museum, the *Elissa,* an iron-hull, 411-ton sailing vessel. Built in Aberdeen, Scotland, in 1877, the *Elissa* was used to transport cotton from Galveston to European ports in the 1800s and early 1900s. Later, in the 20th century, the *Elissa* was a transport ship based in Greece, where in 1969 she was saved from a date with the scrap heap by enterprising preservationists who repaired the vessel and guaranteed her safe harbor forever in Galveston. A 20-minute film at the Texas Seaport Museum documents the ship's history and decade-long restoration. Most people who see the film are incredulous that the gorgeous boat docked at the pier is the same waterlogged bucket they've just seen on screen. There are no guided tours of the vessel, but you can climb aboard and view the main deck, the galley, and the crew's eating and sleeping quarters. Maps, models of ships, photographs, and other exhibits at the museum shed light on Galveston's rich shipping history. *Pier 21; 409-763-1877.*

The three-deck **Ocean Star Offshore Drilling Rig and Museum**—a transformed offshore drilling platform—surveys the region's oil history with interactive displays, equipment exhibits, and videos that explain how companies locate petroleum reserves, drill wells, and produce oil in the middle of the Gulf of Mexico. *Pier 19; 409-766-7827.*

■ TEXAS CITY *map page 129, D-6*

In Texas City, across from Galveston, anglers convene daily on the 600-foot fishing pier attached to the **Texas City Dike,** which extends 5 miles into Galveston Bay. Redfish, flounder, and trout are plentiful, and are supposedly safe to eat, though their proximity to the area's huge petrochemical complex does give one pause.

The Seawolf submarine is one of several retired World War II vessels on view in Galveston.

■ MOODY GARDENS   *map page 155, B-6*

The three giant glass pyramids at Moody Gardens—part amusement park, part science museum, and part hotel in one verdant setting—add a splash of the Egyptian to Galveston's southwestern skyline. Beneath the 12-story-high blue-glass Aquarium Pyramid thrive more than 8,000 specimens of aquatic life from the Pacific Ocean, the Antarctic, and the Caribbean: mammals, reptiles, invertebrates, fish, and plants—everything from sharks to penguins to African ferns. Free-flying tropical butterflies and birds fill the air at the Rainforest Pyramid, and fish undulate through quiet pools at the bases of waterfalls. Interactive demonstrations and experiments are the fare at the Discovery Pyramid, which is geared to children. Lush landscaped grounds surround the 303-room Moody Gardens Hotel. *1 Hope Boulevard; 409-744-4673.*

■ PORT ARTHUR TRIANGLE   *map page 129, D-5/6*

Port Arthur and its sister cities, Beaumont, 17 miles east, and Orange, 22 miles northeast, form what is today called the Magic Triangle, a petrochemical, ship-building, and papermaking complex that was called the Golden Triangle in better days. The area's phenomenal growth began in 1901, with the gushing of the Spindletop well near Beaumont. During World War I, the Golden Triangle refined and exported more oil than any other place on the globe. But the Triangle peaked soon after, and has since suffered economic decline. These days, Beaumont, Port Arthur, and Orange, with their rusting refineries and boarded-over downtowns, are known mostly as the home of Texas Cajuns, who are related to Louisiana's old Acadian culture.

Port Arthur sits at the southeasternmost point of Texas, 20 miles off I-10, the highway that frames East Texas in the south. This is the hometown of the rock chanteuse Janis Joplin, the legendary athlete Babe Didrikson Zaharias, the former Dallas Cowboys and Miami Dolphins coach Jimmy Johnson, and Joe Ligon of gospel's Mighty Clouds of Joy.

A number of Vietnamese refugees came to the area in the late 1970s, drawn by a climate similar to their homeland. When they set themselves up as commercial fishermen, they clashed both economically and culturally with the area's already established fishermen. Today, the animosity has pretty much died out, and the Port

Clouds obscure the sunset east of Galveston at the Bolivar Lighthouse.

Arthur Chamber of Commerce points with pride to two relatively new religious landmarks. The pagoda-like Vietnamese monument to **Mary, Queen of Peace** (801 Ninth Avenue; 409-983-7676) contains a statue of the Virgin Mary three times life-size, built by parishioners of the Queen of Vietnam Martyr's Catholic Church in 1982. **Buu Mon Buddhist Temple** (2701 Procter Street; 409-982-9319) was a Baptist church 40 years ago, but became a Buddhist temple in 1987. Visitors are welcome at services, and tours are arranged by appointment to view the statue of Buddha and the drums and bells used in religious ceremonies.

Many Cajuns settled in the Bayou country of rural Louisiana when they were forced out of Nova Scotia in the 18th century. By the 1840s, some had drifted into the Beaumont–Port Arthur area to work as fishermen and farmers. Later, they went to work in the Louisiana oil fields and refineries after oil was discovered there in the 1920s. When refineries were built on the Texas Gulf Coast, many more moved to Texas to work in them.

Cajun culture shows up most often in Beaumont and Port Arthur place names and in occasional encounters with Cajun speech patterns (Cajun is a mix of Acadian French, Creole French, standard French of the 1800s, and English, mixed with African, American Indian, and Spanish words). One does encounter the Cajun sensibility on certain menus in this region of Texas and throughout parts of the American south. To find Cajun cuisine, look for any eatery offering andouille sausage, gumbo, or dishes with crawfish, shrimp, oysters, fish, turtles, frog legs, or alligator.

To get a sense of how Cajuns lived in this region in the 1800s, stop by **La Maison Beausoleil,** an early 1800s Cajun dwelling from southern Louisiana that was dismantled in 1985, barged down the Gulf Intracoastal Waterway, and rebuilt across from Port Arthur in Port Neches. The small, two-story wood house contains handmade furniture from the 1800s—beds, rockers, armoires—as well as cooking utensils and hunting implements. The house is open for tours on weekends only. *701 Rue Beausoleil, Port Neches; 409-832-6733.*

■ TRAVEL BASICS

Getting Around: Interstate 610 and Route 8 surround Houston, both highways providing access to downtown and most of the surrounding neighborhoods. Interstate 45 enters Houston from the northwest and cuts a mostly straight line through the city all the way down to Galveston, where it terminates. Interstate 10

Like New Orleans, to which it is sometimes compared, Galveston has its own Mardi Gras.

provides a clear way east to Louisiana and west past San Antonio. As for public transportation, the more than 1,000 buses of Houston's **Metro** (713-635-4000) system travel to the downtown area, Hermann Park, Rice University, Memorial Park, Bellaire, East Houston, and beyond. There is weekday express service to Bush Intercontinental and Hobby Airports every 25 minutes from 6 A.M. to 7 P.M.

Climate: The average winter highs in Houston are in the mid-60s, but highs up to 87 are possible. Winter lows average in the mid-40s, but the temperature can drop as low as 9 degrees. Summer highs average in the low 90s, but the high has reached 106 degrees in August. Summer lows average in the mid-70s, with lows of 45 degrees possible. Rain averages 46 inches annually, with most of it falling in May, June, and September. Beaumont and Port Arthur temperatures are similar to Houston's, but their average annual rainfall is over 57 inches, with most of it falling between June and September. Houston and most of southeastern Texas endure intense humidity all year long, except for a short spell in winter, when winds push the atmospheric pressure north. In winter, lowered temperature mixed with moist air creates fog, which can sometimes make for difficult driving conditions.

CENTRAL TEXAS

Central Texas is celebrated for its natural beauty, its music, and its laid-back atmosphere. Geography defines this area, or, to be more precise, divides it—with the Balcones Fault—into two separate regions. To the east of the fault line (and, generally speaking, I-35) lies the Blackland Prairie, good cotton country, wet and mild. To its west the land is rougher, whiter, higher, and drier—ranching territory. The flatter, eastern portion of Central Texas mirrors the terrain of East Texas, and the hillier, river-laced western section resembles that of West Texas, but Central Texas stands apart from these two regions, and the rest of the state, for demographic reasons. During the period of the Republic of Texas, German immigrants, some of them freethinkers and revolutionaries, established colonies to the west of what is now I-35, and during Reconstruction, Czech farmers settled in the cotton country to the east.

European immigrants never constituted a majority in Central Texas—Anglo settlers, Latinos, and African-Americans outnumbered them—but the Hill Country retains some largely undiluted vestiges of its European immigrant past. Boerne (pronounced "BUR-nee"), Fredericksburg, and New Braunfels trade on their German heritage with restored vintage buildings, German restaurants, heritage museums, and festivals, and Castroville similarly celebrates its Alsatian roots.

Economically, Central Texas is distinct because the oil money that made East and West Texas rich never influenced the region to any great degree; as a consequence, the distribution of wealth has been more even-handed. Agriculture has been a mainstay, but the growth of the Austin area is largely a product of its urban and cultural assets. The state government is based here, of course, and the University of Texas at Austin has helped to make the city a center of art and education.

High-tech industrial concerns have been a factor in the local economy since the immediate post–World War II era, but in the 1990s they began to proliferate in greater Austin, many of them evolving out of the activities of SEMATECH (an acronym for Semiconductor Manufacturing Technology). The group, founded in the late 1980s, was initially a research and development consortium of

The natural beauty on view in Central Texas includes field after field of springtime bluebonnets.

computer-chip-making companies, including AT&T, IBM, Intel, Hewlett-Packard, Rockwell, and Texas Instruments, as well as 31 universities in 14 states and the U.S. Department of Defense. Today, what is now known as International SEMATECH is a private operation. The Austin-Georgetown corridor of I-35 and about 20 miles along U.S. 183 to the city's northwest, collectively dubbed "Silicon Hills," developed into an intellectual boomtown. The area's increasing population and prosperity transformed the once-harsh Hill Country—west of I-35 and south of the Llano and Colorado Rivers—into a vast resort, with dude ranches and entertainment complexes displacing working ranches and farms whose owners of a century and a half ago fought Comanche Indians and tamed the land.

■ AUSTIN *map page 184, C-2, and page 188*

Long before even these early ranches, Barton Springs, in what is now downtown Austin, supported indigenous prehistoric people, and in 1730 it served as a temporary way station for Spanish missionaries who were moving three missions out of East Texas to, eventually, San Antonio. A century after the missionaries departed, Jake Harrell, said to be the area's first permanent white settler, and a few other traders built cabins and a stockade. At the urging of the Republic of Texas's new president, Mirabeau B. Lamar, who had succeeded Sam Houston, the Texas congressional site-selection committee chose the town then called Waterloo as the capital in 1839, even though it was dangerously close to the western frontier.

Houston favored his namesake city for a capital, but the two men were bitter enemies, and Lamar would not countenance moving the capital to a town named for Houston. So the capital remained in Waterloo, which the Texas Congress renamed to honor Stephen F. Austin, who had died in 1836.

The new capital attracted businesses and residents, leading to a mini-building boom by the mid-1850s. The products of that boom include the Governor's Mansion and a large number of commercial buildings that still stand, particularly along Congress Avenue and adjoining streets from the State Capitol south to the Colorado River. Austin's first railroad arrived in 1871, prompting another boom. Higher education was firmly established in Austin when Tillotson Collegiate and Normal Institute, a college for black students, opened in 1881, followed two years later by the University of Texas. In 1888, a new red granite capitol, the one currently in use, was built.

The crown jewel of Austin's natural beauty, Barton Springs, was acquired by the city in 1918, and 350-acre Zilker Park was developed around it. The New Deal employment programs of the 1930s provided the labor to build the iconic University Tower. After devastating Austin with frequent floods, the Colorado River was tamed, beginning in 1934, with the formation of the Lower Colorado River Authority, which built a chain of seven lakes, collectively known as the Highland Lakes, along the river from Austin in the southeast to Llano County on the northwest, producing not only flood control but also electric power, municipal water supply, and water-based recreational opportunities.

Austin grew tremendously during the late 1970s as a result of two developments of the previous decade. During the Vietnam War, the city became known as the

Creative expression takes place everywhere, in the streets. . .

Haight-Ashbury of the South, an oasis of kindred spirits for those opposed to the war. Somewhat paradoxically, at the same time hippies began crowding Guadalupe Street—the main commercial drag abutting the University of Texas campus—high-tech companies began to form, many of them supported in their early days by Department of Defense contracts. Austin's scientific base grew to include Texas Instruments, Motorola, IBM, and, by the 1980s, Dell and Apple.

As the semiconductor industry moved into high gear, Austin's countercultural types turned their energies to music, opening dance halls such as the now-defunct Vulcan Gas Company and Armadillo World Headquarters. The hippie musicians who played at these venues in the early 1970s were joined by "redneck rockers" or "outlaw cowboys," including singers like Willie Nelson and Waylon Jennings. A distinctly Austin sound may be hard to pinpoint, but the scene generated performance venues and recording studios. Since 1976, the PBS television show *Austin City Limits* has originated from the city, and its guests have included everyone from Fats Domino and Roy Orbison to Emmylou Harris and Garth Brooks. The highly

. . . and at the clubs.

successful South by Southwest (SXSW), an annual showcase for up-and-coming bands, debuted in 1987, further cementing the town's status as a live-music mecca.

In the early 1980s, amid the creative ferment, faceless glass office high-rises began to sprout all over downtown. Developers erected skyscrapers on nearly every square foot of available ground, and growth spun so perilously out of control that the city council passed ordinances requiring structures over a certain height to be stepped back from the street along Congress Avenue so as not to mar the historic character of the skyline near the capitol.

Many out-of-staters began moving to Austin during this same period, attracted by its urban sophistication and high-tech jobs. The economic turndown of the early 21st century has slowed the pace of immigration, but the growth of the past two decades has left some Austinites fearing that their city is becoming too plastic, too fast-paced, and too focused on money. Yet although progress has transformed Austin, the neighborhoods closest to downtown have been preserved, as well as those west and north of the University campus, and on the whole the place has retained its comfortable, small-town feel.

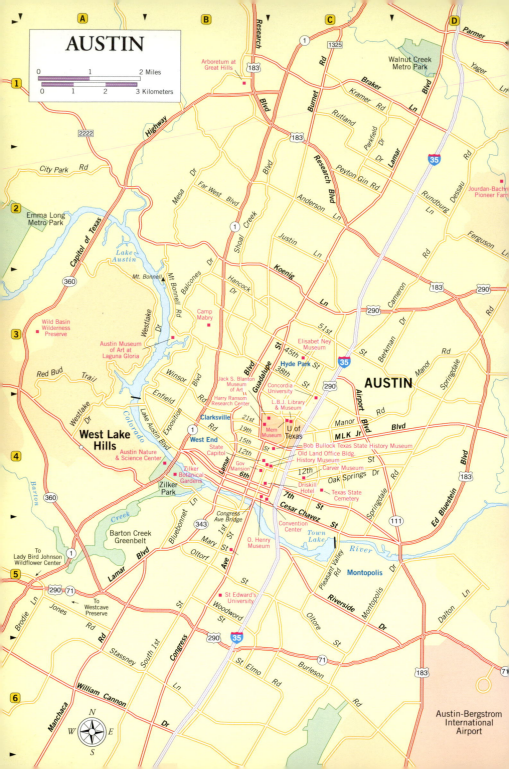

■ **DOWNTOWN** *map page 188, B/C-4*

The most impressive approach to downtown, the city's historic heart, is from the south over the Congress Avenue Bridge, from which you look 11 blocks straight up the wide avenue to the main entrance of the grand Texas State Capitol. Tall modern buildings have reconstituted the architectural mix, but enough of the resplendent commercial buildings of the 1800s have survived to supply a distinctly 19th-century counterpoint, and the set-back requirements keep the new towers from overwhelming the historic ones. Despite the feverish late-20th century building boom, downtown remains a surprisingly drivable area.

Major wheeling and dealing produced the magisterial **Texas State Capitol,** designed by Elijah E. Myers, a Detroit-based architect whose plans for the Michigan capitol had brought him wide acclaim. The government offered the contractor 3 million acres of public land in the Panhandle (which became the XIT Ranch) in lieu of payment for construction. Texas limestone was supposed to be the principal building material, but when this proved unusable—the limestone contained iron pyrites that streaked when exposed to water—the more expensive Sunset Red granite replaced it as the exterior surface. To reduce costs, the government provided the contractor with convicts to quarry the stone, a scheme that provoked the ire of the International Association of Granite Cutters. (The union wasn't any happier when the builder brought in Scottish immigrant stonemasons to cut and work the stone.) Despite the cost-cutting measures, the building, the nation's largest state capitol, is a dazzler. Among the stops on the worthwhile daily tours are the House Chamber, which gives pride of place to the original Battle of San Jacinto flag, and the Senate Chamber, whose glittering chandeliers have dangled from this ceiling since the capitol opened in 1888. Chances are 50-50 the lawmakers won't be in session when you visit: the Texas legislature meets only every other year. *11th Street and Congress Avenue; 512-463-0063.*

The whimsical **Old General Land Office Building,** which dates from 1856, is the oldest extant state office building in Texas. The two-level structure was built for a decidedly routine purpose—to house deeds, surveying notes, maps, land titles, and other public documents—but with its pseudo-medieval elements, crenellations and all, it looks like something out of a Dr. Seuss story. The most famous Land Office employee was William Sidney Porter, better known as O. Henry, who toiled here as a draftsman between 1887 and 1891. Several of his short stories are set in the building, which these days houses the offices of the State Capitol Visitors Center. *112 East 11th Street; 512-305-8400.*

The state's storied past is the star of the Bob Bullock Museum.

Bob Bullock, Texas's 38th lieutenant governor, lobbied hard to establish a museum of state history. Bullock didn't live to see it happen—he died in 1999—but his dream came true in 2001 with the opening of the 176,000-square-foot **Bob Bullock Texas State History Museum.** Four blocks north of the capitol, the museum hosts exhibitions of documents and other materials from regional museums throughout the state. Exhibits include everything from the letters of Sam Houston to ancient Indian artifacts. *1800 North Congress Avenue; 512-936-8746.*

Abner Cook, a leading architect of his day, designed one of Austin's most elegant dwellings, the **Governor's Mansion,** which occupies an entire city block near the capitol. The 1856 mansion has been the home of every Texas governor since the state's fifth, Elisha Marshall Pease. Pease's wife, Lucadia, had a hard time furnishing such a vast spread on the governor's then-paltry pay, so she kept many of the rooms closed. Constructed of bricks made in Austin and wood from nearby pines, the two-story mansion bears the marks of those who have lived here, including Gov. James Hogg—who, to keep his children from speedballing down the banister on their rear ends, hammered tacks into the railing. The nail holes are still visible. The mansion has many fine furnishings, paintings, and antiques, including Sam Houston's bed and Stephen F. Austin's desk. *1010 Colorado Street; 512-463-5516.*

South of the capitol lies **Sixth Street,** formerly the bawdy Old Pecan Street. It's most famous these days for the stretch of live-music venues, cafés, bars, and restaurants along the blocks east from Congress Avenue to I-35. On weekends, the street closes to traffic, creating a festival-like atmosphere—especially at night, when the sounds of blues, jazz, rock, and Caribbean bands pour out of clubs and the smell of barbecue fills the air.

Some of Austin's most interesting architecture can be found on and near Sixth Street. **O. Henry Hall,** now part of the University of Texas, was completed in 1879 as a post office and federal courthouse. James Hill and Abner Cook designed the sumptuous, symmetrical building in Italian High Renaissance style. Its namesake was convicted of embezzlement here in 1898. *Sixth and Colorado Streets.*

John Eberson, one of the early 20th century's leading theater architects, designed the neoclassical **Paramount Theatre,** which opened in 1915 as the Majestic Theater, a vaudeville house. Sarah Bernhardt and the Marx Brothers trod the boards here in the old days, and this remains an active performance venue where acts range from Joan Baez to David Sedaris to Les Ballets Trockadero de Monte Carlo. *713 Congress Avenue.*

The Romanesque Revival–style **Driskill Hotel** reigns over Sixth Street like a dowager duchess. Opened in 1886 by entrepreneur Jesse Lincoln Driskill—busts of Driskill and two sons are carved into the facade—the building, designed by J. N. Preston, was rescued from the wrecking ball in 1969. The hotel has endured numerous face-lifts since then and has played host to A-list movie stars, entertainers, and politicians. Locals say the place is haunted, but Austinites say that about every building in town more than a century old. *604 Brazos Street; 512-474-5911.*

The **Mexic-Arte Museum,** founded by artists in 1984, is one of the country's premier venues for traveling shows of traditional and contemporary art from Mexico and other Latin American countries. The Día de los Muertos exhibit each October and November is sensational. *419 Congress Avenue; 512-480-9373.*

When city engineers redesigned the **Congress Avenue Bridge** in 1980, they inadvertently provided crevices on the underside of the bridge, the makings of a comfy bat nursery. Now the bridge, a few blocks south of Sixth Street, draws a million and a half Mexican free-tail bats each year between March and November. Watching the bats emerge at dusk to catch and eat up to 30,000 pounds of insects has become a steady source of local entertainment. *512-327-9721 (for bat info).*

In 1895, Austin became one of the first cities in the country to light its streets with carbon arc lamps. Seventeen of the original 31 **Moonlight Towers** remain intact today, most of them in the central business district and downtown. (Two can be found near the capitol, at Trinity and West 11th Streets and at Guadalupe and West Ninth Streets.) The towers, whose light has been likened to moonlight (hence the name), were hardly models of efficiency. Each 165-foot-tall tower had to be lit manually, by a worker who would ride to the top of each beacon in a small

(above) The Driskill, saved from the wrecking ball. (opposite) Fireworks over downtown.

elevator. In 1936, mercury vapor replaced carbon, and later a centralized ignition system ended the nightly elevator rides.

The **O. Henry Museum** occupies the tan Queen Anne–style cottage he lived in from 1893 to 1895. The writing desk, books, diary, fine china, family photos, and a piano played by his wife convey the easy domesticity the writer enjoyed before he was jailed—many say wrongly—for embezzling money from an Austin bank. It was in prison that William Sidney Porter changed his name to O. Henry and began writing the stories that made him famous. The museum contains many first editions of his short stories, letters to friends and editors, and copies of *Rolling Stone,* the humorous weekly he started. If the house and its artifacts don't yield the full measure of the man, the enthusiastic curators can easily fill in the gaps. *Brush Square, 409 East Fifth Street; 512-472-1903.*

The maple, cedar, pecan, and magnolia trees of the **Texas State Cemetery** shade the graves of Stephen F. Austin, Barbara Jordan, 11 former governors, many literary and historical celebrities, and more than 2,000 Confederate veterans and their widows. Only those who have been elected to a state office, appointed to a state board, or named in a burial proclamation by a governor or both houses of the legislature may be buried here. *909 Navasota Street; 512-463-0605.*

■ **UNIVERSITY OF TEXAS** *map page 188, B/C-4*
The University of Texas campus sprawls across 360 acres in the center of Austin, but the university's influence extends well beyond its borders—from the artistic and intellectual currents it generates throughout Austin to the economic influence of its 50,000-plus students, many of whom shop and hang out on Guadalupe Street between 21st and 25th Streets. The number of campus buildings is estimated at 120, but new structures are always being erected. The important cultural institutions at UT include the LBJ library and the Texas Memorial Museum. The University Tower supplies the architectural focal point. *Guadalupe and Red River Streets, Martin Luther King Jr. Boulevard, and 26th Street; 512-471-3434.*

Lyndon Baines Johnson (1908–1973) was a complex man, a master legislative strategist whose political undoing was the Vietnam War, a proponent of civil rights who patronized African-Americans, and the champion of some of the most significant social welfare programs in American history. The artifacts and voluminous documents on exhibit at the **Lyndon Baines Johnson Library and Museum** provide some insight into the 36th president's mind and motivations; although his foibles are downplayed, a clear sense of the man—earthy, conniving, sensitive, and wry—emerges. That he was able to function at all may surprise visitors born during the high-tech era. In an age when the average car is loaded with digital gadgets and 12-year-olds wield cell phones, Johnson's black Lincoln limousine and clunky, command-central telephone seem quaintly archaic, though they were state-of-the-art during his presidency. If you schedule a visit to the reading room in advance of your arrival, you can listen to recordings of conversations Johnson had using that telephone. The 30-plus hours of tape recordings include ruminations on Vietnam, economic inflation, and a New York City transit strike. Gordon Bunshaft designed the monolithic travertine building that houses the library; like the limo and the phone, it's a bit of a period piece. *2313 Red River Street; 512-721-0200.*

The **Jack S. Blanton Museum of Art** plays an important role in the cultural life of Austin. Although a teaching school—this is a center for research and training in conservation studies and visual arts—the museum avoids the stifling tendencies of academia, frequently mounting daring special exhibitions. In addition to European holdings rich in Renaissance and baroque works, the museum has a superior sampling of 20th- and early-21st-century American art, and its collection of contemporary Latin American art is one of the largest in the country. *23rd Street and San Jacinto Boulevard; 512-471-7324.*

The French architect Paul Cret's 1936 plans for the **Texas Memorial Museum** called for north and south wings to extend from a central building, a tailored limestone box with subtle art deco flourishes. The wings were scuttled because of funding difficulties, leaving only Cret's alabaster midsection. But the chic interior—with brass doors, glass embellishments, and blood-red marble walls, floors and ceilings— mitigates any sense of abridgement. For many years, the museum presented natural science and cultural history exhibitions, but the focus has now shifted solely to natural science. Among the popular draws are the dinosaur models, including a 30-foot-long mosasaur and a 40-foot-long pterosaur. *2400 Trinity Street; 512-471-1604.*

A copy of the Gutenberg Bible and the world's oldest photograph, produced in France in 1826, are among the rarities in the collections of **Harry Ransom Humanities Research Center,** used mostly by scholars but also open to the public. The formidable photographic holdings consist of two million images, and the center's library has one of the country's most comprehensive collections of English writing from 1475 to 1700. *21st and Guadalupe Streets; 512-471-8944.*

University Tower.

The breathtaking **Littlefield Fountain Memorial,** on the South Mall, reveals the dramatic handiwork of the Italian sculptor Pompeo Coppini, who found his way to Texas (via Connecticut) in 1901, when he learned there might be work there. Coppini had many Texas commissions, but none more famous than this 1933 bronze bubbler, which depicts the goddess Columbia riding on the bow of a battleship led by three hyperactive sea horses. Coppini also sculpted the seven bronze statues on the nearby oak tree–lined mall. *21st Street, South Mall.*

Standing in front of the Littlefield Fountain, your back to 21st Street, the most captivating element on the horizon is **University Tower,** a 310-foot beaux arts citadel designed by Paul Cret and completed in 1937. For three decades, the tower was known mostly for the glorious views from its 27th-floor observation deck, but on August 1, 1966, it became the site of a killing spree by Charles Whitman, an ex-Marine who dragged a battery of rifles to the observation deck and started shooting people until he himself was picked off by a sharpshooter. The observation deck was shuttered from 1966 until 1999, and the university closed it again after the September 11, 2001, terrorist attacks on the United States. *1 South Mall.*

■ HYDE PARK *map page 188, C-3*

The 70-plus sculptures and busts at the **Elisabet Ney Museum** show an artist straining against convention. The career of Elisabet Ney began auspiciously in her native Germany, where she sculpted eminent figures like the philosopher Arthur Schopenhauer and Germany's "Iron Chancellor," Otto von Bismarck. A nonconformist from birth, Ney eventually tired of social mores on the continent and in 1871 moved to East Texas. In the early 1890s, then in her late 50s, Ney designed a house and studio in quiet Hyde Park, calling it Formosa, the Portuguese word for "beautiful." Over the next several years, she would produce some of her most renowned sculptures, including those of Stephen F. Austin and Sam Houston.

Ney was known in Austin for unconventional behavior. She used her maiden name, wore bloomer-type slacks, and, when one of her two children died she cremated his remains in the family fireplace. Her salons were the talk of the town, and from these gatherings of committed art lovers evolved the Texas Fine Arts Association. In 1911, four years after Ney's death, the association turned Formosa into a museum, whose exhibits trace Ney's career. Her studio is set up as she knew it, with sculpting tools, hat, teacup, and other items all in their proper places. The sculptures on view include portrayals of many Texas heroes. *304 East 44th Street; 512-458-2255.*

■ WEST AUSTIN *map page 188, A/B-2*

Several miles northwest of Barton Creek Greenbelt stands **Mount Bonnell.** At 750 feet, the crag offers a sweeping panorama of Austin, the rolling hills to its west, and the Colorado River. You can't get much higher than this in the Austin area, and if the view itself doesn't convince you of that, the 100 steps to the top surely will. The mountain is named after William Bonnell, a journalist and soldier who died during the Texas struggle for independence. *3800 Mount Bonnell Road, off Scenic Drive.*

The historic home of the **Austin Museum of Art** is **Laguna Gloria,** a four-story Mediterranean-style villa built on the banks of the Colorado River by Clara Driscoll Sevier—philanthropist, art lover, and daughter of the developer Robert Driscoll. Sevier chose the 12-acre site because it reminded her of Italy's Lake Como, a favorite vacation spot. In 1916, the San Antonio architect Harvey L. Page was hired to build the 6,600-square-foot villa, which Sevier then surrounded with terraced and sunken gardens that she filled with sculptures, trees, and plants. In 1943, Sevier donated Laguna Gloria to the Texas Fine Arts Association, asking that it be turned into a museum; although the task took 20 years, the house was eventually opened to the public for small-scale shows of paintings and sculpture. Sevier's gift was not the first one she made to support a Texas institution. In 1900, barely out of her teens, she donated $70,000 to help preserve the then-crumbling Alamo; her fight to restore the historic battle site made her a hero among Texans. Laguna Gloria is still used for shows of painting and sculpture, but in 1996 the Austin Museum of Art (which grew out of the Texas Fine Arts Association) opened a 5,000-square-foot downtown space (823 Congress Avenue) to show works in all media. The museum's triennial *New Art in Austin* shows are wildly popular and critically lauded. *3809 West 35th Street; 512-458-8191.*

■ PARKS AND GARDENS

The popular **Zilker Park** is named after A. J. Zilker, who in 1918 deeded land surrounding Barton Springs to Austin. The focus of the 350-acre park—located a couple of miles from the State Capitol—is **Barton Springs Pool** (2201 Barton Springs Road; 512-476-9044), a 3-acre spring-fed swimming hole whose waters are a bone-chilling 68 degrees Fahrenheit year-round. Near the pool's entrance, a bronze sculpture, *Philosopher's Rock,* depicts three beloved personalities of 20th-century Austin: the historian Walter Prescott Webb (the author of seminal works about the Western frontier); the writer J. Frank Dobie (*The Longhorns* and *Coronado's Children*); and the naturalist Roy Bedichek.

In addition to the pool, Zilker Park has hiking and cycling trails, canoe rentals, volleyball courts and soccer fields, and a miniature train ride—the Zilker Zephyr. **Zilker Hillside Theater** (2206 William Barton Drive; 512-477-5335) hosts performances of musical theater and jazz concerts in an amphitheater, and the **Zilker Botanical Garden** (2220 Barton Springs Road; 512-477-8672) holds a rose garden, an herb and fragrance garden, and a butterfly garden, among other natural wonders. The Oriental Garden, a serenely beautiful creation of the landscape architect Isamu Taniguchi, has a thatch-roof teahouse, hand-made lanterns, lotus ponds, waterfalls, and many unique plantings set into a formidable caliche hillside.

The **Umlauf Sculpture Garden and Museum** (605 Robert E. Lee Road; 512-445-5582), in the south end of Zilker Park, has more than 130 works by Charles Umlauf in the house where he lived and worked. Umlauf, who taught in the University of Texas Art Department from 1941 to 1981, created an incredibly diverse body of work that ranged in style from realistic to abstract, using such materials as granite, marble, bronze, wood, and terra cotta. His subjects were equally wide-ranging, from religious figures to nudes, from whimsical animals to family groupings. *2100 Barton Springs Road; 512-472-4914.*

Barton Creek Greenbelt, an 809-acre spread south of Laguna Gloria and west of Zilker Park, has sheer cliff walls, lush vegetation, and several popular swimming holes, making it a great place for jogging, walking, hiking, or just hanging out. You can float the creek by inner tube, inflatable raft, or canoe; though it is mostly dry between August and early March, it swells in the rainy season. *Starts at Barton Springs and follows the creek west.*

In 1965, Lady Bird Johnson, as part of her husband's environmental initiatives, chaired a White House conference on natural beauty in America. Many of the ideas she expressed then about preserving wildflower habitats eventually inspired the creation of the **Lady Bird Johnson Wildflower Center,** which Johnson cofounded in 1982 with the help of a friend, the actress Helen Hayes. The 284-acre center contains 16 gardens filled with 591 different plant species, and four wheelchair-accessible nature trails wind through and around the gardens. The popular Butterfly Garden has a rambling path dotted with seating areas, allowing for the tranquil observation of hundreds of butterflies in their natural habitat. *4801 La Crosse Avenue, off Loop 1 south of U.S. 290; 512-292-4200.*

A 1-mile hike at the 30-acre **Westcave Preserve** leads to a canyon canopied by giant moss-draped cypress trees, where a 40-foot spring-fed waterfall tumbles into an emerald-green pool. Most of the preserve, which is 30 miles west of Austin on the Pedernales River in Travis County, is a prime nesting habitat for the endangered golden-cheeked warbler. Guided tours are conducted on Saturdays and Sundays. *FM 3238 (Hamilton Pool Road) off Route 71; 830-825-3442.*

■ THE HILL COUNTRY   *map page 184, B/C-2/3*

Texans cherish the Hill Country for its scenic, rock-strewn hills, its streams, and its springtime profusion of bluebonnets and wildflowers. The region has been a popular escape hatch for nature-deprived Austinites for decades, but its central location makes it convenient for all the state's residents.

The Hill Country is alive with bluebonnets in the spring; late March and April are usually the best times to view these and other wildflowers.

HILL COUNTRY SCENIC DRIVES

The list of spring-blooming wildflowers in Central Texas includes bluebonnets, Indian paintbrush, Indian blanket, pink evening primrose, Texas bluebells, the Texas mountain laurel, and hundreds of others. In recent years, the Texas Department of Transportation has begun planting wildflower seeds alongside interstate routes. The result is glorious, as the spring blossoms transform otherwise dull highways into roads of blazing color. If possible, plan a visit to the Hill Country in late March or April, when wildflowers are in bloom. Some of the most scenic Hill Country drives are:

▸ Route 29 between Georgetown, 30 miles north of Austin, and Llano (65 miles).
▸ Route 16 between Llano and Kerrville (63 miles).
▸ FM 337 between Medina and Camp Wood, in the far western reaches of the Hill Country (57 miles).
▸ FM 32 (Devil's Backbone) from FM 12 to U.S. 281 (24 miles)

The Hill Country lies in the eastern part of the Edwards Plateau, a 25-million-acre southern extension of the Great Plains. The eastern edge of the plateau is defined by the Balcones Escarpment, a fault line that runs from the Mexican border near Del Rio east to San Antonio, following most of U.S. 90. The plateau is mostly hardscrabble and covered by a thin layer of soil over Austin chalk rock. In areas nearest I-35, where the soils are deeper, vegetation is softer and grows more vigorously. Oaks, shin oaks, Texas mountain laurel, Ashe juniper, hackberry, and Mexican persimmon flourish. Rainfall can be heavy, and with so little soil to absorb water, a heavy rain anywhere in a Hill Country stream's watershed can send a lot of water barreling down the riverbed at once.

■ **THE HIGHLAND LAKES**   *map page 184, B/C-2*

The part of the Hill Country most familiar to Texans is the Highland Lakes area, which stretches from Austin proper to about 70 miles northwest of the city. The seven manmade lakes here lie within a triangle formed by I-35 and Routes 29 and 71. The northernmost lake, Lake Buchanan, extends north of Route 29, and the southernmost, Town Lake, is within the Austin city limits. Power boaters, anglers, and real estate developers favor the lakes close to Austin; Lake Buchanan is the preferred nesting territory of the bald eagle.

A favorite stop in the region is the **Blue Bonnet Cafe,** which has been serving its famous down-home breakfasts, chicken-fried steaks, jalapeño-jelly turnovers, deep-dish plum pies, and other delights since 1929. Breakfast is served all day, and it typically includes omelets, bacon, sausage, hash browns, and biscuits big enough to feed several people. *211 U.S. 281, Marble Falls; 830-693-2344.*

Many travelers to the Hill Country bed down at **Canyon of the Eagles,** a 940-acre resort on Lake Buchanan's northeastern shore. The quiet retreat, a great place for bald-eagle watching, hiking, and swimming, has 64 rooms, a cozy restaurant, 15 miles of trails, and a beach. The resort runs eagle-watching cruises on Lake Buchanan from November through March, wildflower cruises in April and May, and scenic wilderness cruises most of the year. The Vineyard Cruise, between March and May, stops at Fall Creek Vineyard, known for its delicious white wines. *2341 Ranch Road, off Route 29; 512-756-8787.*

Breakfast is served all day at the Blue Bonnet Cafe, where the cinnamon buns are enormous.

■ JOHNSON CITY   *map page 184, B/C-2*

About 50 miles west of Austin and 50 miles due north of San Antonio is Lyndon Baines Johnson country, proclaimed so by large billboards on highways entering Blanco County. **Johnson City,** the county seat and the late president's hometown, wasn't named for Lyndon, but instead for Tom and Sam Ealy Johnson, ancestors who established a settlement there after the Civil War.

Almost every visitor to Johnson City comes to see **Lyndon B. Johnson National Historical Park,** whose 1,570 acres of sights are spread out over a 15-square-mile area. The journey begins in the center of town, at the visitors center on Lady Bird Lane; along with brochures, maps, and information about the park's sights, the amiable staff members dispense tales of Lyndon, his wife, and the other Johnsons.

Across Lady Bird Lane from the visitors center is the president's boyhood home. Johnson lived here from 1913 until 1934, when he married the former Claudia Taylor, known to all as Lady Bird—a nickname she acquired long before she met her husband. The house looks today as it did in Johnson's youth, with furniture from the early 1900s, as well as books, family memorabilia, and photographs. Several blocks away is Johnson Settlement, a ranch house where President

(above) LBJ's boyhood home. (following spread) The president and Lady Bird at their ranch.

How LBJ Lost the '41 Election

In 1941, Congressman Lyndon Johnson ran for the U.S. Senate against Pappy O'Daniel. Each man had pulled every Texas trick to increase his vote total, but Johnson made a fatal mistake that delayed his ascension to the Senate until the end of the decade:

An axiom of Texas politics held that "The lead in the runoff always wins"; in other words, the candidate ahead by the end of Election Day, at which time most of the vote had been counted, almost invariably won because he could "hold out"—delay reporting—enough boxes to keep a reserve to counter changes by the other side; since both sides were changing votes, the one with the lead could keep the lead by changing enough votes to offset the other side's changes. Perhaps the only instance in modern Texas political history in which this rule had been broken was Lyndon Johnson's 1941 race when he had, through overconfidence, allowed all his boxes to be reported early, thereby revealing how many votes his opponent needed to add— and foreclosing his chance to add any more of his own.

—Robert A. Caro, *The Years of Lyndon Johnson: Means of Ascent*, 1990

Johnson's grandparents lived, and alongside it an exhibit hall whose displays and photographs trace the history of Johnson City, from the late 1800s to today. Costumed interpreters wander the settlement and tell stories of cowboys, cattle drives, and farming. An authentic chuck wagon, used during cattle drives to bring supplies to cowboys, rests nearby.

The ex-president's ranch house—Lady Bird continued to live here after his death—is in Stonewall, about 15 miles west of Johnson City, off U.S. 290. Known as the "Texas White House," the two-story dwelling was where LBJ conducted business when not in Washington. Many notables relaxed on the front lawn here, including Harry S. Truman and Adlai Stevenson. The house is not open for touring, but adjacent to the house you can see the restored birthplace of LBJ, and near it the one-room schoolhouse where he received his first school lesson, at age four, and to which he returned as president to sign the National Education Act. Johnson is buried not far away, beneath a tombstone that bears the presidential seal. *Park visitors center, 100 Lady Bird Lane, Johnson City; 830-868-7128.*

How LBJ Stole the '48 Election

In 1948, LBJ ran for the Senate in the Democratic primary against Coke Stevenson, a popular former governor, in an exceedingly nasty campaign. With most of the votes tallied, he still trailed Stevenson by 854 votes. Johnson had tried to buy the election by, among other strategies, paying off political bosses to pad vote totals. Yet...

...although he had paid the highest price in Texas history, he had failed. So now he was trying to steal it.

Some of the men who received...calls [from Johnson operatives, asking them to tweak vote totals] replied that technological considerations prevented them from helping.... San Antonio now used voting machines, and...the results had been recorded....

Now, on Friday morning [six days after the election and after questionable maneuvering by Johnson and Stevenson operatives], the Democratic Executive Committee of Jim Wells County was meeting to make its final certification.... The figure [for one precinct] for Johnson, which had been reported as 765 on Election Night, was now 965—because, according to testimony that would later be given, someone had, since Election Night, added a loop to the "7" to change it to a "9".... Out of 988,295 votes, [Johnson] had won by 87—less than one hundredth of one percent.

—Robert A. Caro, *The Years of Lyndon Johnson: Means of Ascent,* 1990

■ **New Braunfels** *map page 184, C-3*

Popular tourist attractions and small-town charms lure visitors to New Braunfels, about 48 miles south of Austin on I-35. The area's settlement in the mid-19th century originated with the *Adelsverein,* or Association of Noblemen, organized to encourage Germans to emigrate from an overpopulated (as the nobles perceived it) Germany to real estate the group had purchased in Texas. That was the plan, anyway—but the tract the noblemen had secured from Texas land promoters, about 100 miles northwest of Austin between the Llano and San Saba Rivers, was too mountainous for farming and was controlled by the Comanches. So in 1845, the association's commissioner-general, Prince Carl of Solms-Braunfels, bought another 1,300 acres on the Guadalupe River, the land's original purpose being to serve as a way station for settlers trekking toward the larger parcel.

The once-wild terrain around what became New Braunfels has long since been tamed, and today tourists enjoy a locale whose streets are lined with colorful B&Bs, antiques shops, and restaurants, most of them on the **Main Plaza.** Because of the large German population, Braunfelians enjoy some unusual customs—at least by Texas standards—including the autumn Wurstfest, a 10-day blowout honoring a local sausage. At least 150,000 people converge on New Braunfels for the annual festival, gorging on sausage and strudel, pretzels and potato pancakes, sauerkraut, sausage-on-a-stick, and the best of the wurst: a hot dog smothered in onions, chili, and jalapeños. Polka bands oompah, yodelers yodel, and folks dressed up in lederhosen and dirndls dance their hearts out.

■ **FREDERICKSBURG**   *map page 184, B-2*
Prince Carl had neither the training nor the temperament to lead the colonization project, and left after barely a month. His replacement, John Meusebach, by contrast, had studied engineering, forestry, political science, finance, jurisprudence, and economics. He read five languages, spoke English fluently, and had held several governmental posts. In 1845, he bought 10,000 acres for an additional settlement on the banks of the Pedernales River, 88 miles northwest of New Braunfels, and named it Fredericksburg, for Prince Frederick of Prussia.

Deer at Lyndon B. Johnson National Historical Park.

Sweet Painted Churches

Central Texas became a destination for many Slavic peoples hoping to find a better life in America. Between 1851 and 1900, about 250 Bohemian and Moravian communities were established, most of them on the fertile Blackland Prairie, where farming looked promising. The meeting halls of Slavic fraternal associations are still in use in many of these towns, and in Fayette and Lavaca Counties, southeast of Austin, many Slavic communities still celebrate their heritage with annual festivals.

At least 15 churches in Texas, many established by Czechs, are famous for the murals painted on their interior walls. Four churches in the area east of New Braunfels are known as "the painted churches." The oldest is Praha's **Gothic Revival Assumption of the Blessed Virgin Mary,** built in 1895. Gottfried Flury, a Swiss artist living in San Antonio, decorated the interior by marbling the wooden columns and painting the walls with angels and an Eden of palms and leaves, with garlands around the borders and cornices. In High Hill's **Nativity of Mary, Blessed Virgin Catholic Church,** built in 1906, Ferdinand Stockert and Herman Kern of San Antonio marbled the wooden columns and created freehand depictions of angels and religious symbols that include a star of David and a cross with a crown covered with grapes and wheat sheaves and intertwined with flowering vines.

Over at Ammannsville's **Gothic Revival St. John the Baptist Catholic Church,** erected in 1918, an unknown artist stenciled borders and drew leaves and garlands, cherubs, palm fronds, and blossoms. Detailing on the ceiling simulates ribbed vaulting. The original decorator of Dubina's 1909 **Sts. Cyril and Methodius Catholic Church**—whose steeple is topped with an iron cross crafted in 1877 by a freed slave, Tom Lee—is likewise unknown. The artist's work was covered over with white paint in the 1950s but was uncovered and restored in the early 1980s. Tours of these churches can be arranged through the **Schulenberg Chamber of Commerce** (101 Kessler Avenue; 979-743-4514).

Most residents of Fredericksburg, 75 miles west of Austin on U.S. 290, know the story of John Meusebach, but they are more likely to discuss Chester W. Nimitz, the five-star admiral of the Pacific Fleet during World War II, who was born and raised in Fredericksburg. Nimitz attained the rank of fleet admiral shortly after Pearl Harbor was bombed in 1941. After successfully directing the war in the Pacific, he signed the peace treaty for the United States aboard the battleship *Missouri* in Tokyo Bay on September 2, 1945.

The Pedernales, one of the Hill Country's rivers, as painted in 1875 by Hermann Lungkwitz.

Nimitz's accomplishments during World War II are honored at a namesake museum that's part of the 9-acre **National Museum of the Pacific War.** Among the most fascinating exhibits here is a Japanese midget sub used in the invasion of Pearl Harbor in 1941. The grounds also contain a traditional Japanese garden—a gift of the people of Japan—with a waterfall, a pond, and many plants and trees. Adjacent to the garden is the National Memorial Wall, whose plaques honor sailors, ships, and fighting units. *340 East Main Street; 830-997-4379.*

Fredericksburg, a town of 9,300, is one of the Hill Country's most popular destinations. Restored 19th-century stone buildings housing restaurants, biergartens, and arts and crafts shops line seven blocks of **Main Street** (U.S. 290). There are plenty of B&Bs and there's even a store selling locally made dulcimers and psalteries, banjos, mandolins, bagpipes, and other folk instruments. Most of Fredericksburg's sites bear on architectural history, like its many 19th-century "Sunday houses"—small, two-story residences with outside stairways—built by the region's farmers to use when they brought their families into town for market day.

The limestone walls of the former Nimitz Hotel form the National Memorial Wall, which honors sailors, ships, and fighting units that participated in World War II's Pacific Theater.

The octagonal **Vereins Kirche** (Main Street between Adams and Crockett Streets), also called the "coffee mill church," is a reconstruction of the town's first public building, which was used as a school, place of worship, and community meeting house. Today it houses a small local history museum and archives.

To understand what life was like in mid-19th-century Fredericksburg, pay a visit to the **Pioneer Museum Complex** (309 West Main Street; 830-997-2835), a restored eight-room house, store, barn, smokehouse, and log cabin. Seven miles east of town, you can take self-guided tours at **Wildseed Farms** (U.S. 290; 830-990-1393), said to be one of the largest working wildflower farms in the country; the flowers bloom from spring until first frost, usually in early November.

■ LUCKENBACH   *map page 184, B-2*

Luckenbach, founded by German immigrants in 1850, little more than a general store and post office, existed in quiet obscurity until the late 1970s. That's when the country song "Luckenbach, Texas" was released by Willie Nelson and Waylon Jennings, idealizing the town as a rural place where people could be themselves. After the song hit the charts, hordes of people descended on Luckenbach every weekend for dancing, drinking, and clowning. Folks who remember the ballad still come by for a look around. There isn't much to see or do in Luckenbach, but touring bands perform on a fairly frequent basis, and on Sunday afternoons, weather permitting, local musicians cut loose in an alfresco jam session. The town also hosts an acclaimed annual chili cook-off. *FM 1376, 4 miles southwest of U.S. 290.*

■ **ENCHANTED ROCK STATE PARK**   *map page 184, B-2*
Enchanted Rock is named for a bald mountain of pink granite that rises 425 feet above Sandy Creek. Geologists estimate that Enchanted Rock is at least a billion years old, and archaeologists believe the area around it may have been inhabited thousands of years ago, but in more recent times native peoples have avoided the rock because of its supposedly supernatural properties. One such property is a creaking and groaning sound that geologists have attributed to expansion and contraction caused by temperature changes. Superstitions notwithstanding, Enchanted Rock is a favorite destination for climbers, hikers, campers, and stargazers. The view from the top is magnificent in clear weather. *FM 965, 18 miles north of Fredericksburg; 915-247-3903.*

Texas doesn't always pop to mind when people think of wine, but grapes grow well in the Hill Country, aided by warm days and cool nights; the sandy, loamy soil; and the not-too-dry, not-too-wet rainy season. Among the notable Hill Country wineries are **Fall Creek Vineyards** (1820 County Road 222, Tow; 915-379-5361), which produces fine rieslings and chenin blancs; **Becker Vineyards** (Jenschke Lane off U.S. 290; 830-644-2681), 3 miles west of Stonewall and recognized for sauvignon blancs, cabernet sauvignons, and merlots; and **Bell Mountain Vineyards,** (463 Bell Mountain Road; 830-685-3297), 14 miles north of Fredericksburg off Route 16, known for its chardonnays, rieslings, merlots, and cabernet sauvignons.

■ **KERRVILLE**   *map page 184, B-2/3*
There's a saying in Kerrville that people here "lose their hearts to the hills." The natural beauty and tranquility of this area do set hearts pounding, but these days those affected tend to be either the very young or the very advanced—there are 15 summer youth camps in and around town, and 68 percent of the population is made up of senior citizens. The age gap doesn't seem to bother anyone, though, as both young and old can be seen enjoying recreational activities on the Guadalupe River and hiking over the endlessly rolling green hills.

In clear weather, the view from Enchanted Rock is magnificent.

Refugees of Germany's failed revolution of 1848 settled Kerrville, only to find themselves in the midst of another national conflagration. Shortly after their arrival the question of Texas's secession from the United States emerged. The immigrants voted to stay in the Union, and their resistance didn't end when they lost the statewide vote. In 1862, the Confederacy declared Kerr and two adjoining counties in revolt. Sixty-seven of the area's Unionists met on August 1 and headed for Mexico, hoping to escape the Confederate draft. A week later, Confederate troops attacked them near Brackettville, 50 miles north of the Rio Grande. Nineteen Unionists were killed in the fighting, and nine more were executed after capture. Of those who escaped and attempted to cross into Mexico in October, eight died and 20 reached Mexico. At war's end, the remains of the Unionists killed in what Confederate forces called the Battle of the Nueces were buried at Comfort, 19 miles east of Kerrville on I-10. The monument placed over their shared grave still stands.

Kerrville locals crowd into antiques shops, art galleries, restaurants, and cafés along Main Street (also called Junction Highway). Among the fine specimens of late-19th-century architecture is the old Kerrville Post Office, now the **Kerr Arts & Cultural Center** (228 Earl Garrett Street; 830-895-2911). Farther afield is the **Cowboy Artists of America Museum** (1550 Bandera Highway; 830-896-2553), a repository for recent and historical works about frontier life. In the spring, Kerrville is awash in bluebonnets; the Kerrville Chamber of Commerce (1700 Sidney Baker Street; 830-792-3535) has information about the best places to see them.

■ HILL COUNTRY WEST   *map page 184, A-3*
The part of the Hill Country west of Kerrville is a popular place for river-running inner tubers. The Medina, Frio, and Nueces Rivers, so small here they would be called creeks east of I-35, provide recreation all summer. **Garner State Park,** 8 miles north of Concan on the Frio River, is one of the Hill Country's loveliest natural get-away spots. In hot summer weather, the Frio, shaded by huge cypress trees, beckons hot and tired Texans to its cool waters, where they swim the river, glide across its surface in inner tubes or canoes, or chug along its course in paddleboats. Hikers can lose themselves on nearby nature trails, and during summer, there are dance parties at night and miniature golf during the day. Both campsites and cabins are available. *From U.S. 83, turn east on FM 1050 and drive to Park Road 29; 830-232-6132.*

■ TRAVEL BASICS

Getting Around: The major east-west routes through Central Texas are I-10, which enters from the west, plunges southeast into San Antonio, then turns east toward Houston, and U.S. 290, which begins at I-10 about 33 miles northeast of Kerrville and travels east through Fredericksburg, Johnson City, and Austin before continuing on to Houston. A scenic alternative is Route 71, traveling northwest from U.S. 290 southwest of Austin, then to Llano and Fredonia.

The principal north-south highway is I-35, moving from Waco through Austin to New Braunfels on its way to San Antonio and Laredo. A scenic alternative to I-35—a good choice if time is not pressing—is U.S. 281, which comes south on the west side of I-35 through Lampasas and Burnet, proceeds through the Highland Lakes area to Johnson City and on to San Antonio, and then continues to the Mexican border.

Running through the middle of some of the prettiest parts of the Hill Country, 25 to 35 miles west of U.S. 281, is Route 16, which goes from Llano through Fredericksburg and Kerrville, then swings eastward into San Antonio. The main north-south route through the western part of the Hill Country is U.S. 83.

Austin's **Capital Metro Bus** (512-474-1200) runs throughout downtown, the University of Texas campus, and the Capitol complex, and serves most residential neighborhoods. Capital Metro also runs the **Dillo,** whose reproduction trolley cars, dating from the 1930s, traverse downtown and the Capitol complex area. Capital Metro's **The Flyer** buses serve downtown and to the University of Texas and the Capitol complex.

Climate: Summer high temperatures in Austin average 90-plus degrees Fahrenheit, but the thermometer can rise to 110. Winter highs in Austin average a little above 60 degrees, but it's not unusual for temperatures to soar into the 90s in February. The average winter low is in the upper 30s. Austin's annual precipitation averages 32 inches, with most of the rain falling in May and June and the least in December and January.

Temperature and precipitation ranges are similar in the Hill Country and the Kerrville area, though the average precipitation drops as you travel west of Kerrville. In the Hill Country, flash floods are common during spring rainstorms.

S O U T H   T E X A S

From San Antonio southward, there is no East or West Texas, only the more homogenous South Texas. Route 90 is the region's northern limit west of San Antonio, I-10 its limit east of the city. As the state narrows abruptly from here to its southern tip, few trees grow except mesquite and oak. The area is a collection of plains of varying types, and the landscape is a gently rolling one, parts of which are sometimes green, thanks to coastal rains, irrigation, and the Rio Grande.

South Texas is one of the more stable areas of Texas, both economically and culturally. Unlike Dallas, Houston, and Central Texas, the southern portion of the state has witnessed little immigration from other states. Most new residents of South Texas come from Mexico, as has always been the case. And though South Texas is the state's poorest region, large numbers of natives have stuck by their hometowns. To many South Texans, a high-paying but far-away job simply can't compete with family ties and a familiar ambience.

Three cities form a triangle in South Texas: San Antonio, at the northern apex; Laredo, at the southwestern corner; and Corpus Christi, the southeastern base. Interstate 35 connects San Antonio to Laredo, and I-37 connects it to Corpus Christi, a port, refinery, and naval operations town. A highway network connects Laredo and Corpus Christi, but their most celebrated link is the Texas Mexican Railway (known as the Tex Mex), established in 1881 to carry coal from Laredo-area mines to the port. Laredo is today the primary rail port of entry for Mexican goods under the North American Free Trade Agreement (NAFTA), putting the Tex Mex in the catbird seat as cross-border trade continues to increase.

■ SAN ANTONIO   *map page 220, and page 223*

In 1691, Domingo Terán de los Ríos, the governor of Spanish-colonial Texas, arrived in what is today San Antonio and encountered friendly Payaya Indians living along the river. Because the meeting occurred on Saint Anthony's Day, Terán named both the site and the river San Antonio de Padua. (The Indians called the river Yanaguana.) Hearing that these Indians were friendly, a Franciscan priest established the mission of San Antonio de Valero along the San Antonio River in 1718. Spanish soldiers also founded a presidio there that year. To further cement their claim to the area, the Spaniards in 1731 added a civilian settlement, the Villa

Evidence of the Mexican influence on San Antonio is can be observed on many levels, including the abstract, seen here in the colors and shapes of the city's postmodern main public library, designed by the Mexico City–based architect Ricardo Legorreta and completed in 1995.

San Fernando de Béxar, to the religious and military components of San Antonio, populating the Villa San Fernando with 56 immigrants from the Canary Islands. Descendants of those settlers still reside in San Antonio. Four additional missions followed, though their religious function diminished as Indian interest in adhering to Catholic faith and Spanish rule waned. By 1801, Mission San Antonio had become the garrison for a cavalry from Mexico's Alamo de Parras (today's Viesca).

The city of San Antonio became part of Mexico after the Mexican Revolution of 1821; that same year, Stephen F. Austin received a land grant from the new government to bring 300 Anglo families to Texas. When General Santa Anna abolished the 1824 Mexican constitution, these people—along with many Hispanic Texans—refused to recognize his presidency, an act of defiance that led to the Texas Revolution in 1836. By 1836, 3,500 Anglos lived in the city.

After Texas won its independence at the Battle of San Jacinto later in 1836, the next immigrants to arrive in San Antonio were German settlers. Following the state's annexation by the United States, Anglos settled the city in greater numbers, and by 1860, San Antonio's population was 8,200. Although growth slowed during the Civil War, when the fighting ended San Antonio became a ranching center, and served as the starting point for major cattle drives to Kansas.

Both Texas in general and San Antonio in particular have on occasion been a place of refuge for Mexicans protesting their own government's oppression. The principal event in modern Mexican history, the Revolution of 1910, was declared in San Antonio by the exiled Francisco Madero, who served as Mexico's president from 1911 to 1913. But San Antonio was also a place of refuge for many Chinese as well. After they helped build the transcontinental railroads in the mid-1800s, many Chinese stayed in Texas; others migrated to Mexico. In 1882, the U.S. Congress passed the Chinese exclusion law, which effectively barred the exiles from returning to the United States. When Pershing's troops invaded Mexico in pursuit of Pancho Villa, many of the Chinese who had gone there helped the American forces with food and supplies, in payback for which Pancho Villa lynched many Mexican-Chinese. As a result, Pershing secured an exception to the exclusion law to permit him to bring 527 Chinese-Mexicans back with him for their protection. Most of them settled in San Antonio.

With almost 1.2 million citizens, San Antonio today is the hub of South Texas and a town where Mexico's cultural influence remains unusually strong. For

Getting ready for San Antonio's annual Fiesta Parade.

Downtown San Antonio in the late 1880s.

instance, the mayor may claim to be San Antonio's most powerful resident, but his or her stature will always be rivaled by that of the Mexican consul—an important business figure because of the city's role in cross-border trade. The consul, who is appointed by the Mexican president and confirmed by the Mexican senate, is also an important ceremonial figure because two Mexican holidays, Cinco de Mayo (May 5) and Dieciséis de Septiembre (September 16)—Mexican independence days—play as big a role in civic life as does the Fourth of July. On these days, the consul makes speeches to civic clubs, rides floats in parades all over town, and is serenaded by mariachis. But the consul isn't a key figure in San Antonio's biggest spectacle, Fiesta Week, whose climax is the Battle of Flowers parade, usually around April 21. That celebration commemorates the independence of Texas from Mexico.

The significance of the city's Mexican ties was demonstrated when Mexico's then-President Carlos Salinas requested that the NAFTA signing ceremony take place here; he and U.S. President George Herbert Walker Bush traveled to San Antonio in 1992 for the event. It's also telling that on the city's largely Anglo North Side, most enterprises transact business in both English and Spanish.

San Antonio's economy depends a great deal on the military: one army and two air force bases are located there. The army base, **Fort Sam Houston,** was established in 1876, and is, among other things, a center for military medical training. The city's active-duty military population of about 62,000 is supplemented by

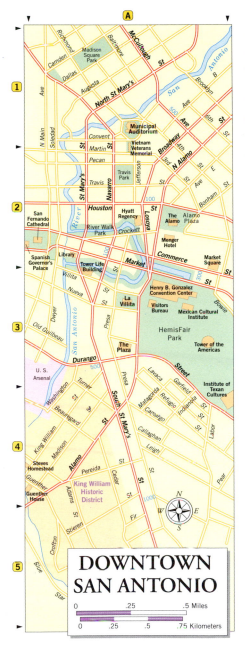

DOWNTOWN SAN ANTONIO

0   .25   .5 Miles

0   .25   .5   .75 Kilometers

25,000 active civilian base employees and by 75,000 retired military and civilian base employees.

The military plays a pivotal role in San Antonio's economy, but so does tourism. In general, the city draws three types of tourists: Texans who come to shop and sightsee; conventioneers; and visitors from across northern Mexico, especially during Christmas and Holy Week. Northern Mexicans who can afford them often buy San Antonio vacation homes, send their children to the city's private schools and universities, consult its doctors—and, quite often, retire and die in San Antonio.

■ **DOWNTOWN** *map page 220, B/C-4/5 and page 223, A-2/3*
San Antonio's architecture has not been smothered by the anonymous modernity that marks Dallas and Houston—primarily because the city was almost unaffected by the oil boom of the 1970s and 1980s that financed so many of those cities' architectural behemoths. The most impressive edifice downtown—only a couple of hotels rival it for size—is the 30-story **Tower Life Building** (310 South St. Mary's Street), which opened in 1929 as the Smith-Young Tower. The eight-sided Late Gothic Revival brick structure was designed by the local

father-son architectural firm Atlee B. and Robert M. Ayres. Five 18th-century missions and the Spanish Governor's Palace survive from that distant era, all of them open for public inspection. But for most visitors, the first stop is the most famous of the missions, which for the past two centuries has gone by the name Alamo.

The **Alamo,** Texas's most sacred shrine and the state's leading tourist attraction (annual visitation: more than three million), is on downtown's eastern side. Once known as the Spanish Franciscan Mission San Antonio de Valero, the Alamo was built of adobe and stone at its original location in 1718. The mission was moved upriver in the 1720s, and the chapel collapsed in 1744. Work on the current building began in the 1750s, but the building was not yet finished when the Spanish secularized some of their colonial missions, including Mission San Antonio, in the 1790s. After serving as a Mexican garrison in the early 19th century, it had fallen into disuse by 1836, when it was occupied by Texas revolutionaries. And it was there, in early 1836, that 180 of them made a 13-day stand against an army of several thousand, led by the self-appointed Mexican president and commander-in-chief, Antonio López de Santa Anna.

One of the earliest known photographs of the Alamo, this shot was taken in 1871, when the former mission was serving as a storage facility.

Three million people visit the Alamo each year.

Operated today by the Daughters of the Republic of Texas, who saved it from ruin a century ago, the Alamo has become a battleground again, this time a cultural one. The site contains the Alamo itself as well as, beyond its front door, a sidewalk, a small street, the flagstone Plaza, and finally a full street, Alamo Street. But recent historical research has shown that the whole area was a cemetery for Indians in the days when the Alamo was a mission. In honor of the dead, Fiesta Week parades no longer pass through the area, and periodically there are proposals to close Alamo Street to traffic.

The historic mission church contains artifacts associated with the revolution's leaders, such as weapons used in the 13-day siege, William Barret Travis's ring, and Davy Crockett's buckskin vest. In the Long Barrack Museum, housed in the former priests' quarters, are more artifacts. A 17-minute film, *Introducing the Alamo*, runs three times every hour in the museum's Clara Driscoll Theater. *Alamo Plaza at Alamo and Houston Streets; 210-225-1391.*

The 316-room **Menger Hotel,** just steps from the Alamo, was built 23 years after the famous battle, in 1859. William Menger, a German immigrant who made a small fortune from his brewery, financed it, and though he hired the San Antonio architect John Fries to build the hotel, its design was partially Menger's. Early

DEFENDING THE ALAMO

The Texan marksmanship, the speed, continuity and fury of their fire, were frightful. Soldiers fell by the score. But the number of their comrades was great, and gaps were closed, and presently there was a great swarm so near the bases of the walls, that the artillery above could not be traversed downward to bear on them. Suddenly a breach was made on the north side, and another on the south, and soldiers poured in to capture the Alamo plaza. The defenders fell back to the convent and its patio, and to the roofless church. The army turned their own cannon on them, and squad after squad advanced to take room after room in the convent cells, killing all whom they trapped in each. The Mexican bayonets whistled and darted in the early sunlight that rayed into the convent patio. The ground was strewn with dead attackers and defenders. But still the army strove and, when all was silent in the outer courts and rooms, threw its remaining power against the church, which was the last stronghold of the Texans. The main doors were forced, and everywhere—in the nave, the baptistry, the transepts, the sacristy, with their heaps of long-fallen stone and weedy mounds of earth, under the light morning sky within the open walls—the victory was won man by man until after an hour not one defender was seen alive anywhere in the profaned and mouldered mission.

—Paul Horgan, *Great River: The Rio Grande in North American History,* 1954

guests of the hotel included both Robert E. Lee and Ulysses S. Grant (though not at the same time, one presumes), and Sarah Bernhardt, Babe Ruth, and Mae West dropped by during the hotel's first century. The most celebrated guest, though, was Theodore Roosevelt, who lodged here while in San Antonio in 1898 to recruit and train the First United States Volunteer Cavalry, better known as the Rough Riders, for the Spanish-American War. And recruit he did, mostly in the bar at the Menger, if the tales are true—gathering 1,200 men with such stated occupations as oarsman, policeman, cowboy, "down-and-outer," musician, Ivy League athlete, and ex-marshal of Dodge City. The Rough Riders were so popular with residents that Roosevelt had to post guards to keep civilians from overrunning the fairgrounds where "Teddy's Terrors" were drilling. The Riders shipped out to Cuba, but their horses didn't; they fought the war, including the famous charge up San Juan Hill (actually Kettle Hill), as infantry. Many did not return. *204 Alamo Plaza; 210-223-4361.*

Col. Roosevelt organizing his Rough Riders, 1898, old Fair Grounds, San Antonio, Texas. In the distance can be seen the tents of Col. Roosevelt, Col. Wood and Maj. Brody.

Photo by Brack.

Teddy Roosevelt's Rough Riders, seen here at San Antonio's old Fair Grounds prior to their participation in the Spanish-American War, were a big hit with the locals in 1898.

On the downtown's western edge is **Market Square,** a restoration of an old farmers' market and surrounding buildings, some from as early as 1840. Some shops and galleries open onto the brick walkways, and other are in the enclosed **El Mercado,** the place to take the kids to buy piñatas and other industrially made "craft" goods. Still more shops are in a separate building across San Saba Street to the west. In a 1920s-era building is the **Centro de Artes del Mercado,** where music and dance performances and gallery shows take place. Around lunchtime in the summer, entertainers perform in the square. *Market Square, bounded by I-35 and Santa Rosa, West Commerce, and Dolorosa Streets; 210-207-8600.*

La Villita (Spanish for "Little Town"), four blocks from the Alamo, is a pleasant place for a quiet stroll on tree-shaded, brick- and tile-paved streets lined with European-influenced buildings, many from the 19th century. In the past, the structures sheltered Mexican, German, Swiss, and French families. Today the restored limestone and clapboard cottages house restaurants, craft and gift shops, and art galleries. In some, visitors can watch craftsmen at work. *Bounded by San Antonio River, Nuevo, South Alamo, and South Presa Streets; 210-207-8610.*

The streets of San Antonio become a colorful marketplace during Fiesta Week.

The **San Antonio River** snakes through the city for 15 miles, while advancing a mere 6 miles from north to south. The Indian name of Yanaguana translates as "drunken old man going home at night"—an apt recognition of the river's many curves. Unlike Waco's Brazos River, or the Trinity River in southeast Texas, the San Antonio River wasn't easily navigated, and though it provided water, its meandering course through the city resulted in a confusing street layout with few grids or patterns. And from the start, the river provided excellent opportunities for people-watching. In his book *Antonio de Béxar,* the poet Sidney Lanier described the view in 1872 from the Commerce Street bridge as including "all manner of odd personages and 'characters' ":

> Here hobbles an old Mexican who looks like old Father Time in
> reduced circumstances. There goes a little German boy who was cap-
> tured a year ago by Indians. Here is a great Indian fighter . . . there a
> portly, handsome buccaneer-looking captain—and so on through a
> perfect gauntlet of people who have odd histories, odd natures or
> odd appearances.

After a flood in 1921 killed 50 people and caused millions of dollars in damage, city officials proposed building an underground channel for the river through downtown and covering it with concrete. Enraged residents, led by the San Antonio Conservation Society, persuaded the city to turn their sow's ear into a silk purse. The combined beautification and flood-control plan, executed under the aegis of the Depression-era Works Projects Administration, also called for the building of retaining walls, walkways, and footbridges. Extensive landscaping followed.

Today El Paseo del Rio, or the **River Walk,** is lined with restaurants, hotels, and souvenir shops that sell items like Alamo snow globes—miniaturizing a meteorological event that occurs in real life about once a decade. Cypress, oaks, and willows shade the waterway, passenger barges chug quietly along, crowds promenade back and forth, and music emanates from the many clubs here. The feel is similar to that of New Orleans's French Quarter, only without the Gallic flavor. Because the river runs about 20 feet below street level at most points downtown, getting to the River Walk is like finding a subway. There are 35 entrances, most of them at street-corner bridges on the business district's south side. *Extends south from the Municipal Auditorium to the King William Historic District.*

San Fernando Cathedral, the Gothic Revival anchor of Main Plaza, lies due west of the River Walk. The cathedral was constructed between 1868 and 1873 as an addition to the front of the original 1749 Spanish Baroque church, built to serve the Canary Islanders who populated the area's first civilian settlement. It was from the top of the original church that Santa Anna displayed the red flag—signaling "no mercy"—during the Battle of the Alamo. The cathedral is still active today, with hundreds of marriages, funerals, and baptisms taking place here each year. *115 Main Plaza; 210-227-1297.*

At the River Walk's northern end is **Southwest School of Art and Craft,** in buildings that formerly housed the Ursuline Academy and Convent, founded in 1851. The clock tower here is blank on its north side, local legend says, because the Reconstruction-era nuns who commissioned the work didn't want to give Yankee soldiers the time of day. The school's Ursuline Sales Gallery sells handcrafted ceramic, glass, and wood items, plus folk art, jewelry, and handmade paper. *300 Augusta Street; 210-224-1848.*

In the northeastern corner of the twisting River Walk is the **Landing** (Hyatt Regency Hotel,123 Losoya Street), the restaurant and club that hosts weekly broadcasts of "Riverwalk, Live from the Landing," a Public Radio International program of classic jazz performed by the Jim Cullum Jazz Band.

(following pages) Shops, bars, and restaurants line the 2.8-mile-long River Walk.

■ **KING WILLIAM HISTORIC DISTRICT** *map page 223, A-4*
Beginning in the 1870s, wealthy German merchants and assorted other moneyed types built grand homes in a 25-block area south of downtown now known as the King William Historic District. The main street of the neighborhood, originally called Kaiser Wilhelm, was later Anglicized to King William Street. (And with anti-German sentiment running high during World War I, the street was temporarily called Pershing Street.) Most of the mansions here playfully mix architectural styles, from beaux arts to neoclassical to Early American. Many of the grandest estates are hidden behind elaborate fences, most of them erected not as status statements but as a means of avoiding unwanted visits from wild dogs, skunks, and the occasional pig.

When Carl Hilmar Guenther, the head of Pioneer Flour Mills, moved to San Antonio from Fredericksburg in 1860, he chose a site on a crook of the San Antonio River for what has become one of the district's most famous mansions. No visible surface at the three-level **Guenther House** was left unembellished—even the window cornices are gold-leaf. Filled with exquisite Victorian-era furniture, European tapestries, and splendid antiques from the late 1800s and early 1900s, this is one of the finest examples of Victorian sensibility in Texas. Two restaurants, one on the ground floor and one on the third-floor roof garden, serve breakfast and lunch. *205 East Guenther Street; 210-227-1061.*

The **Steves Homestead,** one of the few homes in the King William Historic District open for touring, has always been something of a trendsetter. Not only was its eclectic architecture—a successful blend of the French Second Empire and Italian Villa styles—copied by other well-to-do San Antonians, but the estate was the city's first to have a telephone (in 1881) and among the first with electric lights (in 1894). Completed in 1876, the house, occupied by Edward Steves, a lumber magnate, is thought to have been designed by Alfred Giles, a locally renowned architect. That neither client nor presumed architect was American-born might explain the many exotic touches, among them the slate mansard roof and the delicate floral stenciling on the ceilings. *509 King William Street; 210-225-5924.*

Although most of the homes here are privately owned and cannot be visited, you can pick up a walking-tour brochure at the **San Antonio Conservation Society** (107 King William Street; 210-224-6163). The **King William Association** (210-227-8786) conducts tours of several houses on the first Saturday in December and sponsors garden tours and a fair in the spring.

The Steves Homestead is one of many grand late-19th-century homes in the restored King William Historic District.

■ OLD SAN ANTONIO *map page 223, A-2*

The **Spanish Governor's Palace** is all that remains of the old Plaza de Armas (Military Plaza), a military post and parade ground constructed in 1722. For most of the 1700s, the Spanish governors lived behind the palace's hand-carved doors. In the 1850s, the open plaza became the center of the city's government, a municipal market and open-air restaurant, and a place to buy vegetables, hay, wool, hides, songbirds, or ready-to-eat chili.

The design of the original Plaza de Armas has been lost, and only the Spanish Governor's Palace remains in place—a taste of the elegance of aristocratic Old Spain on the raw frontier of New Spain. The palace turns a flat, stark-white face to the public, with its thick, lime-plaster stone walls and small windows covered by wrought-iron grilles. The restored interior has such details as great hooded fireplaces and copper and brass pots and pans in the kitchen. The U-shaped structure curves around a serene walled courtyard bright with trees and flowers. *105 Plaza de Armas; 210-224-0601.*

The Governor's Palace: a taste of the elegance of Old Spain amid the raw frontier of New Spain.

Roughly 10 blocks east of the palace, in 15-acre **HemisFair Park** (South Bowie and Durango Streets), are several leftovers from San Antonio's 1968 international exposition, which commemorated the 250th anniversary of the city's founding. The remnants include the 750-foot **Tower of the Americas** (600 HemisFair Park; 210-207-8615), one of the tallest stand-alone structures in America. The tower's observation deck has a revolving restaurant and spectacular views of San Antonio.

The expo's Texas Pavilion houses the **Institute of Texan Cultures** (801 South Bowie Street; 210-458-2300), whose exhibits examine the history and people of Texas, from Indian tribes to Spanish colonists to Italian farmers and cowboys.

Perhaps the most arresting relic of HemisFair is Juan O'Gorman's mural *Confluence of Civilizations in the Americas,* which illustrates the melding of civilizations in the Western Hemisphere. The mural, on the front of the Lila Cockrell Theater, is near the River Walk.

Across I-37 from HemisFair Park is the **Alamodome** (which isn't a dome at all), the huge rectangular sports arena where NBA's San Antonio Spurs play. Sporting exterior detailing that must have been inspired by Chartpak tape, the odd-looking edifice has a 300-foot-tall mast at each corner, which anchors supporting cables connected to the roof. The mast-and-cable system eliminates the need for interior columns, however, and improves visibility for fans. *I-37 and Market Street.*

The Tower of the Americas towers over the odd-looking Alamodome.

■ **FOUR MISSIONS**   *map page 220, C-5/6*

Four missions, all younger than the Alamo, stand along the San Antonio River in South San Antonio. Though operated by the National Park Service, they remain active parishes. Mission San José serves as visitors center (210-932-1001) for the four.

The mid-18th-century **Nuestra Señora de la Concepción de Acuña,** constructed of stone, mixes Moorish, Renaissance, Gothic, Romanesque, and American Indian influences. Frescoes painted in the 1750s adorn the walls here, and though many of them have faded, one showing God as a mestizo has been beautifully restored on the library ceiling. *807 Mission Road.*

San Juan Capistrano was more simply designed than the other missions; a planned larger chapel was never completed. A small museum with exhibits about mission archaeology now occupies the *convento* (priests' quarters). The *acequia,* or stone irrigation canal, which provided water for the corn, beans, squash, sweet potatoes, and sugarcane grown in the mission's extensive farm fields, has been partially restored. *9101 Graf Road.*

Mission San José y San Miguel de Aguayo, known as "Queen of the Missions," at one time sheltered 300 Indian converts. The rose window here is a postcard favorite. Each Sunday at noon, worshipers pack the sanctuary for a Mariachi Mass. *6702 San Jose Drive.*

QUIET TO THE PAST

There are mysteries held within a family and there are mysteries held within the deeper soul of a nation. We were of a people that had seen the ground beneath our feet renamed several times over the last five hundred years, a Mestizo nation derived partly by intrepid travelers who had left their Spanish homeland far behind—across a formidable span of ocean—and people who believed they had been living in these lands since the time of the world's creation.

But apart from the mute testimony of the mission ruins, and the quiet, slowly ebbing presence of the ruins of San Antonio, no one, either family or schoolteachers, had told me that the city we lived in was already nearly three hundred years old before I was born. . . . Over the entrance to the Spanish Governor's Palace in downtown San Antonio, you can still see the Hapsburg coat of arms, colors and symbols of the Spanish royal family in the eighteenth century.

And for centuries before the Europeans had arrived, Indians had lived in these same territories, migrating on foot with the cycle of seasons, following the circuits of the planets, the serpentine sky dance of the moon and Venus, awed by the majestic, incremental movements of the deeper, distant stars. They fished the same creeks, the ones we called Cibolo, the Salado, and the Coleta. . . .

It wasn't just our family that had remained quiet to this past. It was as if all the Mexicanos had forgotten it.

—John Phillip Santos, *Places Left Unfinished at the Time of Creation,* 1999

San Francisco de la Espada moved to San Antonio from East Texas in 1731. The original chapel, built in the mid-1700s, was in ruins by 1778; the present one dates only from 1886. The most rural of the missions, Espada is known for its acequias, which have been used continuously since they were built. *10040 Espada Road.*

■ **MUSEUMS, PARKS, AND GARDENS** *map page 220, B/C-4*
In 1981, the Lone Star brewery complex was transformed into the **San Antonio Museum of Art.** Galleries in buildings erected between 1895 and 1904 exhibit Greek and Roman antiquities and European and American painting and sculpture. The museum's most popular draw is its 33,000-square-foot Latin American Art Center, built in 1998 to exhibit pre-Columbian, folk, and modern art from Mexico and Central America. *200 West Jones Avenue; 210-978-8100.*

Mission San José (1848–49), by Seth Eastman.

When Marion Koogler McNay died in 1950, her will stipulated that her Spanish Eclectic mansion become the **McNay Art Museum.** An art teacher, art lover, and heir to a Kansas oil fortune, McNay had amassed an impressive collection of post-impressionist paintings that included works by Gauguin, Cézanne, Matisse, Picasso, and van Gogh. Her 24-room house, designed by Atlee B. and Robert M. Ayres, is a perfect showcase for these intimate masterpieces and for the rest of the McNay collection, which includes American art from the early 1900s to the present. Twenty-three acres of landscaped gardens surround the museum. *6000 North New Braunfels Avenue; 210-824-5368.*

The **San Antonio Botanical Gardens** has 33 acres of splendid flora and fauna from all over the globe. Some of the most far-flung species coexist in the Conservatory, a collection of glass structures housing different ecological environments. Designed by the acclaimed environmental architect Emilio Ambasz, the Conservatory buildings are built around a tropical lagoon brimming with marine plants and other watery wonders. Elsewhere in the gardens grow the native plants of the three natural regions that converge in the San Antonio area: the southern forests of East Texas, the rocky Hill Country, and the thorn scrub of the Brush Country of South Texas. The visitors center, near the entrance, is in a restored 1896 carriage house that was rescued from demolition in downtown San Antonio. *555 Funston Place, at North New Braunfels Avenue; 210-207-3250.*

The attractions at spacious **Brackenridge Park,** 2 miles north of downtown San Antonio, include the **Witte Museum** (3801 Broadway Street; 210-357-1900), a history and science museum with traveling exhibits, a theater, and hands-on exhibits; the **Japanese Tea Garden** (3800 North St. Mary's Street; 210-207-3210), a rock quarry converted into a lush garden, complete with lily ponds and a waterfall; and the **San Antonio Zoo** (3903 North St. Mary's Street; 210-734-7184), which has an amazing 3,500 animals, including such exotics as the Andean condor, a blue poison dart frog, and a Hoffman's sloth, an unusual mammal from Central Brazil that spends its entire life hanging upside down.

■ CASTROVILLE   *map page 240, B-1*

Castroville, about 24 miles west of San Antonio on U.S. 90, looks like a little Rhine Valley village, complete with a protective grouping of low hills to the west. Nestled into a curve of the Medina River, Castroville was settled in 1844, mainly by Alsatian farmers brought to Texas by colonizer Henri Castro. Alsace, sandwiched between France and Germany, borrows cultural elements from both cultures, and a few descendants of the original settlers here still speak the German-influenced Alsatian dialect. A couple of Alsatian restaurants, a bakery, and a meat market provide a taste of the old country.

Ninety-six historic structures, most of them built between 1844 and 1880, still stand in this town of about 2,600 people; many are typical Alsatian cottages, characterized by thick lime-plaster limestone walls, steeply pitched roofs, scant ornamentation, and often a gallery or porch across the front. Two noteworthy structures are the **St. Louis Catholic Church** (1306 Angelo Street), which was built between 1868 and 1870, and its predecessor, the tiny **first St. Louis Church** (600 London Street). On the grounds of the Moye Conference and Retreat Center, the first church was completed in 1846.

The **Landmark Inn,** a former store, home, and hotel built in 1849 on what became the San Antonio–El Paso road, once again houses guests as part of the state park system. *402 East Florence Street; 830-931-2133.*

■ From San Antonio to Laredo

To leave San Antonio heading south for Laredo on I-35 is to make a quick transition from the relatively lush Hill Country into the parched terrain of the southern Brush Country. The 154 miles between San Antonio and Laredo cross a region where scrubby trees—mesquite, small live oak, and post oak—compete with cactus and thickets of catclaw, huisache, and cenizo for scant rain and stream water. Many of these plants also inhabit West Texas's severely arid Chihuahuan Desert.

Despite the generally dry conditions, there are places in the gently rolling Rio Grande Plain where farming is profitable because of irrigation, a few constant streams, and lucky patches of soil. **Poteet,** 28 miles south of San Antonio on Route 16, supports a thriving strawberry industry, while **Dilley,** 70 miles south of San Antonio on I-35, has a monument to its primary crop, the watermelon. The area around **Crystal City** and **Carrizo Springs,** 45 miles west of Dilley, is known as the Winter Garden area because it has an almost 300-day growing season: spinach, carrots, cabbage, and other vegetables grow here in winter and early spring as well as in summer. Crystal City was so proud of its spinach 60 years ago that it erected a statue of Popeye, the spinach-chomping cartoon sailor.

Crystal City is also known for having been an organizing center in the 1960s and 1970s for Mexican-Americans seeking a voice in government. Although the majority of Crystal City residents were Hispanic, Anglos dominated the local government organizations. José Angel Gutiérrez became a leader in the Chicano civil-rights movement of the 1960s, organizing, among other things, the Mexican American Youth Organization at Crystal City High School in 1967 and La Raza Unida political party in 1970.

■ Laredo *map page 240, A-4*

Laredo, at the terminus of I-35, is the principal land port for goods going into or coming out of Mexico. This was true before NAFTA was signed, and is even more the case today. A fourth international bridge was added in 2000 to ease the congestion from truck traffic, which has greatly increased since the treaty went into effect. Laredo is also a classic Texas border town. Stone and adobe are its oldest building materials, and its finest structures are in the Porfirian or late-19th-century Mexican style. The city's newest and most prosperous residential sections are on its northern and eastern edges. Commercial areas lie between the newer sections and downtown.

Berry good berries at the Poteet Strawberry Festival.

Founded by the Spanish in 1755, Laredo was not a part of Texas until the Mexican War—and according to a popular view, it isn't quite a part of the United States yet. Nor is Nuevo Laredo, the city on the south side of the Rio Grande, wholeheartedly a part of Mexico, even though it was founded by refugees when Laredo became part of the United States. That Laredoans consider the two to be one city, ignoring the minor detail that an international border separates them, is evident from the literature distributed by the Laredo Development Foundation, which reads, "Laredo and Nuevo Laredo are actually one city divided only by the Rio Grande."

Laredo's downtown business district does not cater to the American trade. Instead it serves the flow of Mexicans who enter on foot over what is called "the old bridge" over the Rio Grande, one of 21 along the Texas-Mexico border—and one of four in the Laredo area. Signs in downtown stores are often in Spanish, and though cashiers ordinarily speak some English, like their customers they live on the southern side of the Rio Grande. Pesos are used as often as dollars downtown; announcements posting the exchange rate are as common as time-and-temperature signs elsewhere, and when the rate is volatile they are watched with greater concern.

Local residents and Mexican motorists do their shopping in the city's suburban-style shopping malls. They're unusually well stocked—one of the benefits of the Mexicanization of retail commerce is that specialty merchandise is available in Laredo that would not ordinarily reach a town of its size—the population is only 188,000). The Wal-Mart store here is one of the largest in the United States.

A bit of old Laredo can be seen in the **San Agustín de Laredo Historic District,** roughly bordered by Iturbide, Santa Ursula, Convent, and Water Streets. The structures don't date back to the town's founding, but they do reflect the Spanish Colonial architectural tradition, particularly the Gothic Revival **San Agustín Cathedral** (200 San Agustín Avenue), built between 1872 and 1877, and the **Museum of the Republic of the Rio Grande** (1005 Zaragoza Street; 956-727-3480). The 1834 stone-and-adobe house the museum occupies served as the capitol of a short-lived republic in 1840, when Mexican federalists rebelled against the centralist government of Santa Anna. In an echo of the Texas rebellion four years earlier, they declared a portion of northern Mexico and the part of Texas south of the Nueces River to be a republic, with Laredo as its capital. The "nation" lasted for 283 days before coming to a bloody end. The museum contains artifacts—weapons, flags, saddles, housewares from frontier homes, spent artillery, and archival materials—that reflect the era.

■ FROM SAN ANTONIO TO CORPUS CHRISTI

If you choose the other leg of the South Texas triangle when leaving San Antonio—I-37 from San Antonio toward Corpus Christi—you'll travel from the eastern section of the Brush Country toward the Gulf Coast, where the terrain gradually flattens into the Coastal Prairies. This is a greener land than that farther west, the result of increased rainfall and humidity brought by the prevailing Gulf breezes. Farming is the main industry here, but there is cattle ranching in the lush coastal pastures.

For a more leisurely approach to the far reaches of South Texas, head east from San Antonio on I-10 to Schulenberg, roughly 100 miles, and then drive south on U.S. 77. The drive is pleasantly meandering, passing through towns that reflect the rich ethnic fabric of south Texas. U.S. 77 and U.S. 281, which plunges directly south from San Antonio, were at one time the main routes into and out of the Rio Grande Valley. Rice crops and petrochemical production provide a two-pronged economic prop for the middle Gulf Coast.

WOMAN'S WORK

Mr. Thompson had never been able to outgrow his deep conviction that running a dairy and chasing after chickens was woman's work. He was fond of saying that he could plow a furrow, cut sorghum, shuck corn, handle a team, build a corn crib, as well as any man. Buying and selling, too, were man's work. Twice a week he drove the spring wagon to market with the fresh butter, a few eggs, fruits in their proper season, sold them, pocketed the change, and spent it as seemed best, being careful not to dig into Mrs. Thompson's pin money.

But from the first the cows worried him, coming up regularly twice a day to be milked, standing there reproaching him with their smug female faces. Calves worried him, fighting the rope and strangling themselves until their eyes bulged, trying to get at the teat. Wrestling with a calf unmanned him, like having to change a baby's diaper. Milk worried him, coming bitter sometimes, drying up, turning sour. Hens worried him, cackling, clucking, hatching out when you least expected it and leading their broods into the barnyard where the horses could step on them; dying of roup and wryneck and getting plagues of chicken lice; laying eggs all over God's creation so that half of them were spoiled before a man could find them....

It was his dignity and reputation that he cared about, and there were only a few kinds of work manly enough for Mr. Thompson.

—Katherine Anne Porter, *Noon Wine,* 1937

■ VICTORIA   *map page 240, D-2*

Victoria, 63 miles south of Schulenberg along U.S. 77, was home to the Texas-born writer Katherine Anne Porter for several years in the early 20th century while she taught dramatic arts, singing, elocution, and dancing to support herself and her father. *Noon Wine,* set on a South Texas dairy farm and considered among the best short novels ever written, concerns a taciturn Swedish hired hand whose past comes back to haunt him and the Thompsons, the couple (said to be based on Porter's own parents, though she denied it) that takes him in.

Almost a century later, the area near Victoria became a hotbed of archaeological activity when, in the summer of 1995, divers with the Texas Historical Commission found the wreck of the *La Belle,* French explorer René-Robert Cavelier, Sieur de La Salle's ship, in the middle of Matagorda Bay a few miles east of Victoria, where it had sunk in 1685. The muddy bottom of the bay had miraculously preserved many parts of the wooden ship and its cargo, which turned out to be precious: cannons, swords, guns, coins, glass beads, jewelry, bottles of wine, bronze bells, pottery, and much more. It turned out to be one of the most significant marine archaeological finds in history. La Salle had been sent to the region by Louis XIV, charged with the task of stopping Spanish encroachment along the lower Mississippi. The explorer set out with 300 colonists aboard, but the team missed Mississippi by 470 miles and ended up instead on the Gulf Coast—where most of the 300, including La Salle, died as the result of illness, malnutrition, and treachery.

Not long after the discovery of the *La Belle,* the commission pinpointed La Salle's colony on a private ranch a short distance inland on the banks of Garcitas Creek. The commission staff moved operations there and excavated the French colony site, as well as that of a Spanish fort that had been built atop the French site a few years after the colony expired. Most of the artifacts removed from *La Belle* are undergoing conservation at the Conservation Research Laboratory at Texas A&M University in College Station, but several items from the doomed ship are on display at the Bob Bullock Texas State History Museum in Austin.

■ GOLIAD   *map page 240, D-2*

Goliad, 25 miles southwest of Victoria at the junction of U.S. 77 and U.S. 59, is one of the oldest towns in Texas, with a compelling history. Goliad has known several names since 1749, the year the Spanish founded a mission site there and built the nearby La Bahía presidio to guard it.

In 1810, Mexico began its struggle for independence with an abortive uprising led by Father Miguel Hidalgo of Dolores, in today's Hidalgo state. Texas then experienced an unsuccessful rebellion of its own: the Gutiérrez-Magee expedition, an invasion from Louisiana by troops mostly of American extraction. Their aim was to make Texas part of the United States. The Gutiérrez-Magee expedition reached La Bahía and took over its fort in November 1812. Its invaders withstood a siege, routed their enemy, and in February marched out and took San Antonio, where they held out until August, when they were crushed. After independence from Spain was won, the congress of the state of Coahuila, which ruled over Texas, granted La Bahía municipal status and gave the settlement a patriotic name: Goliad is an anagram for Hidalgo (though to get the point, you've got to remember that the letter H is silent in Spanish).

Goliad's placid downtown exhibits few traces of the town's long and colorful history.

But the little town is best known for an episode that occurred two decades later. Col. James Fannin of the Texas independence movement was quartered at Goliad in February 1836 with about 500 troops, the largest revolutionary force in Texas, when Lt. Col. William Barret Travis, facing certain death at the Alamo, pleaded for support. Fannin dawdled for weeks, then reluctantly set out to join the besieged Alamo garrison.

When one of his wagons lost a wheel, Fannin turned his troops around. On March 19, two weeks after the Alamo fell, he and his men left for the coast. En route they encountered and fought Mexican troops for a day, then surrendered. The captives were returned to the presidio at Goliad, and on March 27, Palm Sunday, about 400 of them were executed. A large monument about 2 miles south of Goliad on U.S. 183 marks the spot where their remains were buried in a mass grave shortly after independence was won at San Jacinto by Texans whose battle cry was "Remember the Alamo! Remember Goliad!"

Goliad State Historic Park (108 Park Road 6, off U.S. 183/77A; 361-645-3405), a quarter mile south of Goliad on U.S. 183, contains a 1936 Civilian Conservation Corps reconstruction of the **Nuestra Señora del Espíritu Santo**

mission and a museum. Also at the park is a reconstruction of the house in which Gen. Ignacio Zaragoza was born in 1829. Zaragoza led Mexican forces to victory against the French in the Battle of Puebla on May 5, 1865—an event celebrated in Cinco de Mayo festivals all over Mexico and Texas. The house contains displays and artifacts that explore the general's career and the shared history of Mexico and Goliad.

Nearby is **La Bahía presidio** (U.S. 183/77A), which has a small museum with artifacts relating to La Bahía history; **Fannin Battleground State Historic Site** (Park Road 27 off U.S. 59) is 9 miles east of Goliad.

■ ARANSAS NATIONAL WILDLIFE REFUGE
map page 240, D-3

One of the natural glories of the middle Texas coast is the Aransas National Wildlife Refuge, a 70,504-acre sanctuary about 50 miles southeast of Goliad—and the temporary resting place for hundreds of species of migrating birds, including the endangered whooping crane. A flock of the 5-foot-tall birds winters here annually, attracting hundreds of birders each year. Aransas is on the Central Flyway, a major bird-migration route, and on the Great Texas Coastal Birding Trail, which links 308 wildlife-viewing sites along the Gulf Coast. Maps, along with information about the birds likely to be found at each site and the best season to visit, are available at Texas Department of Transportation Travel Information Centers. *Refuge entrance, FM 2040 (off Route 35, take FM 774 for 9 miles and FM 2040 for 7 miles); 361-286-3559.*

From Aransas, U.S. 77 parallels the coastline, from 20 to 25 miles inland, until it reaches the Rio Grande at Brownsville, at the southernmost tip of Texas. As the highway makes its descent, it divides rural South Texas into the **Coastal Prairie,** which is a farming and ranching region, and the **Rio Grande Plain,** a drier area where only ranching is possible. Rainfall and dirt make a visible difference: the area east of the line is wet and black, while to the west the terrain is mostly caliche—bleached white soil—where mesquite, cactus, and brush thrive.

La Bahía presidio was built by the Spanish to protect the mission they had founded at Goliad in 1749.

(above) Corpus Christi Bay Bridge.
(opposite) Aransas National Wildlife Refuge is known for its flocks of migrating birds, but the refuge also holds many reptiles, amphibians, and mammals, including the javelina.

■ CORPUS CHRISTI *map page 240, D-4*

Corpus Christi owes its rise to a boundary dispute. When Texas became a republic in 1836, it announced that the Rio Grande was its southern border, but the fledgling nation was unable to back its claim with force. Mexico maintained that the Nueces River, which runs roughly the same course as I-37, was the appropriate international line. Corpus (Anglo Texans usually dispense with the second part of the name) was established where the Nueces reaches the Gulf. It was a de facto border town with an avenue to the sea—a natural headquarters for smugglers. By signing the treaty ending the Mexican War in 1848, Mexican officials acknowledged the Rio Grande as Texas's official southern border, and with elimination of the threat of Mexican invasion, Corpus Christi began developing into a major port.

The Mexican-American middle class developed a keen sense of its rights early in the 20th century, leading to the founding of two Hispanic-rights organizations in Corpus. Offended by the tradition of Anglo "bossism" and by discrimination based on ethnic background, Mexican-Americans founded the League of United Latin-American Citizens, the first national Mexican-American civil-rights organization, in Corpus in 1929. Out of that emerged the American G.I. Forum, organized in Corpus in 1948 to obtain equal rights from the federal government for Mexican-American veterans. Its mission expanded to include equal governmental rights for all Hispanic-Americans.

Corpus is one of the calmer cities in Texas, not known for booms, busts, or explosive population growth. Between 1980 and 2000, Brownsville's population increased by more than 60 percent; both Arlington and Plano, in the Dallas–Fort Worth area, more than doubled. But during the same period, the population of Corpus grew slightly more than 19 percent—from 232,000 to 277,000. Many locals would like to see it stay that way. "Politicians always hope for growth, so that they can pay off the debts in 20 years that they've made today," says Corpus defense attorney Douglas Tinker, whose past clients include members of the Branch Davidians and the woman accused of murdering the Tejana singer Selena in the mid-1990s. "But as for me, I hope the city doesn't grow too much."

The USS Lexington, *docked in the bay near downtown, is now a floating museum.*

Downtown Corpus grew up facing its beaches, but following a 1919 hurricane most new construction headed inland, to a bluff overlooking the bay. When people in Corpus talk of "downtown" and "uptown," they're referring to the split-level business district, whose waterfront is protected by a 2-mile seawall and laid out along spectacular Shoreline Drive. Some local boosters claim—incorrectly—that Gutzon Borglum, who created the sculptures on Mount Rushmore, designed the Corpus Christi seawall. The real story is that Borglum submitted a design for the entire bayfront area to Corpus Christi officials in 1928, but the voters refused to finance it. Corpus's seawall, constructed 10 years later, was designed and built by a Dallas firm.

Traveling south, Shoreline Drive morphs into Ocean Drive, where some of Corpus's most lavish residences are located. Despite the name, Ocean Drive doesn't face the ocean; it doesn't even face the Gulf. The drive, along with the rest of the Corpus waterfront, faces Corpus Christi Bay.

Three land projections, known as T-heads and L-heads because of their shapes, protrude from the coastline into the Gulf. Pleasure craft and bay shrimp boats dock on the outthrusts, which have many restaurants and bait shops. Locals go to the docking points to buy shrimp fresh from the bay.

The aircraft carrier **USS *Lexington,*** one of five warships stationed in Corpus, was purchased by the city when it was decommissioned in 1990. The ship, larger than three football fields, was active in the South Pacific during World War II. Now in the bay near downtown, it has become a magnet for tourists. The onboard museum exhibits photographs, memorabilia, and artifacts donated by the men who served aboard the *Lexington* from 1943 to 1990, and the deck holds restored aircraft used in military engagements from World War II on. *2914 North Shoreline Boulevard, off Route 181; 361-888-4873.*

There are no beaches worthy of the name on the mainland here; beachgoers travel across the J. F. Kennedy Causeway (Park Road 22) to **Mustang Island State Park** (Route 361, north off Park Road 22; 361-749-5246) or to Padre Island National Seashore (continue south on Park Road 22). As elsewhere in Texas, the beaches are perfect for strolling or, where permitted, beachfront drives. A word of caution, though: in the water or on the beach, stay away from jellyfish. There are plenty of them, and two of the Texas varieties can sting.

Feeding the birds on Padre Island.

■ PADRE ISLAND NATIONAL SEASHORE   *map page 240, D-4/5*

Padre Island stretches 130 miles from Corpus Christi south to Port Isabel, making it the nation's longest coastal barrier island. Of that stretch, the northern 130,355 acres constitute Padre Island National Seashore, a slim 70-mile ribbon edged with glorious, unspoiled white-sand beach along the Gulf of Mexico. The entrance to the National Seashore, which is on North Padre Island, is 10 miles down the island from the JFK Causeway. The beach is backed by salt-tolerant grass, which anchors the dune ridge that rises to as much as 35 feet, and the grass-covered western slope of the ridge falls into marshy tidal flats, which extend into salty, shallow Laguna Madre. At least 600 species of wildflowers and other plants flourish here.

More than 350 bird species—sandhill cranes, pelicans, peregrine falcons, and ospreys—have been sighted on the island, and white-tail deer, bobcats, javelina, coyotes, and five species of endangered sea turtles make Padre Island their home. Among the many rodents here is the Padre Island kangaroo rat, which lives off seeds and sea grasses and can sometimes be seen scurrying about rapidly in the sand. There are also bats, ground squirrels, and raccoons. Dolphins circle the island coast, as do jellyfish.

The visitors center, a mile past the park's entrance, has brochures, a snack bar, and bathhouse. Two campgrounds are nearby—one primitive, one with showers. If you plan to hike farther south, be aware that there is no shade or water along the way and, in warm weather, mosquitoes abound. *Visitors center, Park Road 22, 10 miles south of the JFK Causeway; 361-949-8068.*

■ **KING RANCH**   *map page 240, C-4*

Any map of Texas shows a blank spot, nearly 70 miles long and about 30 miles wide, running along the Laguna Madre from a point that starts about 20 miles south of Corpus Christi. This seemingly empty area, traversed by U.S. 77, takes in almost all of two counties, and parts of four. One of the counties, Kenedy, has only 415 residents, yet the county covers 1,945 square miles of territory—about one and a half times the size of Rhode Island, and only slightly smaller than Delaware.

King Ranch cowboys move cattle during the late 1930s.

The legendary King Ranch—the model for the Benedict ranch in Edna Ferber's 1952 book *Giant* and the 1956 movie based on it—accounts for most of the blank spot. This 825,000-acre spread owes its existence not only to Texas's quixotic 19th-century economy, but also to an important figure of the period.

Richard King was the son of Irish immigrants. Born in New York in 1824, he left home at the age of 11 to work as a cabin boy on an Atlantic Coast freighter. In 1842, while working on a river steam boat, King befriended Mifflin Kenedy, another riverboat sailor. Five years later, the two went into Mexican War service transporting troops and supplies on the Rio Grande. In 1850, they became business partners, and for the next 20 years they operated riverboats along the lower Rio Grande.

Three years after forming his partnership with Kenedy, King paid a Mexican family $300 for a 68,500-acre ranch—more than 107 square miles—on Santa Gertrudis Creek, about 120 miles north of the border. In 1858, the rancher and shipper and his wife built a house on the Santa Gertrudis grant, at a site picked by an army visitor with an engineer's eye, Lt. Col. Robert E. Lee. While establishing himself in ranching, King kept his hand in the shipping business he owned with Kenedy. The two prospered during the Civil War when the Confederate government contracted with them to supply European buyers with cotton, and the Rio Grande and Texas Gulf coast became the main arteries of Southern trade. After the war, the two men divided their holdings. King died in 1885 in San Antonio. His youngest daughter, Alice Gertrudis King, married his executor, attorney Robert Kleberg, and their descendants operated the ranch for many years.

OIL COMING IN

So now the stink of oil hung heavy in the Texas air. It penetrated the houses the gardens the motorcars the trains passing through towns and cities. It hung over the plains the desert the range; the Mexican shacks the Negro cabins. It haunted Reata. Giant rigs straddled the Gulf of Mexico waters. Platoons of metal and wood marched like Martians down the coast across the plateaus through the brush country. Only when you were soaring in an airplane fifteen thousand feet above the oil-soaked earth were your nostrils free of it.

—Edna Ferber, *Giant,* 1952

A worker holds up minerals extracted from the King Ranch.

Oil saved the King empire from bankruptcy during the Great Depression, and by 1953, 650 oil- and gas-producing wells had been drilled on King Ranch lands. As a result, the ranch prospered and expanded. The old Santa Gertrudis grant became the nucleus of operations for more than 1.2 million acres spread through the United States, Cuba, Australia, Brazil, Argentina, Venezuela, and Spain. It also became a horse-breeding ranch. The most famous Thoroughbred out of the King Ranch stables, Assault, won racing's Triple Crown in 1946.

King Ranch also left its name on the map of Texas. King, Kenedy, and Jim Wells counties, and the towns of Alice, Sarita, and Kingsville, are named for players in the King Ranch dynasty. Today, King Ranch Inc. is run not from the palatial 1915 "Big House," west of Kingsville, but from a corporate suite in Houston. Ranch tours take visitors past cattle and quarter horses, and videos at the visitors center chart its 150-year history. *Route 141 west, in Kingsville; 361-592-8055.*

DON PEDRITO OF FALFURRIAS

About 40 miles south of Alice on U.S. 281 lies Falfurrias, location of the principal shrine to one of the more curious and enduring figures in South Texas history, Don Pedrito Jaramillo. He was a thin, white-bearded man, with a haunting, Yoda-like face that still stares out from family altars across South Texas—usually in a pose in which the Don is seated in a chair, a newspaper in his hand. He was Tarascan Indian, born in the middle of the 19th century near Guadalajara. In 1881, when he came from Mexico to the Los Olmos Ranch, just east of what would in two years become the town of Falfurrias, only one doctor lived in rural South Texas. Pedro Jaramillo, who had earlier heard a voice telling him he had received the gift of healing from God, filled the gap.

Curanderismo, still widely practiced today, is a combination of mysticism, indigenous herbalism, and lay Catholic ritual, and Don Pedrito, as he was affectionately called, was a master practitioner. Don Pedrito visited ranches through the region between the Nueces River and the Rio Grande, either walking or riding a donkey. Often he supplied at no cost the remedies that he prescribed, and he distributed food to those in need, paying for it with small donations received through the mail. His methods were unusually simple, even by standards of his mysterious craft, and in keeping with its traditions, Don Pedrito never accepted anything more than nominal sums as his fees. Don Pedrito died in 1907, and he is buried where he lived, about 2 miles east of Falfurrias. His grave has become a shrine—a pilgrimage site for those who revere him and seek his aid.

The most historic of the King Ranch towns is **Alice,** about 45 miles inland from Corpus Christi. Alice, which is far enough south to grow tall palms along its streets, is a ranching center and a hub of the oil and gas industries. The seat of Jim Wells County, Alice was central to the final vote-fixing shenanigans (see page 208) that catapulted Lyndon Baines Johnson into the U.S. Senate in 1948.

■ RIO GRANDE VALLEY   *map page 240, C-6*

The Lower Rio Grande Valley at the southern tip of Texas is a collection of 40 towns—some shoulder to shoulder—in three Texas counties, Cameron, Hidalgo, and Willacy. Some of the area's highway markers point to the region itself, and not its separate towns; to most Texans, the Valley—as they call it—is one place, sprawled across city limits signs.

But it is not a valley. It's a subtropical alluvial plain, about 100 miles long and 50 miles wide, surrounded by flatlands, not mountains. The name was given to the region by the promoters who lured Midwestern farmers—by the trainloads—to locate here in the early 20th century. The Valley is in fact a river delta, an area of soils made rich by the flow of the Rio Grande, irrigated by waters that are banked at Falcon Reservoir, west of the region.

The Falcon Dam is fed regularly by releases of water from the even larger Amistad Dam, about 220 miles upriver at Del Rio. At least that is the way it's supposed to work. However, both Mexico and Texas draw from the Rio Grande for municipal and agricultural purposes; an international agreement stipulates the amounts that both countries may withdraw and how much they must release for downstream uses. The Brush Country along the Rio Grande suffered a prolonged drought that began in 2000, and farmers on the Valley's Texas side protested because Mexico had not released its agreed-upon share of water. Some years were so bad that Texans didn't have sufficient amounts of water to plant crops. There were times when the Rio Grande was totally dry at its mouth.

The town of **Harlingen** is the site of the Valley's chief airport, the usual arrival point for visitors flying in to **South Padre Island,** about 40 miles southeast on the Gulf. This is a town not to be defined by its population count. As promotional brochures state, "Tourism is the only industry on South Padre Island," and the place has very few permanent residents—2,500, according to the 2002 estimate. What it does have are about two dozen hotels, motels, and condo rentals, with a total of 4,500 places to sleep.

Valley Agriculture

Onions, lettuce, carrots, broccoli, greens, cucumbers, sugar cane, tomatoes, cabbage, and most of the aloe vera sold in the United States flourish in the valleys of the Rio Grande, where a 330-day growing season makes agriculture the prime component of the region's economy. The Valley is also a greenhouse for ornamental plants and trees. Locals cultivate poinsettias, avocados, and papayas in their gardens, and the region blossoms with bougainvillea, hibiscus, oleander, and other bright foliage along the roadways, in yards, and even at places of business. The prize of Valley horticulture, however, is not decorative plants but grapefruit and oranges.

The Valley's citrus industry was established early in the 20th century, and its success led to its nickname, Magic Valley. Citrus growers produce oranges, but they don't sell many for eating: Texas oranges aren't as pretty as their Florida and California competitors, and they tend to be harder-skinned. Most Valley oranges wind up as orange juice. Valley grapefruit, on the other hand, are prized, mostly because of their yellow skins and red pulp. The redder varieties—the Ruby Red, the Star Ruby, and the Rio Ruby, all three of which were developed in Texas—are sweeter than their white-pulped cousins. Red pulp also indicates the presence of a significantly higher level of Vitamin A than white pulp.

The island, reached by a 2.6-mile causeway from Port Isabel, was a refuge for pirates and Karankawa Indians. Early attempts to promote its 34 miles of beach were stymied because developers could not obtain hurricane insurance coverage until legislative acts in the 1970s forced insurers to offer it. Today, some of the island seems almost overdeveloped, but there are no souvenir shops, T-shirt stands, or movie theaters at the **Laguna Madre Nature Trail** (7355 Padre Boulevard). The 1,500-foot boardwalk, next to the Convention Center, traverses marshes and wetlands, allowing for viewing of sea birds and marine life in their natural habitat. **Breakaway Cruises** (Sea Ranch Marina, 1 Sopadre Boulevard, slip 27; 956-761-2212) operates dolphin and sunset cruises aboard glass-bottom boats and larger craft, providing an aquatic perspective on the island.

Although off the beaten path, South Padre Island is hardly isolated, and chain and fancier eateries can be found along Padre Boulevard, the main drag. Lodgings

Pirates and Native Americans were among the first inhabitants of South Padre Island.

in South Padre are either on the Gulf, on the inner island, or bayside—bayside facing the Laguna Madre, the narrow stretch of water between the island and the mainland. Swimmers and surfers seek out Gulf digs, but bayside lodgings are preferred by fishermen, especially those who, despite restrictions and prohibitions, aim to catch red drum, a type of channel bass whose habitat is the Laguna waters.

■ EDINBURG   *map page 240, C-6*

Edinburg calls itself the Gateway to the Valley, and it does serve that purpose for land travelers. Nearly 150,000 "winter Texans"—mainly Midwestern retirees who spend their winters in motor or trailer homes—come down U.S. 281 to the Valley every November and return north every March. Because winter residents return to the same park every year, a small-town atmosphere prevails. Shuffleboard and bridge tournaments are popular, and residents often organize square-dance teams, exercise classes, bingo games, even yoga and quilting sessions.

■ FROM MCALLEN TO BROWNSVILLE   *map page 240, C/D-6*

U.S. 281 brings travelers south into the Valley, but U.S. 83 is its belt line, connecting the most important Valley towns: **Mission,** the birthplace of the legendary Dallas Cowboys coach Tom Landry, on the western edge of the region, and **McAllen,** less than 10 miles east.

Nearly shoulder to shoulder east of McAllen are **Pharr, San Juan, Alamo, Donna, Weslaco, Mercedes, La Feria,** and Harlingen. Most of the towns have an all-American, Main Street look but have only nominal attractions for the traveler—except San Juan, whose lure is the **Virgin of San Juan del Valle** (U.S. 83 south, take the San Juan Road Exit and make the first right), a 1980 statue inspired by a similar one Mexico. Pilgrims to the shrine include migrant workers seeking benediction before and after their forays to harvests in the American Northwest and Midwest.

U.S. 83 runs 10 miles north of U.S. 281, which takes an east-west route at the tip of the Valley, paralleling the Rio Grande. The settlements along U.S. 281 are much smaller than those on U.S. 83, and include a half-dozen *colonias,* or in Spanish, "neighborhoods." The colonias aren't ordinary neighborhoods, however, and explaining what they are requires an understanding of events that occurred in Mexico between 1917 and 1992.

The Mexican Constitution in 1917 guaranteed all Mexican citizens the right to own a plot of land. Newcomers to the cities used that right to claim plots of unused land. Ordinarily, a hundred or more homeless families would pick out a tract on the outskirts of a town and—following another Mexican tradition—begin building their homes on it, with their own hands. While occupying the land and building on it, they often kept the legitimate owners and policemen away with armed force. Invariably, the developments were not provided with water, sewer, and utility lines at their onset. Yet with the passage of time, the squatter-residents legalized their stay and regularized services.

Recent immigrants to the Valley from Mexico have tried to recreate a similar pattern in Texas. Landowners have cooperated by offering tracts for sale—without sewer lines and other common services. Some of the tracts offered have been as small as 60 by 100 feet, at prices that everyone could afford. Because city and county governments weren't able to fund the laying of lines across the Valley—and it's not their legal responsibility, anyway—during the immigration crush of the 1980s, Texas voters approved a $100 million referendum to provide vital services to the colonias. In the wake of that grand disbursement, various legislative measures were passed in an attempt to prevent the rise of new colonias.

If the border's history is an indication of what might happen in the future, the new regulations aren't likely to succeed. Many colonias have grown so large over the last several years that the U.S. Bureau of the Census includes them in the list of unincorporated areas to be treated as identifiable concentrations of population.

■ SANTA ANA NATIONAL WILDLIFE REFUGE
map page 240, C-6

On the south side of U.S. 281, a little east of Hidalgo, is the 2,000-acre **Santa Ana National Wildlife Refuge.** The park preserves the natural habitat of the Valley before it was developed. Despite its small size—2,088 acres—the refuge is rife with birders and botanists. Almost 400 bird species nest here over the course of a year, including many rare species from Mexico. Texas ebony grows in the preserve, and even the endangered ocelot and jaguarundi—American and South American wildcats, respectively—survive in its thick growth. The park has an open-air butterfly garden, one of the most productive in Texas. At least 300 species of lepidoptera are known to settle here during the peak butterfly months of October and December. *U.S. 281, 7 miles south of Alamo; 956-784-7500.*

Another natural gem in the area is the **World Birding Center** (956-584-9156), a chain of nine prime birding sites, most of them within the 80 miles between South Padre Island and Mission, ranging in size from 1,000 acres to 10 acres. The sites feature blinds and towers to help visitors spot such rarities as green jay, rose-throated becard, and masked tityra. The center's headquarters, at **Bentsen–Rio Grande Valley State Park** (FM 2062, 3 miles south of Mission), has maps, bird lists, directions, and additional information on bird sites.

Brownsville, at the junction of U.S. 77/83 and U.S. 281, is the largest city in the Valley (its population is close to a million), and the southernmost city in Texas, lying at essentially the same latitude as southern Florida. It is a deep-water port, through a 25-mile channel to the Gulf. Its shrimp-fishing fleet of almost 200 boats annually hauls in the fifth-largest catch in the United States, a fact reflected in menus all over town.

The first gunfire of the Mexican War was heard here in 1846, when the United States, having acquired Texas, decided to test its contention that the state's border was the Rio Grande, not the Nueces River. To this end, the army established a post here, Fort Taylor, on the north bank of the Rio Grande. But in April 1846 Mexican troops lobbed shells at the fort, killing its commander, Maj. Jacob Brown. The fort then became **Fort Brown,** and the city itself followed suit by adopting his name.

In May of 1846, conflict between the armies was renewed at **Palo Alto,** 15 miles northeast of Brownsville, at the intersection of FM 1847 and FM 511, where Gen. Zachary Taylor won an artillery duel against Mexican soldiers. The outbreak of the Mexican War is dated by some accounts to the shelling of Fort Taylor/Brown, and by others to the artillery match at Palo Alto. The Palo Alto location is under development as a National Historic site. The interim visitors center can be reached at 956-541-2785.

Twelve miles east on Route 4 is a historical marker noting the May 12–13, 1865, **Battle of Palmito Ranch**—the last land battle of the Civil War—fought a month after the Confederacy's surrender at Appomattox. On May 11, a Union force on the Gulf Coast sent 300 mostly African-American troops to accept the surrender of the Confederate troops at Fort Brown. The Union commanders presumed that the Confederates holding Fort Brown knew of the Appomattox surrender and would promptly turn over their command.

Bird lovers sight rare and endangered species at the World Birding Center.

The Feet of a Laborer

Domingo gazed up at the sky as he climbed the aluminum ladder, stepping lightly on each rung. The white clouds floating over the Rio Grande Valley appeared close enough for a man to reach out and touch with his hand. Sweat was streaming down his face, and the band of his hat was drenched. His machete hung off the back of his belt. The ladder wobbled slightly as he hacked at broken branches, and he thought he might have been more secure on the rungs if he had climbed barefoot. He would have done this, but he was embarrassed to show his tired cracked feet in front of la señora. They were the feet of an old man who had worked his whole life like a mule. Some of the jobs he took paid very little, but he felt fortunate to still be working. No one could say he had ever backed down from a day's work.

—Oscar Casares, "Domingo," in *Brownsville*, 2003

Some reports indicate that the Confederates had not heard of the South's surrender and resisted. Confederate officers at Fort Brown, however, knew full well that the eastern armies had surrendered, but had resolved to continue fighting in spite of it. After several skirmishes, they routed the Union forces at Palmito Ranch on May 13, killing 30 Union soldiers and capturing 115. A few days later, federal officials arranged a truce with the die-hard Confederate officers.

■ Visiting Mexico

If you're visiting South Texas, you'll probably want to set aside a morning or afternoon—probably not more—to visit one of the cities on the Mexican side of the Rio Grande. Access is easy, language and currency are no barriers, and some are well stocked with merchandise that is hard to find elsewhere.

Entering Mexican border towns in the past was simplicity itself. You paid a nominal toll or turnstile fee on the American side of an international bridge and walked or drove across. Since September 11, 2001, however, reentry to the United States has become more regimented. U.S. Customs prefers to see a valid U.S. passport or a certified copy of a birth certificate and a current photo ID issued by a government agency. Travelers who are not American citizens will need to carry entry documents to show to U.S. immigration agents upon returning north across the Rio Grande.

Drivers should check their policies: some American insurers don't cover border-town accidents. (When renting a car in, say Austin, a rental company will often require you to stipulate that you will *not* drive within 50 miles of the border.)

Though it takes less than 10 minutes to enter Mexico from Texas by car, it's probably best to walk if you don't plan to bring back any bulky or heavy items. U.S. customs inspections are sometimes thorough, and motorists often find themselves waiting in long lines to reenter the United States.

Most Texans visit border towns to buy liquor and cigarettes, which are much cheaper south of the border. Each adult returning from Mexico is permitted to bring one liter of liquor—subject to a $1 tax—and one tax-free carton of cigarettes. Non-Texans visiting the border towns are usually more interested in the works of Mexican artisans—most towns have a street lined with arts and crafts shops. Many Americans also visit Mexican pharmacies, where antibiotics are sold more freely than in the states. A note of caution, however: in Mexico, narcotic drugs are restricted, just as in the United States, and black-market sales are more severely punished there than in this country.

■ TRAVEL BASICS

Getting Around: Interstate 10, at the northern edge of South Texas, comes into San Antonio from the northwest. U.S. 83 comes into Laredo from the western side of the Hill Country, and then parallels the Rio Grande to Harlingen, where it joins U.S. 77 to continue south to Brownsville. Interstate 35 comes south out of San Antonio and ends at Laredo. Interstate 37 travels southeast from San Antonio to Corpus Christi. U.S. 281 runs north to south; it joins I-37 for a short distance before dipping south through Alice to the border, below McAllen. San Antonio's **VIA Metropolitan Transit** (210-362-2020), provides daily bus service to the airport, downtown, and most suburban neighborhoods.

Climate: San Antonio summers are hot and humid, with average highs of 90-plus degrees Fahrenheit and average lows in the mid-70s. In winter, average highs run in the mid-60s, with lows around 40 degrees. Rain averages 31 inches per year, with most of it falling in May and June. Laredo's average and extreme temperatures, high and low, run about 5 degrees hotter than San Antonio's all year. Laredo's precipitation averages only about 20 inches per year, most of it in September. Corpus Christi's average highs in summer are in the low 90s, with average lows around 75. Winters are balmy: highs from 65 to 70 degrees, and lows seldom below 45.

THE PANHANDLE
AND NORTHERN TEXAS

Far northern Texas is almost entirely rural, too far from big cities to be a weekend getaway for urbanites. The area contains a couple of spectacular locales, but scenic beauty is the exception here, not the rule, and there are only three rivers of any significance: the Canadian River and major forks of the Red and Brazos Rivers. A patient observer will spot antelope and deer in canyons, or "breaks," though deer are more common in South and Central Texas. Furtive coyotes, which ranchers have always regarded as pests, roam much of the area. Some landowners trap or shoot them—poisoning them is now illegal—and hang their carcasses on fence posts, a warning to other coyotes to pick a different spread.

Save for the occasional windmill, oil-well pump jack, grain elevator, or center-pivot irrigation sprinkler, little punctuates the skyline. The view is plain sky meeting a flat expanse, the same panorama that Capt. Randolph B. Marcy of the U.S. Army observed while on an 1849 surveying expedition of the Llano Estacado ("Staked Plains"):

> When we were upon the high table land, a view presented itself as boundless as the ocean. Not a tree, shrub, or any other object either animate or inanimate, relieved the dreary monotony of the prospect. It was . . . the dreaded Llano Estacado…a land where no man, either savage or civilized permanently abides…a treeless, desolate waste of uninhabited solitude, which always has been and must continue uninhabited forever.

Despite Marcy's estimation that the region was unfit for human habitation, it eventually was settled, though its population remains sparse to this day. In physical terms, northern Texas comprises two regions: the Panhandle, which stretches from the state's northern border south to U.S. 180, and the sector north of that highway east from U.S. 83 to the west side of Fort Worth. The area Marcy described—still called the Llano Estacado but also known as the South Plains—is in the southern part of the Panhandle, west of the city of Lubbock.

Dust storms over northern Texas can transform light into dark in a flash.

PANHANDLE PREFERENCES

People accustomed to mountains and tree cover go crazy out here. But I just hate trees and mountains. I went to Virginia once. I felt so fenced in by the landscape I could scream. When I was in Chicago, the skyscrapers made me feel the same way. I can't imagine spending your life in a place where you can't see for miles in all directions.

—Bill Green, curator of history at the Panhandle-Plains Historical Museum in Canyon, as quoted in Robert D. Kaplan's *An Empire Wilderness,* 1998

The Panhandle "has weather," locals note enthusiastically. Dust storms turn the sky black, and strong winds can cause temperatures to drop as much as 40 degrees Fahrenheit in two hours. Around here, that's called a "norther." Hail, tornadoes, dust storms, or strong winds are almost always stirring, and snow falls in the Panhandle at least once a year, sometimes as late as May.

Because frontiersmen were cowed by the weather—and by the Comanches, who controlled the Panhandle until 1874—this was the last part of Texas to be settled. The largest Panhandle towns, Amarillo and Lubbock, didn't exist until the late 1880s, and even when oil was discovered here—at the Panhandle Field in 1910, and at other finds thereafter—boomtowns did not spring up like the ones that materialized after the big strikes in East and West Texas.

Although it doesn't physically resemble the Panhandle, the section of Texas west and north of Fort Worth is linked to the Panhandle by history and tradition. The terrain here is rolling and sometimes hilly—this is prairie land, for the most part, and the plains are low ones. Wichita Falls, with about 105,000 residents, is this area's largest city.

Most people approach the Panhandle heading west out of Fort Worth, so we begin this chapter following the two main routes—first U.S. 180 and then U.S. 287. From there, we head on to the Panhandle itself, traveling west through the Caprock escarpment, then north to Lubbock, the Palo Duro Canyon, Amarillo and points beyond.

(following spread) Claims about its supposedly healing waters made the town of Mineral Wells rich in the early 20th century. The wells are gone now, but the Mineral Wells Rodeo still attracts Texans from all over the region.

■ WEST ALONG U.S. 180

■ WEATHERFORD *map page 275, E-4*

Several urban myths have attached themselves to Parker County's seat, Weatherford, about 30 miles west of Fort Worth on U.S. 180. Abraham Lincoln supposedly holed up here after "pretending" to be assassinated, and a murderous werewolf allegedly lurks in a swamp on the outskirts of town. More verifiable is that this is the hometown of the late actress Mary Martin. The mother of Larry Hagman, who played the infamous J. R. Ewing on *Dallas,* Martin is honored in front of the **Weatherford Library** (1214 Charles Street) with a bronze statue of her as Peter Pan, the role she created on Broadway. No statue honors Jim Wright, the former Speaker of the U.S. House of Representatives, who was elected to Congress from Weatherford but retired in disgrace following an ethics scandal.

The Texas architectural firm of Dodson and Dudley topped the Victorian-Gothic **Parker County Courthouse** (1 Courthouse Square) with an eye-catching four-faced clock tower. The sturdy white- and red-trim structure was completed in 1885. Also of architectural note is the **Texas Pythian Home** (1825 East Bankhead Drive), 3 miles east of Weatherford between U.S. 180 and I-20. The castle-like structure was built between 1907 and 1909 by the Knights of Pythias as a home for dependent widows and orphans. Mary Martin is buried at Weatherford's **Greenwood Cemetery** (Front and North Mill Streets), as are Oliver Loving and Bose Ikard—two legendary trail drivers of the late 1800s whose activities inspired part of Larry McMurtry's book *Lonesome Dove.*

■ MINERAL WELLS *map page 275, D-4*

As you head west along the 19 miles from Weatherford to Mineral Wells, the landscape becomes increasingly flat and barren. The area's money comes from cattle and the oil, gas, gravel, and clay extracted from the surrounding countryside. In the late 1800s, Mineral Wells evolved into a prime tourist destination, all because J.A. Lynch dug a well for drinking water. What came out of the ground smelled foul and tasted even worse, but Mrs. Lynch, who was ill, drank it anyway. Miraculously, her health improved, and as word spread about the Lynch "medicinal well," people descended on the town to partake of the liquid, claiming it as a cure for everything from rheumatism to insanity. Many of the pilgrims came to drill wells themselves, and by 1883 more than a hundred wells were operating.

During its early-20th-century heyday, Mineral Wells was a popular spa resort.

By 1891, the railroad had arrived, bringing even more health seekers. Three decades later, 400 wells were producing water in Mineral Wells, and Crazy Water Crystals, produced by evaporating the water, were being promoted on NBC Radio broadcasts from the lobby of the seven-story **Crazy Water Hotel** (U.S. 180 and U.S. 281), which was completed in 1927. The 14-story **Baker Hotel** (U.S. 180 and Northeast First Avenue), designed in a style described by one historian as "Spanish Colonial Revival Commercial Highrise," opened its even posher doors two years later. Everybody who was anybody stayed at the Baker during its heyday, including Helen Keller and performers like Will Rogers and Jean Harlow.

The magic water business was killed by the Depression, and clampdowns by the government on claims for health cures, and by improvements in the quality of conventional medical care. The Crazy Water was eventually converted into a retirement hotel, and the Baker has remained shuttered since it ceased operations, though it still dominates the town's skyline. Contemporary science, though, has validated some of the claims made for Mineral Wells water: one study showed that the output of four wells bore traces of lithium, a mood regulator, and that water from two of those wells contained potent amounts of the natural drug.

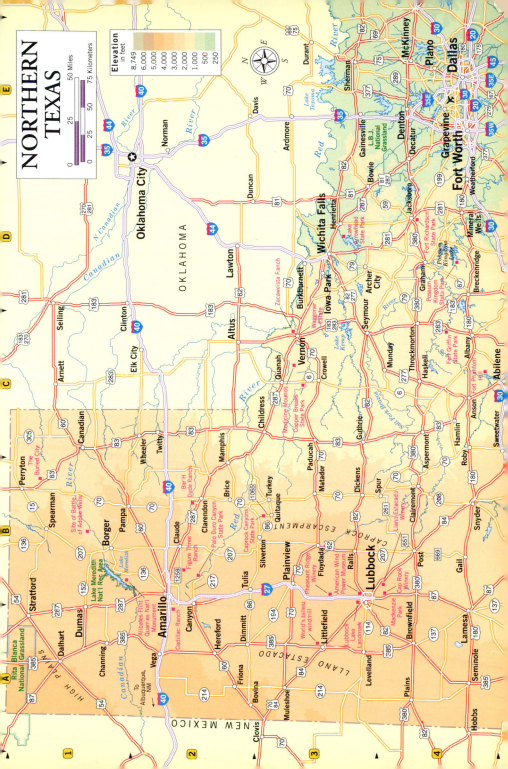

■ **BRECKENRIDGE**   *map page 275, D-4*
Breckenridge, about 98 miles west of Fort Worth on U.S. 180, turned dizzy during an oil boom that followed discoveries in the late 1910s. By 1920, the town was becoming overrun by the usual cast of speculators, oil workers, and supporting players, among them bootleggers, prostitutes, and gambling-parlor operators. The population jumped twenty-fold—from 1,500 to 30,000—between 1920 and 1921. The party lasted three years, with about 200 wells operating in Breckenridge itself during this period. But activity tapered off appreciably by the end of the 1920s, and as the Depression dawned the population had dropped by 75 percent.

Life in contemporary Breckenridge, population 6,000, proceeds at a more regulated pace, though remnants of the boom days exist. The 1920 First National Bank Building now houses the **Swenson Memorial Museum** (116 West Walker Street; 254-559-8471), a repository of local artifacts such as barbed-wire and cattle-brand displays. The museum's **J.D. Sandefer Oil Annex** (113 North Breckenridge Avenue), tells the oil-boom story; it's named for Jefferson Davis Sandefer Jr., a wealthy oilman who was part of the 1920 influx.

AUTUMN ON THE BRAZOS

Usually, fall is the good time to go to the Brazos, and when you can choose, October is the best month—if, for that matter, you choose to go there at all, and most people don't. Snakes and mosquitoes and ticks are torpid then, and maybe gone if frosts have come early, nights are cool and days blue and yellow and soft of air, and in the spread abundance of even a Texas autumn the shooting and the fishing overlap and are both likely to be good. Scores of kinds of birds, huntable or pleasant to see, pause there in their migrations before the later, bitterer northers push many of them farther south. Men and women are scarce.

Most autumns, the water is low from the long dry summer, and you have to get out from time to time and wade, leading or dragging your boat through trickling shallows from one pool to the long channel-twisted pool below, hanging up occasionally on shuddering bars of quicksand, making six or eight miles in a day's lazy work, but if you go to the river at all, you tend not to mind. You are not in a hurry there; you learned long since not to be.

—John Graves, *Goodbye to a River,* 1960

To take the measure of regional geography, visit **Possum Kingdom Lake,** a fine 14,000-acre clear-water lake enclosed by dramatic bluffs. The deep lake lies between and slightly north of Mineral Wells and Breckenridge in a state park. Many scuba divers have descended 150 feet and more; anglers here typically catch striped bass and catfish. *Park Road 33, 17 miles north of U.S. 180's Caddo Exit; 940-549-1803.*

■ NORTHWEST ALONG U.S. 287

An alternate route into the Panhandle is U.S. 287, which heads northwest out of Fort Worth. The first town of much size you'll encounter is Wichita Falls, on the Wichita River about 110 miles from Fort Worth. The Wichita Falls area was set-tled by the Wichita Indians, whom the Spanish first encountered in 1541. The name "Wichita" comes from a Choctaw word that translates as "big arbor," a refer-ence to the thatched conical huts the Wichitas built. The tribe's two names for itself were translated as "first people" and "raccoon eyes," the latter a reference to the members' face-painting technique.

■ WICHITA FALLS   *map page 275, D-3*
The 5-foot-high waterfall that gave Wichita Falls its name washed away in a flood in the late 1800s, though it was replaced 100 years later with a 54-foot-high, three-tiered cascade in a city park. The area has endured other meteorological catastro-phes as well, including one of the state's worst tornadoes, which took place on April 10, 1979. The twister rampaged through the middle of town, killing 42 peo-ple, injuring 1,740, destroying more than 3,000 homes, causing $400 million in damage, and leaving 20,000 people homeless. This wasn't the first tornado to touch down here. In April 1964, seven people were killed and 111 injured by another twister. Northwest Texans, especially those in the Red River Valley, learn to live with the threat of tornadoes. They hunker down in a bathtub—bathtubs are heavy and not easily swept into the air—pull a mattress over the top, if there's time, and wait for the danger to pass.

More grueling than riding out a twister is the **Hotter 'n' Hell Hundred** bicycle race, a 100-mile endurance test that for some sadistic reason is held in August, when temperatures hit 100 degrees or higher. Mellower activities in Wichita Falls include the **Farmers Market,** held from May through September except Sundays, at which you can pick up everything from local strawberries to okra and black-eyed peas.

■ **ARCHER CITY** *map page 275, D-3*

Archer County, which surrounds Wichita Falls' western side, has surprisingly verdant stretches, and a trip to Archer City, roughly 25 miles south of Wichita Falls on Route 79, provides a fine introduction to the region.

The city—the hometown of Larry McMurtry, who used it as the model for the town of Anarene in his book *The Last Picture Show*—has earned the nickname "Book City" for its many bookstores. The small **Three Dog Books** (107 East Main Street; 940-574-4797), for instance, specializes in "rare and interesting" books.

McMurtry himself moved back to Archer City from the East Coast in 1987 and opened **Booked Up** (216 South Center Street; 940-574-2511), a used-book store that occupies four buildings downtown. His shop, a renowned stop for bibliophiles visiting the region, is open for business on Thursdays, Fridays, and Saturdays and by appointment.

Local history can be sampled at the **Archer County Historical Museum,** which is inside the former town jail. Exhibits include artifacts from the frontier days: dishes, antiques, saddles, guns, clothing, early photographs, and farming equipment. *400 West Pecan Street; 940-574-2489.*

■ **VERNON** *map page 275, C-3*

Vernon, about 50 miles west of Wichita Falls, is the home of the 520,000-acre Zacaweista Ranch, one of the largest expanses of private property in the United States. The spread is part of the Waggoner Estate, begun in 1849 by Daniel Waggoner and his son, W. T. Waggoner. Father and son made a fortune driving cattle, and their heirs' wealth increased when oil was discovered in Electra, a few miles east of Vernon, in 1911.

Today, the mainstays of the Waggoner enterprise are ranching, oil, and horse-breeding. Electra Waggoner Biggs, daughter of W. T.'s son E. Paul Waggoner, became a sculptor best known for *Into the Sunset*—her statue of Will Rogers on horseback, a copy of which stands in front of the Will Rogers Memorial Auditorium and Coliseum in Fort Worth; another of her Will Rogers statues adorns the Texas Tech campus in Lubbock.

The area around Wichita Falls reports more tornadoes than anyplace else in the world. This one, photographed in 1947, killed 167 people across the border in Oklahoma.

Quanah Parker.

Vernon's role as headquarters of the Waggoner operation isn't the town's only claim to fame. Vernon Savings & Loan was one of the high-profile establishments involved in the savings and loan scandals of the 1980s. Vernon is also known as the birthplace of two music legends: Roy Orbison, the singer-songwriter who hit his stride in the 1960s; and Jack Teagarden, the jazz trombonist, who performed with Benny Goodman, the Dorsey brothers, Bix Beiderbecke, and Louis Armstrong.

The **Red River Valley Museum** (4600 College Drive; 940-553-1848) sheds light on the town's musical celebrities with exhibits, photographs, memorabilia, and archives.

■ QUANAH   *map page 275, C-3*
Quanah, 30 miles west of Vernon, was named in 1881 after Quanah Parker, a Comanche whose fame in the state is exceeded only by the heroes of the Texas Revolution.

Quanah never lived in Quanah, but the town's founders, probably inspired by the relative isolation of the place, felt a strong connection with the region's Comanche past. A sense of that heritage can be experienced southeast of the town at the mysterious **Medicine Mounds** (FM 1176, 5 miles south of U.S. 287). The

The Last Comanche

Quanah Parker first became a household name in Texas because he was the son of Cynthia Ann Parker, probably the best-known woman in Texas during the latter half of the 19th century. In 1836, at the age of nine, Cynthia Ann had been captured by the Comanches during an East Texas raid in which her father was killed. Parties of whites who traded along the Canadian River in far North Texas spotted her five years after her kidnapping, and again seven years later. She told them that she had married Peta Nocona, a Comanche notable; that she was the mother of two sons, including young Quanah; and that she had no desire to return to the remnants of her birth family. (Nocona, a town of 3,240 about 50 miles east of Wichita Falls on U.S. 82, is named for Cynthia Ann's husband.)

Nevertheless, white Texans continued to keep an eye out for her, and to report sightings. In 1860, at the Battle of Pease River, she was recaptured, along with her infant daughter, Topsanah, and Topsanah's father, Peta, was killed. The following year, the Texas legislature voted a league of land and a pension to Cynthia Ann, who had been returned to her Texas relatives. But she could not adjust to the life she found with them, and her attempts to escape were foiled. In 1864, her daughter died, and a few weeks later, 37-year-old Cynthia Ann was laid in her grave too. It was said that she died of a broken heart.

Quanah Parker's age at the time he was orphaned has not been accurately established. By some accounts, he was eight; by others, 13. By the early 1870s, he was a leader among his band, the Quahadi Comanches, who did not accept treaties with the United States. Parker was reported as a participant and sometimes as a leader of horseback raids on settlements as far south and west as Fort Stockton. In 1874, he joined with leaders of the Kiowa and Cheyenne in one of the last Indian battles in Texas, at Adobe Walls, near today's Amarillo. The Indians were vanquished and surrendered the following year. Quanah Parker took up residence on an Oklahoma reservation, making the transition with seemingly little difficulty and helping his people adjust to their new way of life. In his last years, he became a reluctant celebrity of the region. He died in 1911.

mounds, four cone-shape hills created by the Comanches, rise from 200 to 350 feet above the surrounding plains. The mounds are believed to be ceremonial sites on top of which sacred potions were mixed and then left to be blessed by powers that the native peoples believed lived in the sky.

■ THE PANHANDLE

Literalists insist that the Panhandle includes only the topmost Texas counties, the ones between the New Mexico and Oklahoma state lines. This area is also called the North Plains. From Route 86 down to U.S. 180 is known as the South Plains. The North Plains and the South Plains taken together are the High Plains. The multiple labels tend to confound outsiders.

The chief difference between the South Plains, whose anchor city is Lubbock, and the North Plains, whose hub is Amarillo, is how the weather affects agriculture. The North Plains region is wheat territory, the South Plains cotton and grain sorghum country. On the North Plains, freezes come too soon, and thaws too late, to make cultivation of cotton possible. South Plains cotton, usually planted in May or June, is harvested as late as Christmas.

■ THE CAPROCK *map page 275, B-2/3*

The High Plains are so named because, although the terrain is flat, most of the region resembles a giant mesa. These plains lie atop an escarpment called the Caprock, which is characterized by abrupt shifts in elevation of 200, 500, and in some places as much as 1,000 feet above the rolling plains to the east. From space, the Caprock, which geologists hypothesize is a consequence of erosion, looks something like the Great Wall of China, zigzagging north and south across the Panhandle for 175 miles.

You can trace this course by driving east on U.S. 180 from the town of Lamesa, heading north at Gail, northeast from Post to Spur, and north up Route 70 to Matador, Turkey, and Clarendon. Along most of the route, in front and to the left, you'll see the Caprock's rise, forming a one-sided canyon. Drive up onto the crest, and flatness and sky overwhelm the senses. Look back over your shoulder, and you'll see the world at the Caprock's feet, a land of tiny tractors and dry-land farming. Up here is land so flat and even that one town is simply called Levelland.

The superiority of life on the Caprock shows itself in statistics: according to the U.S. Census Bureau, Caprockers enjoy the highest per capita income and educational levels in Texas. Mechanized, irrigated family farms, plus a few oil and gas discoveries, have made it so. During the oil boom of the 1970s and early 1980s, when much of Texas succumbed to money fever, this country maintained its equilibrium. Experiencing no flush of capital or rush of immigration from elsewhere, it remained as truly Texan as it ever was. Nobody wore cowboy boots for show, and Caprock dwellers never told Texas jokes, if only because they've always known that nothing is as hilarious as Oklahoma.

The unimaginable expanses of flat, dry land and the endless sky proved inspirational to famed artist Georgia O'Keeffe, who lived in the Panhandle on and off from 1912 to 1918. Born in Wisconsin and educated in Virginia, Chicago, and New York, she supervised the teaching of art in the Amarillo public schools from 1912 to 1914. After teaching stints at universities in Virginia and South Carolina, she was hired in 1916 to teach at West Texas State Normal College (now West Texas A&M University) in Canyon. While she was living in Canyon, she found her artistic voice, expressing her love of the Panhandle landscape in many of the works she created during her years in Texas.

■ **LUBBOCK** *map page 275, B-3*
Named after Tom S. Lubbock, an honored officer of the Confederacy and signatory of the Texas Declaration of Independence, the city of Lubbock is laid out in numbered and lettered streets as straight and square as the fields that run up to its limits. The older homes here are mainly of the Prairie and Victorian styles, and commercial buildings of red or yellow brick reflect staid mid-20th-century tastes. Lubbock was established in the early 1890s, as land-hungry settlers began pushing onto the South Plains, which by then were free of Indians. Promoters sold lots slowly in the unremarkable little town until the railroad arrived in 1909, after which Lubbock soon became a marketing and transportation hub. Following World War II, Lubbock became one of the country's fastest-growing cities, its population hitting 130,000 by 1961. The population today is a little more than 200,000.

Cotton is Lubbock's mainstay. The United States produces about a quarter of the world's supply of cotton; Texas produces more than any other state; and about half the Texas yield comes from the South Plains. So does most of its export crop. Some of the cotton exported from Lubbock goes by truck and train to Galveston, and from Galveston into the Gulf of Mexico, and then travels overseas. But most of the cotton goes on railcars to the Los Angeles area, from where it is sent across the Pacific to looms and factories in Asia.

(following pages) When seen from space, the 175-mile-long Caprock looks like the Great Wall of China.

IRRIGATION AND PUMPS

Anyone who drives across the South Plains is sure to notice V-8 engines standing at the edges of fields, sometimes housed in tin shacks. These engines power water pumps, hundreds of feet below ground, that bring water from the Ogallala Aquifer up to farms. The ability to tap this underground water source made large-scale farming possible on the High Plains.

Those who fly across the region notice a variation on "crop circles"—discs of green amidst brown fields. But these are not the work of aliens—they're produced by automated center-pivot sprinklers that slowly turn, bestowing aquatic blessings on all plants within their radius. (For some days or weeks after a rain, riders in the sky will also notice sunlight glinting off irregularly shaped pools of water across the High Plains. These naturally occurring pools are called "playa lakes," or "playas.")

Unfortunately, the Ogallala Aquifer is being pumped dry. With many aquifers, water that is pumped out is replaced by rainwater that percolates back into the formation. Rainfall in the High Plains, however, averages less than 20 inches a year, and because of the area's geology, the little that does fall doesn't adequately replenish the aquifer. Governmental and quasi-governmental agencies are expending considerable effort to promote water conservation. Among the efforts: encouraging farmers to convert old-style sprinkler systems—which spray water into the air, where most of the moisture evaporates in the dry summer heat before it hits the ground—to drop-tube systems, which release water immediately above the crops. Ongoing aquifer-replenishment experiments include pumping water from playa lakes into the aquifer. But farmers continue to pump water out of the aquifer faster than it is being replaced, and water tables are dropping, causing some cotton farmers in the High Plains to return to dry-land farming.

There is speculation that if the Ogallala goes completely dry, the South Plains may revert to the grassland prairie it was more than a century ago. T. Boone Pickens, a Texas oilman and wheeler-dealer who owns land above the Ogallala, may be the person who can make that happen sooner rather than later. In 2000, he announced a scheme to pump water out of the aquifer and sell it to cities far removed from the High Plains—something he can do legally because of Texas's archaic groundwater usage laws and because one of the Panhandle's water-conservation agencies granted him a permit to do so. Surveys taken in 2000 and 2001 reveal popular disapproval of the scheme, but Texas law would still let him do it as long as he has a permit.

Cotton is today harvested by machines that pull the whole boll in which the fibers rest, rather than picking the fibers away, as when the crop was gathered by hand. Harvested cotton is packed into modules about 10 feet high and as long as 50 feet, and left in the fields until processing plants, called gins, can accommodate them. At the gins—750 are scattered across the South Plains—the fiber is separated from bolls and seed and packed into bales; bales bound for export are reduced in size at facilities called compresses.

Lubbock is home to **Texas Tech University**, which enrolls about 27,000 students. ("Tech" is not an abbreviation: the school was founded in 1923 as Texas Technological College, but was renamed Texas Tech in 1969.) The university, with its impressive Mission-style architecture, lies on the north side of town, on a campus so big that students use cars and bicycles to change classes. A statue of comedian Will Rogers on his horse, Soapsuds, sculpted by Electra Waggoner Biggs, greets visitors east of Memorial Circle, inside the main entrance at University and Broadway.

Tech's excellent ranching-history museum, the **National Ranching Heritage Center,** interprets the evolution of ranching from the 18th through the mid-20th century. Ranchers have donated 37 buildings and other structures, which the museum has refurbished and filled with appropriate furnishings and equipment. Shelters range from the primitive (like dugouts, burrowed into the ground, which were used for lodging before a permanent house was built) to the sophisticated (a three-story Victorian house, complete with gingerbread trim). Smokehouses, oat bins, a blacksmith shop, and six windmills illustrate other aspects of ranch life. *3121 Fourth Street; 806-742-0498.*

Windmills have played an important role in Texas history. Moving cattle onto the High Plains in the late 1800s wasn't easy. A rancher couldn't raise cattle unless his land had a water source—ranchers at the time had to cluster around the few constantly flowing rivers and streams. In the 1860s, railroads introduced windmills in Texas as a means of providing water for steam locomotives. Windmills caught on with farmers and cattle raisers in East Texas, and quickly began to appear elsewhere in the state. Ranchers discovered that they could divide their acreage into pastures with barbed wire (invented in the early 1870s by Joseph F. Glidden) and provide water to remote streamless pastures with windmills, thus separating their herds and improving their stock. By the 1880s, windmills and barbed wire migrated onto the High Plains, and the southern transcontinental railroad was completed across Texas, ending the need for cattle drives.

HERD OF TEXAS CATTLE EN ROUTE FOR ELLSWORTH—Kansas Pacific Railway.

This 1874 illustration shows a herd of Texas cattle en route to Kansas.

The **American Wind Power Center and Museum,** in a city park, is a good place to explore the incredible variety of windmills and learn how they revolutionized ranching and made farming possible on the High Plains. At last count, the museum had more than 100, both inside and outside—it's enough to give Don Quixote nightmares. Many of the antique windmills, including one that is more than 100 years old, are inside. *Mackenzie Park, 1701 Canyon Lake Drive, east of I-27 between U.S. 62 and U.S. 82; 806-747-8734.*

Your historical perspective may broaden considerably at the **Lubbock Lake Landmark,** an archaeological and nature preserve on 300 acres of a site that has shown evidence of human habitation going back at least 11,500 years. Excavation of the area in 1936 yielded the bones of extinct mammals—giant armadillos, mammoths, camels, and other creatures—as well as artifacts from every cultural period since humans first appeared in the area. Signs along a 0.75-mile trail explain the sights along the way, and a nature walk provides the environmental perspective. *Landmark Lane, North Loop 289, north of Clovis Highway (U.S. 84); 806-742-1116.*

Cotton and cows are not the only agricultural products raised around Lubbock: wine grapes also grow here. In the 1970s, a few risk-takers planted vineyards, believing that the area's loamy soil, warm days, cool nights, and low humidity, aided by the use of drip irrigation, would produce superior grapes. Three wineries have won numerous awards in wine competitions not only in Texas, but also in California and Europe. **Cap Rock Winery** (U.S. 87 and Woodrow Road; 806-863-2704), known for its cabernet sauvignons and merlots, and **Llano Estacado Winery** (FM 1585; 806-745-2258), which produces excellent chardonnays and dessert wines, are open daily for tours and tastings. **Pheasant Ridge Winery** (Route 3, Exit 14; 806-746-6033), which makes a full range of red and white wines, opens its tasting room on Fridays and weekends.

WINDMILL MAN

The Cutaway foreman at the time was Hermann Slike, a crusty old German-Texan with nostrils like the entrances to twin caves.

"You know anything about windmills?" he asked the Dutchman. . . . There wasn't a cowboy in the outfit who'd voluntarily work on the mills, and when one or two was forced to get up on the towers with their grease cans they cursed Slike from breakfast to bunkhouse and, after one man was blasted by a lightning bolt, a Cutaway cowboy had only to hear the word "windmill" and he would quit. There were tall weeds around windmills, good places for rattlesnakes, and a tool dropped in the weeds was there forever. . . . So Slike himself had spent many lonely hours on greasy ladders skinning his knuckles on recalcitrant metal and worn gears. . . .

"We'll, we'll try you out. I need a good windmill man. Hell, I'd take a bad windmill man. Most important man on a ranch if you ever seen cows dead from thirst. Cows got a drink. . . . The cattle business is a business and water is the name a the cattle business."

. . . It didn't take long to see that the crane-shanked Dutchman was a little crazy but indispensable and that he earned his seventy-five a month. In the distance riders would often see his lanky figure balanced atop a rickety mill, or his cranky wagon dusting across a pasture, and they would thank God they were horseback cowboys and not windmill monkeys.

—Annie Proulx, *That Old Ace in the Hole*, 2002

Lubbock is also known for music. From the South Plains have come rock and roller Buddy Holly and country stars Waylon Jennings, Mac Davis, Tanya Tucker, and Jimmy Dean, all of whom are memorialized with bronze plaques in the **Walk of Fame** (6th Street at Avenue Q), a downtown attraction anchored by a bronze statue of Buddy Holly himself. The **Buddy Holly Center** (1801 Avenue G; 806-767-2686), including the Texas Musicians Hall of Fame, has exhibits about Holly's life and short career, along with ones about other Texas musicians.

■ LITTLEFIELD   *map page 275, A-3*
Littlefield, roughly 38 miles northwest of Lubbock on U.S. 84, is known for its replica of the **world's tallest windmill** (132 feet tall), which was built in 1887 on the XIT Ranch—the ranch established on land that was traded by the state of Texas as payment for the construction of the State Capitol. Its location in a canyon was the reason for the windmill's height: it had to be tall enough to catch the wind. The original windmill toppled during a windstorm in 1926; the replica was built in 1969. *Historical marker at U.S. 84 and Delano Street.*

■ PALO DURO CANYON   *map page 275, B-2*
An imaginary dividing line between the South Plains and the North Plains runs west to east through a point no farther north than the town of **Canyon,** a college and tourist town 16 miles south of Amarillo on I-27. Exhibits at the superb **Panhandle-Plains Historical Museum** (2503 Fourth Avenue; 806-651-2244), on the West Texas A&M University campus, one block east of U.S. 87, reflect the region's history and art. The museum also contains an entire Panhandle town and a two-room log ranch house built in the late 1870s.

Canyon's primary attraction—and the source of the town's name—is Palo Duro Canyon, a 120-mile-long, 20-mile-wide, 800-foot-deep break in the tabletop-flat terrain. About 10 miles east of town, the canyon reveals the handiwork of four geological ages. For centuries this has been a refuge from the severity of the plains, with evidence of habitation going back at least 12,000 years. The canyon had water and greenery, and it provided early inhabitants with shelter from the cold winds that blew on the flatlands above. The efficient Comanches occasionally used it as a bison slaughterhouse, with the mounted warriors stampeding the animals over its cliffs.

Windmills revolutionized farming in Texas by bringing water to drought-plagued regions.

BUDDY HOLLY

Buddy Holly was born in Lubbock on September 7, 1936, and in his five or so years of recording (1954–59), he changed the face of rock and roll. In the process, he established the rock-band prototype: guitar, bass, drums, vocals.

Until he heard Elvis Presley, Holly was a dyed-in-the-straw hick, playing bluegrass and country music even while transforming the music into something rawer, more exciting. By the time Holly headed to Nashville and began recording for Decca Records, however, he had chosen the rock and roll path. On January 26, 1956, Holly recorded "Blue Days," "Love Me," and the Jimmy Ainsworth–Earl Lee cut "Midnight Shift" at the Nashville studio of the legendary producer Owen Bradley. "Midnight Shift," a harder rockabilly cut, wouldn't see daylight until two years later, in part because his record company didn't know what to make of Holly. Owen Bradley continued to record Holly throughout 1956, but Decca eventually released him from his contract.

Holly figured that was it for his career, but he nonetheless put together the Crickets, with drummer Jerry Allison, bassist Larry Welborn, and rhythm guitarist Niki Sullivan—all of Lubbock. On February 25, 1957, the quartet set to wax "That'll Be the Day" and "I'm Lookin' for Someone to Love," both major hits for Buddy Holly and the Crickets.

Holly was a perfectionist both as a songwriter and in the studio; the results were heard on the subsequent singles "Peggy Sue," "Not Fade Away," "Everyday," and "Oh Boy!"—all released in short succession from September to November 1957. Each track is a rock classic—simple, clear, powerful. "Maybe Baby" and "Rave On" followed in early 1958, and by the middle of that year, the Crickets were superstars with number-one, million-selling records, European tours, and guest shots on Ed Sullivan's popular television variety show. Meanwhile, Holly had met and married Mary Elena Santiago, whom he met in New York City while recording a record without the Crickets.

In January 1959, Holly headed out on a package tour with Ritchie Valens, the Big Bopper, and the Belmonts. The plane carrying Holly, Valens, and the Big Bopper went down on February 2 near Mason City, Iowa, in a snowstorm, killing all aboard. Holly's fame only grew in death, though it wasn't until March 1980 that a statue of Lubbock's favorite son was erected in front of the Lubbock Civic Center.

—Robert Wilonsky

The Comanches resided in the canyon, hidden from the American cavalry, until 1874, when Col. Ranald Mackenzie and his troops discovered their secret, invaded their canyon-floor camps, slaughtered 1,400 of their horses, and forced their owners to return to Oklahoma on foot. Two years later, the cattleman Charles Goodnight, a trail driver and the inventor of the chuck wagon, moved cattle into the canyon. Soon after, he acquired a partner—the Englishman John Adair—with whom he established the JA Ranch, which eventually covered more than 1.3 million acres both in the canyon and on adjoining land.

Visiting the 18,000-acre **Palo Duro Canyon State Park,** much of which was developed in the 1930s by the Civilian Conservation Corps, is a great way to appreciate the natural wonders of Palo Duro Canyon. There are 16 miles of scenic drives, and many trails—some difficult, other less so—that wind around the park's otherworldly rock formations. Horseback-riding is popular, and there are camping facilities. A museum here has exhibits on the canyon's flora and fauna, and in summer the park's open-air theater presents *Texas Legacies,* a romantic rendering of the state's history. *Route 217, 8 miles east off I-27; 806-488-2227.*

An unforgettable way to experience the canyon scenery and its almost supernatural tranquility is on an outing with the folks from **Cowboy Morning Breakfast.** The trip begins at 8:30 A.M. at the Figure Three Ranch, on the canyon's north edge. Staffers in cowboy get-up transport guests in an authentic chuck wagon to the north rim of the canyon, where they enjoy spectacular morning scenery while devouring a traditional cowboy breakfast of eggs and sourdough biscuits, with hot gravy, sausage, coffee and juice. Breakfast is served from April through October; reservations are essential. *FM 1258, 27 miles southeast of I-40, Exit 77; 806-944-5562.*

The red sandstone cliffs of **Caprock Canyons State Park** are similar in color to the pinkish-orange escarpments in Palo Duro Canyon. Roughly 50 miles southeast of Palo Duro Canyon, the park contains more than 15,000 acres that were part of the JA Ranch. The ranch's legacy is not only the park, but also the official state bison herd, which includes descendants of bison saved from slaughter in the 1880s by Goodnight. Graceful, fleet, distinctively marked pronghorn antelopes also inhabit the park, along with deer, raccoons, coyotes, bobcats, and opossums; golden eagles are often spotted soaring overhead. Ninety miles of trails range from easy to extremely difficult. The Caprock Canyons Trailway, a former railroad, is now a 64-mile-long trail that stretches from the town of South Plains to Estelline. *FM 1065, 3.5 miles north of Route 86; 806-455-1492.*

Scenic drives and trails penetrate the isolated wilderness of Palo Duro Canyon State Park.

■ **AMARILLO**   *map page 275, A/B-2*

"The only thing between Amarillo and the North Pole," goes a Texas summation about this town known for icy weather, "is a barbed-wire fence, and it's down." The landscape is flat, and the streets are laid out in straight north-south and east-west grids. When 40 mph winds blow through Amarillo's streets during "northers," the barbed-wire quip speaks a truth.

Yet if the North Plains climate is hostile to warm-weather crops like cotton, it's not unfriendly to agriculture in general: North Plains farms produce wheat, corn, and sugar beets. Ranching is also a much bigger business on the North than on the South Plains, and the state's largest cattle auction is held in Amarillo.

Established, as was Lubbock, in anticipation of the Fort Worth and Denver railroad's arrival in the Panhandle in the late 1880s, Amarillo began life as a cattle-loading and distribution center. But it is perhaps best known for its role as a way station on old U.S. 66, which ran along the city's northern edge on its way west to Los Angeles. In its heyday, Route 66 fostered dozens of service stations, motels, and restaurants; one commentator dubbed Amarillo "the world's biggest truck stop." Interstate 40, built during the 1960s through the center of town, left U.S. 66 a city route. The motels with Western-theme signs have aged, the eateries are second-rate, and there's an on-again, off-again red-light district that sometimes finds itself out of commission because Amarillo's policy is to arrest not only prostitutes, but their clients as well.

Amarillo, with 176,000 residents, enjoys a reputation as a conservative cowboy town, and it certainly has that look, with jeans- and Stetson-wearing men visible everywhere. It was most assuredly a cow town when its population was less than 10,000 and cattle marched on its outskirts on their way to railheads farther north. But today's cowboys are few and far between; most of the aforementioned men are manual laborers, farmers, or lawyers.

Class differences are evident between cowboys and their bosses, cattlemen. The cowboy still lives in a "line camp" (usually a farmhouse that once belonged to a cattleman's family) and drives his pickup into town once or twice a month to go shopping. Cattlemen—who wear starched jeans—can be found at the **Amarillo Livestock Auction** (100 Manhattan Avenue; 806-373-7464) on Tuesday mornings, where they buy and sell cattle, usually in lots, at auction. There's no admission fee, and nobody looks askance at people dressed like city folk.

Auctions take place in the ring, a dirt-floor area above which the auctioneer sits at a microphone, calling out prices to the audience, which takes its seats around the ring above floor level. As the cattle are displayed and the auctioneer makes his calls, prospective buyers raise their hands or shout assent to a purchase. After the auction has concluded, they load up the cattle and take them to their new home— or to a slaughterhouse.

Live auctions occur less frequently than in days past, because it is easier for cattlemen to tune into auctions broadcast via satellite and make a purchase by phone. But cattle folk are still social types, and the stockyards area, in addition to the auction ring, has several restaurants where the satellite bidders stop by, even on days when there's no auction. That's partly because no technology has yet replaced the rancher's most important associate, the banker, who holds notes on a rancher's cattle, and sometimes his land. (If you don't know from cattle, the conversations taking place here over platters of chicken-fried steak might as well be in Greek.)

■ DRIVE-BY AND OTHER ART

Amarillo is known to aficionados of eccentric art as the easel of Stanley Marsh 3. (It's pronounced "three," not "the third"; he was named Stanley Marsh III by his millionaire oilman father, but he considers "III" pretentious.) Marsh is the person responsible for **Cadillac Ranch,** the place where 10 vintage Cadillacs were planted, fins-up, in a row along I-40 west of Amarillo. Marsh provided, as he puts it, "the money, the beer, and the flatbed" for hauling the cars to the site. His partners in the 1974 project—from Ant Farm, a San Francisco-based arts consortium—conceived and executed it, using Caddies made between 1949 and 1963, with huge tail fins. The cars face west and lean at "the same angle as the Cheops pyramid in Egypt"; they are also covered with layers of graffiti, which disturbs Marsh not one bit. In 2003 the cars were painted black in honor of Ant Farm member Doug Michels, who died that year. *I-40, about 8 miles west of Amarillo; you can't miss it.*

Ozymandias is Marsh's own brainchild. The artist commissioned the sculptor Lightnin' McDuff to create two enigmatically shaped "legs of stone" in the "desert" south of town—one 24 feet high and the other 34 feet high. Marsh then created a fake historical marker at the site that explains the "discovery" of the ruins by the poet Percy Bysshe Shelley and how they inspired the creation of his poem, *Ozymandias. I-27, at Sundown Lane, 1 mile south of Loop 335.*

(following pages) A cowboy at work on the Smith Ranch, near Amarillo.

Bottoms up: not all Texas art hangs in museums, as the tail fins at Cadillac Ranch attest.

Then there are the **yard signs**—5,000 diamond-shape signs similar in size and shape to informational road signs—that Marsh arranged to have made and placed around residential Amarillo during the 1990s. Some of the signs carry mottos or slogans, and some are pictorial. The first sign, "Road does not end," was placed at the entrance to Marsh's ranch. A picture of Marilyn Monroe was installed on Monroe Street. One sign states, "Hot pepper," while another opines, "He's either a madman or a poet." Amarilloans, a largely conservative and demonstrative lot, are not neutral about the signs: they either hate them or find them highly amusing.

Not all of Amarillo's art is of the drive-by variety. Though its holdings are hardly humdrum, the **Amarillo Museum of Art** supplies a more conventional experience. The permanent collection emphasizes regional art, but there are also many fine paintings by American modernists and significant works by early- to mid-20th-century American photographers. The museum's 24,000-square-foot steel-and-brick structure, designed in the mid-1960s by Edward Durrell Stone, is as eye-pleasing as the collection. *2200 South Van Buren Street; 806-371-5050.*

■ CLARENDON *map page 275, B-2*

For a close up view of traditional ranch life in Texas, visit the **Bar H Dude Ranch** near Clarendon, about 55 miles southeast of Amarillo. Bar H is both a working ranch and game preserve. Guests can either help ranch hands perform chores such as fixing fences and herding cattle, or watch them do so from the safe distance of a well-positioned lawn chair. Horseback riding and hiking through the tranquil surroundings are encouraged. The hospitality is exceptional, and the chuck wagon breakfasts (biscuits, gravy, and sausage) and dinners (grilled steaks and hamburgers) are hearty. *FM 3257, 2 miles north of U.S. 287; 806-874-2634.*

■ THE ALIBATES FLINT QUARRIES NATIONAL MONUMENT

map page 275, B-1

The Alibates Flint Quarries National Monument, 25 miles northeast of Amarillo, provides insight into the lives of the indigenous people who occupied this area for thousands of years and who fashioned the oddly colored flint from these quarries into tools and weapons. The flint was widely traded by the prehistoric stoneworkers, and shards have been found as far north as Montana and Canada. The monument spans 300 acres of 250 to 300 horseshoe-shaped quarry pits. The flint was named for a rather mysterious character named Allie Bates, probably the son of a local rancher, who is believed to have lived in a dugout nearby on the Canadian River. The remains of the dugout are still in the park. The monument has neither a visitors center nor exhibits and is open only to guided tours, for which reservations are required. *Cas Johnson Road, off Route 136; 806-857-3151.*

■ LAKE MEREDITH NATIONAL RECREATION AREA

map page 275, B-1

Roughly 45 miles north of Amarillo is one of the Panhandle's most popular destinations, Lake Meredith National Recreation Area. More than a million people visit the lake and its environs annually to swim, hike, fish, and camp. It's especially popular among birders, who come to see the estimated 200 bird species known to nest here, including grebes, mergansers, cormorants, and Canada geese.

The small town of Fritch, on the east side of Lake Meredith, has restaurants and motels as well as the **Lake Meredith Aquarium and Wildlife Museum** (101 North Roby Street; 806-857-2458), which displays specimens of indigenous critters and fish. *Recreation Area: Route 136; 806-857-3151.*

■ **PERRYTON** *map page 275, B-1*

Perryton, 115 miles northeast of Amarillo—at the very top of the state—is the ranch home of John R. Erickson, creator of Hank the Cowdog. Erickson, a former cowboy and ranch manager, has been writing since 1982 about Hank the Cowdog, the "smelly, smart aleck Head of Ranch Security" at M-Cross Ranch. Erickson's popular children's book series playfully evokes the Panhandle—and the Texas—of the American imagination: a High Plains landscape more sky than land, a remote ranch where cattle and cowboys roam and coyotes and rattlesnakes lurk, where fierce winds whip up on a moment's notice and tornadoes are a near-constant threat. The real Texas, as we have seen, comprises much, much more.

■ **TRAVEL BASICS**

Getting Around: U.S. 287 comes out of Fort Worth, proceeding northwest through Wichita Falls on its way to Amarillo before turning north and heading into Oklahoma. Interstate 40 cuts across the Panhandle east-west through Amarillo. U.S. 180 defines the southern boundary of the Panhandle–Northwest Texas area, running almost due west from Fort Worth through a succession of small towns until it passes into New Mexico. Interstate 27 goes north and south only between Lubbock and Amarillo. U.S. 87 comes into the northwestern corner of the Panhandle and travels southeast to Dumas, where it turns south to go through Amarillo; from there to Lubbock it shares part of the route with I-27, then travels south from Lubbock to Lamesa, turns southwest and heads for San Angelo. U.S. 385 traverses the western side of the Panhandle from north to south, coming into the state near its northwest corner, then traveling through no towns of any size on its way to Odessa and points farther south.

Climate: Average summer highs in Wichita Falls range from 92 to 98 degrees Fahrenheit, with spikes as high as 117 possible. Summer lows hover in the 70s, and winter highs are in the 50s. Winter lows average about 30 degrees, but the temperature can drop as low as minus 12. In the High Plains, winds blow constantly, and from every direction. Average summer highs in Lubbock are in the low 90s, and occasionally the mercury tops 110. Summer lows are usually in the mid 60s. Winter highs average in the 50s; winter lows in the upper 20s, with extremes around minus 17. Amarillo's temperatures are typically from 4 to 10 degrees cooler than those in Lubbock.

How much is that bovine in the Mustang. . . ?

P R A C T I C A L
I N F O R M A T I O N

■ AREA CODES AND TIME ZONES

The area codes for major Texas cities are: Austin, 512; Dallas, 214, 469, and 972; El Paso, 915; Fort Worth, 817; Galveston, 409; Houston, 281, 713, and 832; San Antonio, 210.

All of Texas lies in the Central time zone except the counties of El Paso and Hudspeth and the northwestern corner of Culberson County, where clocks run an hour earlier, on Mountain time.

■ METRIC CONVERSIONS

1 foot = .305 meters   1 mile = 1.6 kilometers
Centigrade = Fahrenheit temperature minus 32, divided by 1.8
1 pound = .45 kilograms

■ CLIMATE/WHEN TO GO

That old saying—"if you don't like the weather, stick around a couple of hours"— is especially applicable to Texas. The weather varies enormously with the state's geography, but almost everywhere it is subject to rapid changes as "northers," or cold fronts, blow in.

Still, there are a few general truisms about Texas weather. People do not expect snow in Texas, except in the Panhandle and on the mountaintops of the Trans-Pecos. When it does snow in these areas, mostly between October and May, the snowfalls are not heavy. Rain falls almost year-round east of I-35. West of that divide, rain sometimes comes in spring and summer, and sometimes doesn't come for years. Hail can blanket the northern part of the state any time rain falls. Tornadoes mainly affect northern Texas, usually in the spring; hurricanes affect only the coast in late summer, but once or twice in a decade. Strong winds are a constant feature of the weather along the coast, West-Central Texas, and the Panhandle, but they can also occur across the prairie areas, from about Waco northward, any time between early February and late April.

CITY	FAHRENHEIT TEMPERATURE			ANNUAL PRECIPITATION	
	Jan. Avg. High/Low	July Avg. High/Low	Record High/Low	Avg. Rain	Avg. Snow
Abilene	55 31	95 73	110 -9	24"	5"
Amarillo	49 21	92 66	108 -14	20"	16"
Austin	59 39	95 74	109 -2	32"	1"
Brownsville	69 50	93 76	106 16	27"	0"
Corpus Christi	65 45	93 75	104 13	30"	0"
Dallas	55 35	96 76	113 1	36"	3"
El Paso	56 29	96 68	114 -8	9"	5"
Houston	62 43	92 75	107 7	46"	0"
Midland	57 29	95 69	116 -11	15"	5"
San Antonio	61 38	95 75	108 0	31"	1"

Because much of Texas is subtropical, visitors tend to be more aware of its heat than its cold spells, and heat in Texas is a function of humidity as much as it is the thermometer. The 80 percent mean annual relative humidity of Texas coastal areas becomes suffocating in July and August, when temperatures average in the 90s Fahrenheit. Hundred-degree July and August days in Dallas are scorchers, despite a humidity of about 65 percent. In Presidio, statistically the hottest spot in Texas, July–August temperatures frequently pass 105 degrees F, but the Big Bend area's relative dryness—at about 50 percent humidity—makes the extra heat almost tolerable. Alpine, Marfa, Fort Davis, and Amarillo, because of their clear skies and elevations, are pleasant places even when temperatures surpass 90 degrees F.

Cold months in Texas are mild by comparison to those in the northern reaches of the United States. On southern stretches of the coast and in the Rio Grande Valley, freezing temperatures come only two or three times in a decade. Citrus and palm trees can't survive in northern Texas, but despite periodic freezes, they thrive in the South.

The best months for travel in Texas are April, May, June, October, and November.

■ GETTING THERE AND AROUND

The chief factor influencing travel in Texas is the state's size: 267,277 square miles, 54,000 square miles bigger than France, the largest country in Europe. Though Texas is served by the same air, bus, and rail lines as other states, the distances to be covered give rise to travel considerations that are not universal in the United States.

■ BY AIR

Texas is served by the usual national and international airlines, but for intrastate travel, most Texans fly on a Dallas-based carrier, Southwest Airlines.

Austin-Bergstrom International Airport (AUS), on the site of the former Bergstrom Air Force Base, is 8 miles southeast of downtown Austin on Texas Highway 71 near the U.S. 183 intersection. *3600 Presidential Boulevard; 512-530-2242; www.ci.austin.tx.us/austinairport.*

Dallas-Fort Worth International Airport (DFW), midway between Dallas and Fort Worth, is the main airport for both cities. It is currently the second-largest airport in the United States, served by approximately two dozen domestic and international carriers. *International Parkway, off Route 183 from the south and Route 114 and I-635 from the north; 972-574-3694; www.dfwairport.com.*

Love Field (DAL), 7 miles northwest of Dallas's downtown business district, is the headquarters of Southwest Airlines. *8008 Cedar Springs Road, at Mockingbird Lane; 214-670-6073; www.dallas-lovefield.com.*

El Paso International Airport (ELP) is 5 miles east of downtown, served by half a dozen airlines, mainly domestic. *Airport Road off U.S. 62/180; 915-772-4271; www.elpasointernationalairport.com.*

George Bush Intercontinental Airport (IAH), Houston's international airport, is 23 miles north of downtown near the Sam Houston Tollway (Beltway 8 North) and is served by two dozen carriers, including Continental, which is headquartered here. *2800 North Terminal Road; 281-230-3100; www.houstonairportsystem.org.*

W. P. Hobby Airport (HOU), 7 miles south of downtown Houston, near I-45/Gulf Freeway, is served by domestic flights. *7800 Airport Boulevard; 713-640-3000; www.houstonairportsystem.org.*

San Antonio International Airport (SAT) is in northeast San Antonio between Route 281 and I-410, about 13 miles from the downtown River Walk area. Approximately a dozen U.S. and Mexican airlines fly here. *9800 Airport Boulevard, 210-207-3450, www.ci.sat.tx.us/aviation.*

■ **BY CAR**

It is not sensible to think about travel in Texas without an auto. No city in the state has a subway, and because Texas cities are sprawling, taxi service is expensive and inner-city bus transportation is poor. Visitors who arrive by air are well advised to rent a car.

There are more than 4,000 cities, towns, and settlements in Texas, and there are 72,000 miles of state-maintained highways, designated on maps as interstate highways, federal highways, Texas highways, farm-to-market roads, ranch roads, and park roads. Locating small towns can be a task, because most maps do not include farm-to-market roads; many overlook all but a few state highways as well.

The **Texas Department of Transportation** (800-452-9292) publishes a map with highways, park roads, and farm-to-market and ranch roads, plus topographical features, state and federal park locations, and population figures for towns. The maps are available by mail or at the dozen Travel Information Centers on highways leading into the state.

The *Texas Almanac* (800-826-8911), which is updated every two years, has detailed road maps of each county and includes many local and farm-to-market roads not on the Department of Transportation map.

■ **BY TRAIN**

Amtrak operates daily from Chicago to Dallas, Austin, and San Antonio; daily from Oklahoma City to Fort Worth; and several times weekly from Orlando to Los Angeles, stopping in Houston, San Antonio, and El Paso. *800-872-7245; www.amtrak.com.*

■ **BY BUS**

Greyhound provides service to cities and towns large and small. *800-229-9424; www.greyhound.com.*

■ FOOD

Mexican food is the lingua franca of the Texas food world, and salsa has long since overtaken ketchup as the red sauce of choice in most parts of the state. Tex-Mex— the Anglicized version of traditional Mexican food, which runs to tacos, enchiladas, burritos, flautas, and huevos rancheros—is served in most areas of the state. Tamales—known in Mexican homes as traditional, wrapped-in-a-corn-shuck Christmas Eve treats—can now be found year-round in restaurants and supermarkets, from gringo style (little heat, little flavor) to authentic chile-infused filling so greasy it runs down your arm. Along the Mexican border and in the larger cities, traditional Mexican dishes, including *barbacoa* (traditionally made from a beef head cooked over coals, but now made from chuck roast, lamb, goat, or pork that's oven-roasted for several hours), *tacos de lengua* (tongue), and *menudo* (a fragrant stew made from tripe and touted by some as a hangover remedy) can be found in Tejano enclaves.

The larger cities have *taquerías*, Mexican fast-food joints with a selection of tacos and other simple foods: hot, tasty, cheap, and priced a la carte. Mexican bakeries are worth seeking out in the larger cities for the light *pan dulce* ("sweet bread") and melt-in-your mouth crispy cookies, like the delicate, anise-flavored *biscochitos. Empanadas* (baked turnovers) are plump with pumpkin, apple, caramel, pecan, guava, mango, or other fillings.

The Gulf Coast from South Padre Island to Beaumont is awash in seafood restaurants, many emphasizing local specialties from the Gulf waters: oysters, blue crabs, shrimp, and red snapper. Locals drive down to the fishing-boat docks to get their seafood splashing fresh.

In East Texas, aside from Houston, food runs to Deep South home cooking. Many items are fried, including vegetables—and if the veggies aren't fried, they are usually seasoned with generous hunks of pork. In summer, roadside stands in East Texas are laden with terrific homegrown tomatoes, bell peppers, blueberries, squashes, and peaches.

West of I-35, in the Panhandle and West and West-Central Texas, the emphasis is on beef, often grilled over mesquite wood (using fragrant mesquite for grilling is encouraged by ranchers, who consider the native tree a water-hogging, pestiferous weed). The national dish of West Texas is chicken-fried steak: a hunk of beef generously dredged in seasoned flour and served with mashed potatoes; cream gravy is ladled over everything on the platter.

BARBECUE

Barbecue, also known as barbeque and Bar-B-Q, is a universal constant of the Texas culinary landscape, with at least one place in nearly every town claiming to serve "The Best Barbecue in Texas."

There are essentially two types of barbecue in Texas—pork and beef—with infinite variations on each. Pork is the preferred meat in East Texas. Ribs are the most popular part of the pig east of I-35, a tradition since settlers from the Deep South arrived. East Texas barbecue sauce tends to be sweeter than it is in West Texas, where nothing will do but beef, usually brisket. The supremacy of beef harks back to the days of the open range, when cowhands would butcher a steer and cook its choice parts for hours over an open-pit wood fire. Barbecues came to be social events, the rancher's equivalent of cocktail parties.

East Texas barbecue requires that the meat be slathered in tomato-based sauces while it cooks. In Central and West Texas, barbecue is rarely basted while cooking. If barbecue sauce is used at all, it's added when the meat is served. The distinctive flavor of Central and West Texas barbecue comes from the oak—in some places mesquite—woods used to smoke the meat. In East Texas, connoisseurs fiddle with formulas for the perfect barbecue sauce; in Central and West Texas, they tinker with mixtures of wood.

Barbecue joints—nobody ever calls them restaurants—are fundamental, not fancy. An authentic joint is easily recognizable. Look at its ceiling: if it's clean, the place is probably a fake. If it's smudged and greasy from years of rising smoke, you're in the right place. Most places price their meals by the weight of the meat purchased, with extra charges for side dishes. White bread or saltine crackers, pickles, and onions are usually thrown in for free. Many joints are open only for lunch, and the food is served cafeteria style. The more rural the area, the more basic the barbecue. In western areas of Central Texas, for instance, side dishes are never served.

The most authentic barbecue joints in Central and West Texas started as butcher shops, like **Kreutz Market** in Lockhart (619 North Colorado Street; 512-398-2361) or **Southside Market** in Elgin (1212 U.S. 290; 512-285-3407). One of the Austin area's greatest barbecue joints is **Salt Lick** (18001 FM 1826; 512-858-4959), near Driftwood, southwest of town. The meats are scrumptious, as is the cole slaw. If you can't get to the original location, you can sample some of their delicacies at the Bergstrom airport's food court.

Restaurants in Central Texas tend to be more sophisticated than in rural areas. The larger towns with German populations have a number of cafés specializing in German dishes. Roadside stands in the Fredericksburg and Johnson City areas offer terrific peaches in summer, if the weather cooperates. Specialty jams, jellies, relishes, oils, and vinegars are also produced and sold locally. Look for ethnic bakeries and European-style meat markets: German in New Braunfels and Fredericksburg, Czech in West (17 miles north of Waco on I-35), and Alsatian in Castroville.

In Dallas and Houston, the dining possibilities range from burgers and barbecue to elegant pan-Asian to exotic fare from Morocco, Ethiopia, and Brazil. The Dallas Farmers Market, at the southeast corner of downtown, is a magnet for locals in summer, when East Texas farmers join the market's year-round commercial vendors to present their freshest homegrown produce: black-eyed and cream peas, peaches, tomatoes, bell peppers, chilies, baby okra, yellow squash, miniature eggplants, blue lake green beans, and tiny red potatoes. Cool season turnip, mustard, and collard greens appear in spring and fall; fat, sweet yams arrive in October.

■ LODGING

Dallas, Houston, Austin, and San Antonio accommodations include large convention hotels, chic little boutique hotels, opulent luxury palaces, and chain hotels and motels. San Antonio offers a number of B&Bs and hotels in historic structures. Lodging reservations for Austin should be made well in advance, particularly when the legislature is in session (January through May 31 in odd-numbered years) or when the University of Texas Longhorns are playing a home football game.

All along the Gulf Coast are hotels, motels, and beach houses. Corpus Christi has a large convention hotel on the waterfront, a plethora of typical beach hotels, and chain motels.

Galveston's split personality—part beach playground, part historical port city—is reflected in the beach motels and hotels along the seawall, and historic accommodations on the Galveston Bay side of the island, including several elegant B&Bs in Victorian structures.

Lodging options in the smaller towns throughout East Texas can be spotty, with some moderate- to low-end motel chains along with mom-and-pop independents. Marinas and cabins around the area's many lakes are particularly appealing to anglers and other fans of the region's wildlife. Jefferson has about five dozen B&Bs in vintage houses.

Bed and breakfasts are also found in abundance around Central Texas, particularly in and near the historic German settlements. Fredericksburg and environs alone have almost 300 B&Bs and guest houses. Dude ranches—sometimes called "guest ranches"—cluster in the hills around Bandera (the self-styled "Cowboy Capital of the World") and Kerrville. Sprinkled around the Hill Country are several luxury resorts, complete with golf courses whose greens are caviar to the area's white-tailed deer. Bed-and-breakfasts frequented by birding enthusiasts are proliferating in South Texas, particularly in coastal areas on the major migratory bird routes and in the Lower Rio Grande Valley.

Nine state parks, scattered around the state, have rustic furnished cabins, but guests must bring their own linens, cooking equipment, utensils, and dishes, as well as food. The cabins have heaters but are not air-conditioned, although some have attic fans.

■ RESERVATION SERVICES
First Class Bed & Breakfast Reservation Service. *888-991-6749; www.granbury-lodging.com.*
Gästehaus Schmidt Reservation Service. *830-997-5612; www.fbglodging.com.*
Historic Accommodations of Texas. *800-428-0368; www.hat.org.*

■ HOTEL AND MOTEL CHAINS
AmeriSuites. *800-833-1516; www.amerisuites.com.*
Baymont Inns & Suites. *877-299-6668; www.baymontinns.com.*
Best Western. *800-528-1234; www.bestwestern.com.*
Bradford Homesuites. *888-486-7829; www.bradfordsuites.com.*
Comfort Inn. *800-228-5150; www.comfortinn.com.*
Courtyard. 800-321-2211; *www.courtyard.com.*
Days Inn. *800-325-2525; www.daysinn.com.*
Doubletree. *800-222-8733; www.doubletree.com.*
Econo Lodge. *800-553-2666; www.choicehotels.com.*
Embassy Suites. *800-362-2779; www.embassysuites.com.*
Four Seasons. *800-819-5053; www.fourseasons.com.*
Hampton Inn. *800-426-7866; www.hamptoninn.com.*
Hilton. *800-445-8667; www.hilton.com.*
Holiday Inn. *800-465-4329; www.6c.com.*

Hyatt. *800-233-1234; www.hyatt.com.*
La Quinta. *800-531-5900; www.laquinta.com.*
Marriott. *800-228-9290; www.marriott.com.*
Motel 6. *800-466-8356; www.motel6.com.*
Omni Hotels. *800-843-6664; www.omnihotels.com.*
Quality. *800-228-5151; www.choicehotels.com.*
Radisson. *800-333-3333; www.radisson.com.*
Ramada. *800-272-6232; www.ramada.com.*
Renaissance Hotels. *800-468-3571; www.renaissancehotels.com.*
Rodeway Inn. *800-228-2000; www.choicehotels.com.*
Sheraton. *800-325-3535; www.sheraton.com.*
Super 8 Motels. *800-800-8000; www.super8.com.*
Travelodge. *800-255-3050; www.travelodge.com.*
Westin. *800-228-3000; www.westin.com.*
Wyndham. *800-996-3426; www.wyndham.com.*

■ CAMPING

In state parks, camping facilities run the gamut, from primitive tents-only sites to more sophisticated places that offer water, electricity, and sewer connections. Most parks provide two or more types of camping facilities, and many have screened shelters.

Army Corps of Engineers. *817-334-2705; www.usace.army.mil/inet/functions/cw/cecwo/scdet.htm.*
National Forests in Texas. *936-639-8501; www.southernregion.fs.fed.us/texas/recreation.html.*
National Park Service. *800-365-2267; www.nps.gov/parks/search.htm (park info) and reservations.nps.gov (reservations).*
Texas Association of Campground Owners publishes the annual *Texas RV Travel and Camping Guide,* which can be ordered by phone or online. Reservations must be made directly with the property. *512-459-8226; www.campingfriend.com/taco.*
Texas Parks and Wildlife Department. *800-792-1112; www.tpwd.state.tx.us/park/findapark.htm (park info) and www.tpwd.state.tx.us/park/admin/res (reservations).*
Texas State Parks. *512-389-8900; www.tpwd.state.tx.us/park/facilities/camp.htm.*

■ OFFICIAL TOURISM INFORMATION

Travel Texas. The tourist board publishes the magazine-style *Texas State Travel Guide,* which is filled with information about destinations, attractions, history, state parks, lakes, and other details. *800-452-9292; www.traveltex.com.*
Amarillo. *806-374-8474; www.amarillo-cvb.org.*
Austin. *800-926-2282; www.austintexas.org.*
Corpus Christi. *800-678-6232; www.corpuschristicvb.org.*
Dallas. *214-571-1000 or 800-232-5527; www.dallascvb.com.*
El Paso. *915-534-0600 or 800-351-6024; www.elpasocvb.com.*
Fort Worth. *817-336-8791 or 800-433-5747; www.fortworth.com.*
Galveston Island. *888-425-4753; www.galveston.com.*
Greater Houston. *713-437-5200 or 800-446-8786; www.houston-spacecity.com.*
Highland Lakes. *830-598-7541; www.highlandlakes.com.*
Laredo. *800-361-3360; www.visitlaredo.com.*
Lubbock. *806-747-5232 or 800-692-4035; www.lubbocklegends.com.*
San Antonio. *210-207-6700 or 800-447-3372; www.sanantoniocvb.com.*
Texas Hill Country River Region. *800-678-6232; www.thcrr.com.*
Texas Midwest. *915-676-0329; www.texasmidwest.org.*

■ USEFUL WEB SITES

The Alamo. Historical information, maps, directions. *www.thealamo.org.*
Austinchronicle.com. Online edition of Austin's alternative weekly has features and entertainment listings. *www.auschron.com.*
DallasNews.com. News from Dallas's major daily newspaper. *www.dallasnews.com.*
Dallas Observer. Online edition of alternative weekly newspaper. *www.dallasobserver.com.*
Handbook of Texas Online. An encyclopedia of Texas history, trivia, and lore. *www.tsha.utexas.edu/handbook/online.*
HoustonChronicle.com. News from Houston's major daily newspaper. *www.houstonchronicle.com.*
Johnson Space Center. Mission control for the Space Shuttle and International Space Station programs. *www.jsc.nasa.gov.*
San Antonio Express-News. Web site of *San Antonio Express-News* and TV station KENS 5. *www.mysanantonio.com.*

Statesman.com. Online edition of the daily paper the *Austin American-Statesman*. *www.statesman.com*.

Texas Almanac. Well-researched round-up of all facts Texan. *www.texasalmanac.com*.

Texas Highways Online. The travel magazine's Web site has info about Texas regions, destinations, events, and food. *www.texashighways.com*.

Texas Monthly. Great features on the state, plus travel and food columns. *www.texasmonthly.com*.

Texas Observer. The online edition of the iconoclastic newspaper has news, features, and columns. *www.texasobserver.org*.

■ FESTIVALS AND EVENTS

■ JANUARY

Southwestern Exposition and Livestock Show and Rodeo, Fort Worth. Judging and exhibitions of farm animals—from pigeons to horses and bulls—plus rodeo performances and appearances by country music celebrities. *817-877-2400; www.fwssr.com*.

■ FEBRUARY

Charro Days, Brownsville. In *charreadas,* or rodeos on the original Mexican model, locals wear colonial-era or turn-of-the-19th-century garb; there are also parades and pageants. *956-542-4245; www.charrodays.org*.

    Galveston Mardi Gras. Two weeks of parades, floats, and revelry; it's like New Orleans, but not as grand. *888-425-4753; www.mardigrasgalveston.com*.

    Houston Livestock Show and Rodeo. Parade, country music acts, cowboys, and horses. Begins in late February and continues through early March. *832-667-1000; www.hlsr.com*.

    Southwestern International Livestock Show and Rodeo, El Paso. Parade, exhibits, music acts, and competitions. *915-532-1401; www.elpasostockshow.com*.

■ MARCH

Jaycees World's Largest Rattlesnake Roundup, Sweetwater. Hunters bag snakes, milk them for venom, skin them, and fry their meat. Festivities include a parade and the Miss Snakecharmer Pageant. *915-235-5488; www.rattlesnakeroundup.com*.

South by Southwest Music and Media Conference, Austin. Showcase for a thousand bands (playing blues, pop/rock, punk, country, and other genres) at Austin nightclubs—a must for music critics and record-industry scouts. *512-467-7979; www.sxsw.com.*

Texas Cowboy Poetry Gathering, Alpine. Readings by cowboy-poets (some more cowboy, some more poet) from across the United States and Canada. *915-837-1071; www.alpinetexas.com.*

Texas Dogwood Trails, Palestine. Bus tours through 400-acre Davey Dogwood Park, dogwood excursions on Texas State Railroad, and walking tours of historic buildings. *903-723-3014; www.visitpalestine.com.*

■ APRIL

Easter Fires Pageant, Fredericksburg. A cast of 600 presents a story of Fredericksburg's origins, in which a mother tells her children that Comanche signal fires actually come from the Easter Bunny boiling eggs. *830-997-2359; www.gillespiefair.com.*

Fiesta San Antonio. Nine days of street and river parades, dress balls, mariachi serenades, *charreadas,* and fireworks, commemorating Texas independence. *210-227-5191 or 877-723-4378; www.fiesta-sa.org.*

Houston International Festival. Music, dance, food, and arts and crafts of the world, spotlighting a different country each year. *713-654-8808; www.ifest.org.*

■ MAY

Cinco de Mayo, San Antonio. Celebrations and a parade with Mexican mariachi flair commemorate Mexico's independence from France. *800-447-3372.*

Kerrville Folk Festival. Almost three weeks of live folk, blues, and country music, plus songwriting contests. *830-257-3600; www.kerrvillefolkfestival.com.*

National Polka Festival, Ennis. Three days of nonstop polka music and dancing, plus a parade, Czech food, arts and crafts, and children's activities. *888-366-4748; www.nationalpolkafestival.com.*

■ JUNE

Texas Folklife Festival, San Antonio. Celebrates 40 of the ethnic and cultural groups that make up Texas's population. Crafts, food, music, storytelling, and dances. *210-458-2390; www.texancultures.utsa.edu.*

Viva El Paso! Regional history pageant in an outdoor amphitheater, presented in the evenings through mid-August. *915-565-6900; www.viva-ep.org.*

World Championship Fiddler's Festival, Crockett. A tradition for more than 60 years, with arts and crafts booths and food. *936-544-2359.*

■ JULY

Texas Cowboy Reunion, Stamford. Competitions among working cowhands take place at this event, which bills itself as the world's largest amateur rodeo. *915-773-2411; www.tcrrodeo.com.*

Tops in Texas Rodeo, Jacksonville. One of the larger regional rodeos, with evening events and country music performances. *903-586-2217.*

■ AUGUST

Hotter 'n ' Hell Hundred, Wichita Falls. A 100-mile bicycle race in 100-degree Fahrenheit (more or less) heat. *940-322-3223; www.hh100.org.*

■ SEPTEMBER

National Cowboy Symposium and Celebration, Lubbock. Storytelling, poetry, academic presentations, chuck wagon cook-off and breakfast, forging and shoeing clinics, horse-training seminars, and even a Western fashion show. *806-795-2455; www.cowboy.org.*

Panhandle–South Plains Fair, Lubbock. Authentic regional fair features a week of livestock shows, midway, and country music acts. *806-763-2833; www.southplainsfair.com.*

■ OCTOBER

State Fair of Texas, Dallas. Midway, musicals, livestock competition, auto show. *www.bigtex.com; 214-565-9931.*

Texas Rose Festival, Tyler. Parade with rose-bearing floats, an exhibit of cut roses, art show, beauty contest, and dances. *903-597-3130; www.texasrosefestival.com.*

Wurstfest, New Braunfels. More than 100,000 people come to this event, held in late October and early November, to tipple, two-step, and polka. *830-625-9167; www.wurstfest.com.*

■ **NOVEMBER**

Original Terlingua International Championship Chili Cookoff. Bean, black-eyed pea, and barbecue cook-off. *903-874-5601; www.abowlofred.org.*

Terlingua International Chili Championship. Annual Chili Appreciation Society International cook-off. *817-975-2200; www.chili.org.*

Women's National Finals Rodeo, Fort Worth. The nation's largest and most important rodeo event for women includes competitions in bareback riding, calf roping, team roping, breakaway roping, and even bull riding. *719-576-0900 or 817-625-1025; www.wpra.com or www.cowtowncoliseum.com.*

■ **DECEMBER**

Dickens on the Strand, Galveston. Enjoy parades in Victorian garb, a Dickens costume contest, a Royal Victorian Wedding Ceremony, and other events in the downtown historic district. *409-765-7834; www.dickensonthestrand.org.*

RECOMMENDED READING

■ History

Anglos and Mexicans in the Making of Texas, 1836–1986 (1987), by David Montejano. In his well-regarded book Montejano sheds new light on the place of Mexicans in Texas history.

City on Fire (2003), by Bill Minutaglio. In 1947, two freighters loaded with ammonium nitrate exploded in Texas City. Minutaglio relates this story through the lives of people who experienced the catastrophe.

The Conquest of New Spain (1963), by Bernal Diaz. This memoir of a soldier who accompanied Hernán Cortés is an excellent primer in Mexican history.

The Doomed Road of Empire (1963), by Hodding Carter. A volume in the American Trails Series, this book covers more than three centuries of conflict and drama along El Camino Real—the Royal Road.

Duel of Eagles (1973), by Jeff Long. In this version of the Alamo battle, the soldiers defending the mission are ne'er-do-wells who fall under the spell of Sam Houston.

Gone to Texas: A History of the Lone Star State (2003), by Randolph B. Campbell. An up-to-date, balanced, and inclusive history of the state from the first arrival of humans 10,000 years ago to the early 21st century.

The Great Frontier (1952), by Walter Prescott Webb. The book places Texas and the United States in a European context, comparing frontier individualism with corporate culture.

The Great Plains (1931), by Walter Prescott Webb. This famous study from the early 1930s examines the history of the Texas Plains country, focusing on its native peoples, the cattle industry, and the introduction of water to the region.

Great River: the Rio Grande in North American History (1954), by Paul Horgan. This two-volume history of the Rio Grande looks at the history of the river and its impact on the surrounding region.

History of the German Settlements in Texas, 1831–1861 (1930), by Rudolph Leopold Biesele. Biesele's book explores the German migration to Texas in the 1900s and examines how the newcomers adapted to their new home.

Isaac's Storm (1999), by Erik Larson. Larson's account of the Great Hurricane of 1900, which leveled Galveston, is told through the life of Isaac Cline, the U.S. Weather Bureau's resident meteorologist at the time.

The King Ranch (1957), by Tom Lea. This two-volume history of the fabled King Ranch, illustrated by the author's sketches, describes in fascinating detail the people and events that shaped the development of the huge and highly successful ranching empire.

Krasna Amerika (1983), by Clinton Machann and James Mendl. This unusual book explores the history of Czech settlement in Texas.

Occupied America (1972), by Rodolfo Acuña. In this Latino view of the Southwest, the heroes of the Alamo are not heroes.

Pipe Dreams: Greed, Ego, and the Death of Enron (2002), by Robert Bryce. Only in freewheeling Houston, writes Bryce, could a scandal of the scope and manner of the Enron debacle have occurred.

Sam Houston: A Biography of the Father of Texas (1993), by John Hoyt Williams. The story of the man who defeated General Santa Anna, and served as president of the Republic of Texas, then U.S. senator and governor of the state of Texas.

With a Pistol in His Hand (1973), by Américo Paredes. The story of Gregorio Cortez, fabled hero from the borderlands.

■ CULTURE, MEMOIR

Cowboys and Cadillacs (1983), by Don Graham. A critical and sometimes funny review of Texas as Hollywood knows it.

Deliberate Indifference (1994), by Howard Swindle. Swindle's tome is an award-winning report on and social commentary about the death of an African-American man in the custody of East Texas police.

Friday Night Lights: A Town, a Team, and a Dream (1990), by H. G. Bissinger. A brilliant book that tracks Odessa's obsession with its high school football team.

Goodbye to a River (1960), by John Graves. Before a series of dams was built along the Brazos River, the author traveled the river by canoe, vividly recording the era before the waterway was altered.

Places Left Unfinished at the Time of Creation (1999), by John Phillip Santos. In his autobiography, Santos lyrically reflects on family life, his Mexican heritage, Texas history, and many other topics.

Too Great a Temptation (1994), by Joel Gregory. Purportedly about how the state's most promising preacher came to turn his back on the Baptist hierarchy, this is really an inside look at urban megachurches, from the mechanics of deacons' boards to the details of pledge cards.

Unknown Texas (1988), by Jonathan Eisen and Harold Straughn, editors. A sampler, with excerpts by Sam Houston, Davy Crockett, General Santa Anna, and contemporary Texans Dan Rather and Larry McMurtry.

■ FICTION

All the Pretty Horses (1992), by Cormac McCarthy. In this coming-of-age story, a boy leaves his Texas ranch on horseback and goes to Mexico.

Brownsville (2003), by Oscar Casares. Remarkable stories inspired by the men and women of the border town.

Giant (1952), by Edna Ferber. Ferber's story sketches the members of a ranching family against the backdrop of the oil wildcatting that eventually superseded the cattle-ranching industry.

Lonesome Dove (1985), by Larry McMurtry. McMurtry's American epic tells the story of a cattle drive from Texas to Montana. Part love story, part adventure, part Western, it's a classic, as is his novel *The Last Picture Show* (1966).

Quakertown (2001), by Lee Martin. In this novel set in the 1920s, a black community is duped into relocating to make way for a park.

That Old Ace in the Hole (2002), by Annie Proulx. A 25-year-old scouts Panhandle locations for a hog-farm conglomerate in this evocative novel about the region and its people.

West of the Pecos (1937), by Zane Grey. The quintessential Western writer tells the tale of a young woman who must pose as a man to survive in the Trans-Pecos.

INDEX

COMPASS AMERICAN GUIDES

Alaska	Kentucky	Pennsylvania
American Southwest	Las Vegas	Santa Fe
Arizona	Maine	South Carolina
Boston	Manhattan	South Dakota
California Wine Country	Massachusetts	Tennessee
Cape Cod	Michigan	Texas
Chicago	Minnesota	Utah
Coastal California	Montana	Vermont
Colorado	New Hampshire	Virginia
Connecticut & Rhode Island	New Mexico	Washington
Florida	New Orleans	Washington Wine Country
Georgia	North Carolina	Wisconsin
Gulf South	Oregon	Wyoming
Hawaii	Oregon Wine Country	
Idaho	Pacific Northwest	

Compass American Guides are available at special discounts for bulk purchases for sales promotions or premiums. Special editions, including personalized covers, excerpts of existing guides, and corporate imprints, can be created in large quantities for special needs. For more information, contact your local bookseller or write to Special Markets, Fodor's Travel Publications, 1745 Broadway, New York, NY 10019. Inquiries from Canada should be directed to your local Canadian bookseller or sent to Random House of Canada, Ltd., Marketing Department, 2775 Matheson Boulevard East, Mississauga, Ontario L4W 4P7. Inquiries from the United Kingdom should be sent to Fodor's Travel Publications, 20 Vauxhall Bridge Road, London, England SW1V 2SA.

COMPASS AMERICAN GUIDES

Critics, booksellers, and travelers all agree: you're lost without a Compass.

"This splendid series provides exactly the sort of historical and cultural detail about North American destinations that curious-minded travelers need."
—*Washington Post*

"This is a series that constantly stuns us . . . no guide with photos this good should have writing this good. But it does." —*New York Daily News*

"Of the many guidebooks on the market, few are as visually stimulating, as thoroughly researched, or as lively written as the Compass American Guide series."
—*Chicago Tribune*

"Good to read ahead of time, then take along so you don't miss anything."
—*San Diego Magazine*

"Magnificent photography. First rate."—*Money*

"Written by longtime residents of each destination...these handsome and literate guides are strong on history and culture, and illustrated with gorgeous photos." —
San Francisco Chronicle

"The color photographs sparkle, the archival illustrations illuminate windows to the past, and the writing is usually of the utmost caliber." —*Michigan Tribune*

"Class acts, worth reading and shelving for keeps even if you're not a traveler. "
—*New Orleans Times-Picayune*

"Beautiful photographs and literate writing are the hallmarks of the Compass guides." —*Nashville Tennessean*

"History, geography, and wanderlust converge in these well-conceived books."
—*Raleigh News & Observer*

"Oh, my goodness! What a gorgeous series this is."—*Booklist*

ACKNOWLEDGMENTS

■ FROM THE AUTHORS

From Mary G. Ramos for this edition: During my 18-year tenure on the staff of the *Texas Almanac,* I came to appreciate the work of the Texas State Historical Association and the Texas Historical Commission in gathering, documenting, and disseminating information about the history and culture of this large and complex state. My contributions to this guide would not have been possible without their generosity in sharing this enormous body of knowledge with the public through their publications and Web sites.

From Dick J. Reavis for the original edition: Lots of people write and study about Texas, but not many study and write about Texas all the time. In compiling a book like this, one quickly learns who they are, and even if you've known them for years, you come into a more thorough appreciation of their work. In preparing this book, I've learned from several of these masters of Texas: Jan Reid, Gary Cartwright, Anne Dingus, Mike Cochran, Don Graham, Laura Miller, Richard Zelade, Carol Countryman, John Davidson, Pam Diamond, Stephen Harrigan, Carlos Guerra, Sandy Sheehy, Bryan Woolley, Susan Chadwick, Paul Burka, and Jan Jarboe among them. I hope this guide qualifies me to stay in such company.

■ FROM THE PUBLISHER

Compass American Guides would like to thank Rachel Elson for copy-editing the manuscript, Ellen Klages for proofreading it, and Joan Stout for indexing it. All photographs are by Kevin Vandivier unless noted below. Compass would like to thank the following individuals or institutions for the use of their illustrations or photographs:

Overview
Page 15, Library of Congress

History
Page 24, Center for American History, University of Texas, Austin, Boadsides Collection (CN00834)
Page 26, Texas State Library and Archives Commission, Austin
Page 30, Center for American History, Prints & Photographs Collection (CN00773)

Page 35, Texas Instruments
Page 36, Texas Senate Media Services
Page 39, Enron Corp.
Page 41, Center for American History, The Country Blues (CN01028)

West Texas
Page 51, Brian Kanof
Pages 56–57, Florian Holzherr
Page 61, Marty Harris/McDonald Observatory
Page 67, National Archives, Washington, D.C. (ITC-68-045)
Page 68, Center for American History, Prints & Photographs Collection (CN07532)
Page 72, Center for American History, Prints & Photographs Collection (CN03235)
Page 74, Center for American History, Prints & Photographs Collection (CN08120)
Page 79, Center for American History, Prints & Photographs Collection (CN00081)

Dallas and Fort Worth
Page 89, 7-Eleven, Inc.
Page 91, *The Dallas Morning News*
Page 99, Cesar Mateos/Dallas Museum of Art
Page 101, Hulton Archive/Getty Images
Page 107 (top), Carolyn Brown
Page 107 (bottom), Pete Vollenweider
Page 113, Robert Newcombe/Kimbell Art Museum
Page 115, David Woo
Pages 120–121, North Fort Worth Historical Society

East Texas
Page 126, The Texas Collection, Baylor University
Page 130, Waxahachie Chamber of Commerce
Page 131, Waxahachie Convention and Visitors Bureau
Page 132 (top), Collin Street Bakery
Page 136, The Texas Collection, Baylor University
Page 139, Library of Congress, Prints & Photographs Division (LC-USZ62-110029)

Houston and Galveston
Page 156, Houston Metropolitan Research Center, Houston Public Library
Page 158–159, Library of Congress, Geography and Map Division
Page 161, Hickey-Robertson, Houston

■ ABOUT THE AUTHORS

Mary G. Ramos, who thoroughly revised this edition of *Compass Texas,* is a native of the state's Lower Rio Grande Valley. These days a Dallas-based writer and editor, she began her career as a freelancer for regional and national publications. She was associate editor of the *Texas Almanac* for nine years and its editor for another nine. Her extensive historical research resulted in many features for the almanac, and she is coauthor of *The Texas Almanac's Political History of Texas,* published in 1992. Travel writing and photography projects have taken her to many Texas destinations, as well as Virginia, Maryland, Massachusetts, Colorado, Canada, Mexico, and England.

Dick J. Reavis, the author of this book's original edition, began his career as a journalist with the *Moore County News* in the Panhandle town of Dumas, where he covered everything from stock shows to the wheat harvest to courthouse news. Between 1977 and 1990 he worked in various capacities as a writer for *Texas Monthly,* and in 1987 he drove every road on the state highway department's map of Texas—72,000 miles in all—as the basis for his *Texas Monthly* column, "National Tour of Texas." Reavis is the author of three books: *Conversations with Moctezuma: Ancient Shadows over Modern Life in Mexico* (1990); *Ashes of Waco: An Investigation* (1993); and *If White Kids Die: Memories of a Civil Rights Movement Volunteer* (2001).

■ About the Photographer

Born and raised in Houston, Kevin Vandivier became involved with photography while studying forestry and wildlife game management at Stephen F. Austin State University. He ultimately changed his major to photojournalism, graduating from the University of Texas at Austin. Hired out of school by the *Dallas Times Herald*, he spent a couple of years at the newspaper honing his shooting skills, but, restless for new challenges, moved back to Austin and launched his freelance career. His work has been published in *National Geographic World, Popular Photography, Life, Newsweek, Time, Texas Monthly*, and other publications. Kevin lives in Lakeway, just west of Austin, with his wife, Leslie, and their three children, Shannon, Kaitlin, and Kelly.